D0597112

TODAY the STRUGGLE

LITERATURE AND POLITICS
IN ENGLAND DURING THE
SPANISH CIVIL WAR

By KATHARINE BAIL HOSKINS

UNIVERSITY OF TEXAS PRESS
AUSTIN & LONDON

Standard Book Number 292–78411–2
Library of Congress Catalog Card Number 78–83763
Copyright © 1969 by Katharine Bail Hoskins
All rights reserved

Printed by The University of Texas Printing Division, Austin
Bound by Universal Bookbindery, Inc., San Antonio

PR
478
.S6
H6

Acknowledgments

I wish to thank the following for permission to reprint excerpts from previously published materials:

W. H. Auden for passages from *Letters from Iceland* by W. H. Auden and Louis MacNeice, copyright © 1937 by W. H. Auden and Louis MacNeice, copyright renewed 1965 by W. H. Auden; reprinted by permission of Curtis Brown Ltd.

W. H. Auden and Christopher Isherwood for passages from *The Ascent of F6*, copyright © 1936, 1964 by W. H. Auden and Christopher Isherwood, and from *On the Frontier*, copyright © 1939, 1967 by W. H. Auden and Christopher Isherwood; both reprinted by permission of Curtis Brown Ltd. and Faber and Faber Ltd.

George Barker for passages from "Calamiterror" by George Barker from his *Collected Poems 1930 to 1965*, copyright © 1957 by George Barker. Reprinted by permission of October House Inc. and Faber and Faber, Ltd.

Cambridge University Press for passages from *The Spanish Labyrinth* by Gerald Brenan.

Curtis Brown Ltd. for passages from Roy Campbell's *Flowering Rifle*, reprinted by their permission.

C. Day Lewis for selections from *Collected Poems 1954*, published by Jonathan Cape Ltd. and The Hogarth Press, copyright © 1931, 1966 by C. Day-Lewis. Reprinted by permission of Jonathan Cape Ltd. and Harold Matson Co., Inc. Also for passages from *The Buried Day*, copyright © 1960 by C. Day Lewis, published by Chatto and Windus and reprinted by permission of Harold Matson Company and the Hogarth Press, Ltd. Also for *A Time to Dance*, copyright © 1933, 1961 by C. Day-Lewis. Reprinted by permission of Harold Matson Company.

J. M. Dent & Son Ltd. for excerpts from *The Hitler Cult*, by P. Wyndham Lewis, published by J. M. Dent & Son Ltd. and reprinted by their permission.

William Empson for passages from "Autumn on Nan-Yueh" in *Collected Poems of William Empson*, published by Harcourt, Brace & World, Inc. and Chatto & Windus Ltd. and reprinted by their permission.

Victor Gollancz, Ltd. for excerpts from *More For Timothy* by Victor Gollancz, published by Victor Gollancz, Ltd. and reprinted by their permission.

Graham Greene for passages from *The Confidential Agent*, published by The Viking Press and reprinted by their permission and by permission of Laurence Pollinger, Ltd.

Harper & Row, Publishers for excerpts from *The God That Failed*, edited by Richard Grossman, published by Harper & Row, Publishers and reprinted by their permission; and for excerpts from *The Spanish Civil War* by Hugh Thomas, published by Harper & Row, Publishers and reprinted by their permission.

The Hogarth Press, Ltd., for passages from "Granien" by T. H. Wintringham, from "The New Offensive" by Margot Heinemann, and from "Those With Investments in Spain 1937" by Brian Howard, all from *Poems for Spain*, published by The Hogarth Press and reprinted by their permission.

Hollis & Carter, Ltd., for passages from *Light on a Dark Horse* by Roy Campbell, published by Hollis & Carter, Ltd. and reprinted by their permission.

Arthur Koestler for passages from *The Invisible Writing*, published by William Collins Sons & Co., Ltd. Reprinted by permission of A. D. Peters & Co.

John Lehmann for excerpts from *The Whispering Gallery*, published by Harcourt, Brace & Co., Inc., copyright © 1955, John Lehmann, reprinted by permission of A. Watkins, Inc. and David Higham Associates, Ltd.

The Macmillan Company for passages from "Politics" in *Collected Poems of W. B. Yeats*, copyright © 1940 by Georgie Yeats; passages from "Three Songs to the Same Tune," in *Collected Poems* by W. B. Yeats, copyright © 1934 by The Macmillan Company, renewed 1962 by Bertha Georgie Yeats; passages from "Three

Marching Songs," in *Collected Poems* by W. B. Yeats, copyright © 1940 by Georgie Yeats, all published by The Macmillan Company and reprinted by their permission; also by permission of Mr. M. B. Yeats, Macmillan & Co., Ltd., and A. P. Watt & Son, Ltd.

Macmillan & Co., Ltd. for lines from *The Star Turns Red* by Sean O'Casey, from *Collected Plays*, Vol. II, published by Macmillan & Co. and reprinted by their permission and by the permission of Mrs. O'Casey, St. Martin's Press Inc., and The Macmillan Company of Canada, Ltd.

Charles Madge for four lines from "Letter to the Intelligentsia" reprinted here by his permission.

Methuen & Company, Ltd. and Henry Regnery Company for passages from Wyndham Lewis' *The Revenge for Love*, reprinted by their permission.

Frederick Muller, Ltd., for passages from *The Mind in Chains*, edited by C. Day Lewis, published by Frederick Muller, Ltd. and reprinted by their permission.

Estate of George Orwell, for passages from *Coming Up for Air*, copyright © 1950 by Harcourt, Brace and World, Inc., reprinted by permission of Brandt & Brandt.

Oxford University Press, Inc., for passages from *The Collected Poems of Louis MacNeice*, edited by E. R. Dodds. Copyright © The Estate of Louis MacNeice, 1966. Reprinted by permission of Oxford University Press, Inc., and Faber and Faber, Ltd.

The Oxford University Press for excerpts from *The Poetry of W. H. Auden: The Disenchanted Island*, by Monroe K. Spears, published by The Oxford University Press and reprinted by their permission.

The Public Trustee and The Society of Authors for passages from Bernard Shaw's *Geneva* reprinted by their permission.

Grateful acknowledgment is extended to Random House, Inc. for the use of excerpts from the various volumes of W. H. Auden poetry. Copyright 1933 through © 1966 by W. H. Auden.

Grateful acknowledgment is extended to Random House, Inc. for the use of excerpts from the various volumes of Stephen Spender poetry. Copyright 1930 through © 1955 by Stephen Spender.

Random House, Inc., for *Trial of a Judge* by Stephen Spender. Copyright 1938 by Random House, Inc. Reprinted by permission.

Henry Regnery Company for lines from "The Flight" and "The Sling" from *Selected Poems* by Roy Campbell, published by the Henry Regnery Company and reprinted by their permission.

Pat Sloan for excerpts from "Full Moon at Tierz" by John Cornford from *John Cornford: A Memoir*, edited by Pat Sloan, published by Jonathan Cape, Ltd. and reprinted by their permission.

T. Stanhope Sprigg for passages from *Studies in a Dying Culture* by Christopher Caudwell, reprinted by Stanhope Sprigg's permission.

Julian Symons for passages from his *The Thirties: A Dream Revolved*, reprinted by permission of Curtis Brown Ltd.

Philip Toynbee for excerpts from *Friends Apart*, published by MacGibbon & Kee and reprinted by their permission.

The Vedanta Society of Southern California for passages from *An Approach to Vedanta* by Christopher Isherwood, copyright © The Vedanta Society of Southern California 1963, published by the Vedanta Society of Southern California and reprinted by their permission.

Rex Warner for passages from "Arms in Spain" and "The Tourist Looks at Spain"; also for passages from *The Wild Goose Chase*, reprinted by permission of The Bodley Head, Ltd.

To My Family

Tomorrow, for the young, the poets exploding like bombs,
The walks by the lake, the winter of perfect communion;
Tomorrow the bicycle races
Through the suburbs on summer evenings; but today the struggle.

Today the inevitable increase in the chances of death;
The conscious acceptance of guilt in the necessary murder;
Today the expending of powers
On the flat ephemeral pamphlet and the boring meeting.

Today the makeshift consolations; the shared cigarette;
The cards in the candle-lit barn and the scraping concert,
The masculine jokes; today the
Fumbled and unsatisfactory embrace before hurting.

The stars are dead; the animals will not look:
We are left alone with our day, and the time is short and
History to the defeated
May say Alas but cannot help or pardon.

W. H. Auden, "Spain, 1937"

Preface

This study sprang from an interest in the relation of literature to politics in England. Good authors have been writing with political intent at least since Aristophanes, but I chose to focus my attention upon the decade of the nineteen-thirties because it was the most recent period of intense political activity among British writers, because the issues that excited the activity are not so far removed from those of today as to raise problems of perspective and are in fact still relevant, and because various highly talented authors produced some very interesting work as part of their contribution to the causes they chose to serve.

It is necessary to stress "writing with political intent." If politics is defined broadly as the means by which men in groups order, adjust, and manipulate their mutual and conflicting interests, then a vast body of literature can be said to be *about* politics. For the purposes of this study, I am not concerned with those works that draw upon politics for background or even chief subject matter but are clearly not intended to have practical political effect; I am interested in those works composed by writers who have taken sides and are consciously attempting to use their literary talents in behalf of, or in opposition to, some fairly explicit program or course of action. Conrad and Stendhal found politics a fruitful subject, but their novels hardly serve as prescriptions for political action. If reading Flaubert helped influence certain young Frenchmen to try to remold French society, this was not due to any reformist zeal on the part of the author. Trollope's parliamentary novels are no more seriously concerned with contemporary political issues than his Barsetshire novels are with theological problems.

Serious writers, at least for the past century, have rarely demonstrated any notable satisfaction with things as they are, but most of them have not, even for a time, felt it part of their function to promote change; there is, of course, no moral imperative for a writer to devote himself to a political cause however noble, and indifference or hostility to political action has characterized some of the best modern authors. A writer who has achieved Conrad's aim, "to make you *see*," has achieved much, perhaps as much as can reasonably be asked; but at certain times, large numbers of writers have seemed to feel more was required. This was true in the thirties.

At the beginning of the decade, W. H. Auden sought high sanction, in his "Petition," for "new styles of architecture, a change of heart." While it could well be argued that no first-rate work of literature leaves the "heart" of a sensitive reader quite unchanged, the desire for "new styles" in social architecture represented a shift in emphasis from the literary attitudes of the previous decade. During the next ten years, a good proportion of the most gifted writers in England, as elsewhere, were to dedicate themselves to plans for remodeling society. Not all the recommended styles were strictly new—there was considerable enthusiasm for a kind of Gothic Revival—but they seemed so to their proponents.

The twentieth century has provided a great variety of banners under which "engaged" writers could enlist, but by the thirties the choices seemed to many writers to have narrowed to two, communism or fascism. Socialism in all its guises had been established as a literary cause well before the turn of the century, and the elements of what came to be identified as fascism were of almost as venerable ancestry. In the years immediately before World War I, the milder forms of socialism had become virtually respectable, in England as abroad. On the Left, it was the anarchist faction, derived from Bakunin, which seemed dangerously revolutionary, rather than the soberly parliamentary Marxist majority faction. On the Right, frankly counterrevolutionary royalist or "legitimist" movements had some prominence on the continent, but all such tendencies in England went under the general heading of conservatism.

The most flamboyant precursors of fascism were the Italian Futurists. Futurism began as a literary movement in Italy under the leadership of the poet Marinetti, but it was to find most vivid expression in painting and sculpture. From 1909 into the war years, it was to attract young artists in Italy and France and to influence Ezra Pound and Wyndham Lewis in England. Deriving from Stirner and Nietzsche rather than from Marx and Bakunin, Futurism nevertheless had some surface resemblances to radical movements of the Left, and some of the Futurists had early been associated with Italian anarchism. With their slogans of "Burn the museums!", "Drain the canals of Venice!", and "Kill the moonlight!", the Futurists, like the leftists, extolled the future over the past, the industrial over the pastoral, the machine over the moonlight. But to the leftist ideals of international peace, brotherhood, and justice, however forcibly they might have to be achieved, the Futurists opposed the ideals of "War, the only health giver of the world, militarism, patriotism, . . . the beautiful Ideas that kill, the contempt for women. . . . For art can be naught but violence, cruelty, and injustice."[1]

World War I and its aftermath effected a temporary deflation of socialist and Futurist, as of all prewar, ideals. The Russian Revolution and the aborted revolutions elsewhere split the already faction-ridden Left still further. The French Futurists became part of the Dada and Surrealist movements; in the thirties, the political line of the merged movements became Communist. The Italian Futurists, however, became identified with Mussolini's fascism. As for the major literary talents of the twenties, almost all demonstrated profound disenchantment with political action of all kinds.

The leading writers of the twenties were by no means indifferent to their social and political situation; perhaps no comparable period has seen such a thorough and impressive anatomization and criticism of contemporary society. What was absent was any apparent hope or expectation of improvement. Among British writers, D. H. Lawrence offered his formula for a better world and Wyndham Lewis continued his personal counterrevolution with undiminished vigor, but most of the best writers were preoccupied with illuminating present horrors, not evoking visions of a happier future. The political effect of these nonpolitical excoriations of society has been amply

[1] F. T. Marinetti, "Manifesto of Futurism," first published in *Le Figaro* of Paris in 1909, reprinted by Joshua C. Taylor, *Futurism*, pp. 124–125.

described by writers of the next generation, the fervidly political poets and novelists of the thirties. For them, the works of their elders combined with actual events to convince them at once of the bankruptcy of Western civilization and of the urgent necessity for radical change.

In the thirties, political consciousness among writers became acute and polarized. By mid-decade, those from all areas of the Left had largely united behind the cause of communism, and fascism had won the active support or the reluctant justification of many of those on the Right. Liberals like E. M. Forster were to be heard praising communism, and conservatives like Yeats and Eliot were finding kind words for fascism. Before the decade was over, this political fervor had cooled, and from the perspective of thirty years it has become clear that the excursion into political action of almost all the writers considered in this study was no more than that, a temporary excursion. It would be inaccurate to say that they then turned from politics back to their more personal affairs, because for the best of them politics *was* a personal affair during the thirties. How it became, and how it ceased to be, personal for them is what has chiefly interested me in this study.

I had not been long in pursuit of my subject when it became obvious that if I was to avoid going into three volumes I must find a focal point, and the Spanish Civil War seemed admirable for my purpose. Interesting and important in itself, for the world as for Spain, the Spanish War had enormous symbolic meaning for British as for other writers of the time. Few of the authors to be considered in these pages were awakened to political consciousness by the events in Spain: most of them had been dealing with sociopolitical subject matter for some years before the summer of 1936, but to a considerable degree, they had simply been talking to each other. The "great debate" on the relative merits of communism, fascism, and liberal social democracy had been confined largely to common rooms, political study groups, intellectual journals, and literary drawing rooms. With the outbreak of the Spanish War, the debate moved into the popular press and the pubs, and writers who, for all their talk of mass movements, had been speaking only to a rather select intellectual coterie, found themselves with a large, attentive, and strongly partisan audience.

"See Spain and see the world," wrote Rex Warner. Roy Campbell called Spain "a mirror in a public place," and W. H. Auden described the Spanish conflict as embodying the most private and personal conflicts of himself and his contemporaries. The hopes of the revolutionary, both Left and Right, and the fears of the conservative were acted out on that "arid square, that fragment nipped off from hot/ Africa, soldered so crudely to inventive Europe." How far the "facts" of the Spanish War fit the highly subjective interpretations of British observers cannot be sharply ascertained: contemporary accounts were likely to reflect the prejudices of the reporters; the official pronouncements of both sides showed the time-honored disregard for truth characteristic of wartime propaganda; and later historians have had to make do, as historians generally must, with inadequate and ambiguous evidence. Nevertheless, I have felt obliged to offer in an appendix an earnest, if perhaps foredoomed, attempt to describe what the issues of the war actually were, as background to my discussion of how these issues appeared to British writers.

In selecting writers and works to discuss in detail, I have allowed myself considerable freedom. Neither attempting a complete, nor even necessarily a balanced, picture of British literature during the 1936–1939 period, I have excluded some admirable authors whose works had no appreciable bearing on the Spanish Civil War or the political ferment surrounding it, and among the many whose writing I considered relevant to the subject, I have chosen to discuss only a few closely. Concentrating generally, although not invariably, on works that seem to me to have intrinsic literary merit, I have largely ignored those writers, always the majority in any period, who were merely typical. I have been concerned chiefly with artists of high abilities who, at least during the thirties, dedicated their talents to the propagation of certain social and political ideas. The attitudes of most of the chief figures of this study changed in the course of the Spanish Civil War, and I have felt justified in ranging backward to works composed well before the war and, in some cases, forward to others that postdate it, in order to clarify the development of these attitudes. I have also given close attention to some works of the 1936–1939 period which bear tangentially, rather than directly, upon events in Spain, because I consider them relevant to the issues dramatized in Spain.

The two questions that most occupied me were whether the venture into politics of the writers I have chosen to study had any significant effect upon the events they hoped to mold and whether the use of political subject matter affected the quality of their writing. The answer to both questions proved to be, with some qualifications: not much. The process of enquiry was, however, very rewarding for me.

The proportion of one chapter on right-wing writers to four on those of the left wing reflects, very roughly, the proportion of adherents to these positions among British writers of the late thirties rather than my own personal bias. I do, however, have a bias, and although I have tried to allow for it, I have considered it the part of honesty to make no great effort to conceal it.

Contents

TODAY THE STRUGGLE

Literature and Politics in England during the Spanish Civil War

Chapter I

STIMULUS AND RESPONSE

The first shot of the Spanish Civil War was not heard very far around the world. When Francisco Franco and a group of other generals began their insurrection on July 17–18, 1936, the event struck many observers as simply the latest in a series of Fascist conquests that had been occurring monotonously for the previous several years. Italian forces were in Abyssinia; German, in the Rhineland; Japanese, in Manchuria; Dollfuss was apparently consolidating an Austrian "corporate state." The imminent fall of the Spanish Republic seemed perhaps sad but not very surprising. For those familiar with Spain, the uprising did not even appear very closely connected with the advance of fascism in Europe: military juntas had been overthrowing civil governments in that nation from time to time for over a century, and though the Spanish Falange called itself Fascist, it was only one and, at the beginning of the rising, far from the strongest of the several elements within the Insurgent forces. By the end of July, however, the conflict in Spain had become an international affair in which governments and individuals passionately took sides, and for over two years the Spanish Civil War was, in Stephen Spender's words, "a debate, both within and outside Spain, in which the three great political ideas of our time—Fascism, Communism, and Liberal-Socialism—were discussed and heard."[1]

[1] Stephen Spender, *World Within World*, p. 170.

This debate was not initiated by the Nationalist rising; it had been in progress almost since the end of World War I, but the events of the summer of 1936 dramatized and crystallized the issues as nothing had done before. Most of the writers to be considered in this study had been dealing with sociopolitical subject matter for several years when the Spanish War broke out. For them, the war provided a focus for their ideas, an intensification of their fervor to propagate these ideas, and a much enlarged audience, newly ready to listen. The literary leftists, in particular, found themselves transformed from a small and rather special coterie to spokesmen for a large segment of British public opinion.

Spain was to remain a center of intense concern for Britons of all classes and political persuasions for two years. Even after the victory of the Franco forces was clearly assured and developments in central Europe had drawn international attention to another threatened republic, Czechoslovakia, many members of that large and very motley group who were loosely called "anti-fascist" continued to look to the Spanish Loyalists as symbols of the forces of light in valiant and losing combat against the encroaching darkness.

Two factors were chiefly responsible for the focussing of world attention upon Spain: the genuine, though short-lived, social revolution precipitated in Republican territory by the revolt raised the specter—or hope, depending on the observer's point of view—of communism; and the hardly disguised assistance of Mussolini and Hitler to the Insurgents raised the threat—or hope—of fascism. Outsiders tended to grant their sympathy and assistance on the basis of whether they considered fascism or communism the greater threat to their own countries, and the rather small group who chose not to take sides based their neutrality on the belief that there was little to be preferred in either of the two contending forms of totalitarianism.[2]

The triumph of the Franco forces in Spain has been generally ascribed to the combination of foreign intervention by Germany and Italy and the Non-Intervention policy followed by Great Britain, France, and the United States. German and Italian assistance to the Nationalist insurgents proved to be superior to that which Russia was able or willing to give the Republic. But probably of equal im-

[2] The conflict in Spain was not so easily defined. For an attempt at sharper definition of the issues of the war, see Appendix.

portance to the outcome of the war was the failure of other major powers to intervene, and it was the British government that was chiefly responsible for this policy. Although Non-Intervention was first proposed by the Popular Front Premier Léon Blum, he may well have assumed, as many Labour party people in Britain did at the time, that it would not preclude purchases by the Spanish government of arms for its own defense. What Non-Intervention meant to the British government was that all signatories to the pact were forbidden to supply war materials to either side. This policy was revealed as a dismal joke almost from the beginning of the war, but the British government resolutely maintained the farce throughout the war and were able to insist that the French do the same. However Republican the sympathies of the Popular Front, France was far too apprehensive about Germany to risk a breach with England, and her leaders were convinced that a deep embroilment with the Spanish Republic would entail just this. It was also possible for the British, through the American ambassador, Joseph Kennedy, to dissuade the United States government from yielding to popular pressures to end the embargo.

There were important and influential voices in Britain that actually favored the Insurgents, but the controlling motive in the government was not to help either side but simply to prevent, at all costs, the development of a general war out of the Civil War. To this end, the policy-makers were willing to close their eyes to the flagrant breaches of the Non-Intervention Pact and even to bear with amazingly good grace the attacks on British shipping which were incidental to the Nationalist blockade of Republican ports.[3] The Opposition, having decided in October, 1936, that Non-Intervention was serving merely to aid the Insurgents, supported the Republic actively, although they never took the kind of nonconstitutional action, such as organizing a trade-union boycott on Nationalist trade, which some members advised.[4] There was passionate debate in and out of Parliament on the wisdom of Non-Intervention, and not all of the criticism was from the Left; there were solid Tories who con-

[3] Hugh Thomas describes a Low cartoon of June 16, 1938, in which Colonel Blimp puffs, "Gad sir, it is time we told Franco that if he sinks another 100 British ships, we shall retire from the Mediterranean altogether" (*The Spanish Civil War*, p. 504 n).

[4] Thomas, *Spanish Civil War*, p. 584 n.

sidered shamefully unEnglish their leaders' tame submission to a blockade and their evident unwillingness to offend Germany and Italy. Nevertheless, the government remained firm, and their policy achieved its intended purpose. Hugh Thomas, however, points out that, while Non-Intervention very likely did delay the outbreak of general war,

> this delay, like Munich, was undoubtedly caused by a certain craven indolence on the part of the British Government which did not profit them at all. A general war which broke out over Spain in 1936, 1937, or 1938 would have been fought in circumstances more favourable for the Western democracies than that which came in 1939 over Poland. One alternative to the 'farce of non-intervention,' was, of course (as it was to Munich, to the re-occupation of the Rhineland and to German re-armament), to stand firm and denounce the breach of the agreements. This policy had at least a possibility of upsetting the dictator without a war being needed. But this firmness did not exist.[5]

Although many of their efforts were simply humanitarian, raising funds and collecting supplies to help the innocent victims of the war or to provide medical services, the British supporters of the Republic were primarily concerned with effecting a change in official policy which would permit military assistance to the Loyalists, and Non-Intervention was their major target. They were able to marshall impressive forces for the cause. With all respect for the propaganda skills of the Republican apologists, it must be said that their work was made easier by a wave of spontaneous popular indignation over the Franco uprising, markedly greater than any inspired by the Japanese invasion of Manchuria, the Italian attack on Abyssinia, or Hitler's repressions in Germany. Arthur Koestler suggests that this feeling arose not only because Spain was so near at hand and the atrocities of the war were so public and so widely reported but also because of an awakening of historic memories with the appearance of Moorish troops and the spectacle of "a mercenary horde, the Foreign Legionaries of the Tercio, who killed, raped, and plundered in the name of a Holy Crusade, while the air smelt of incense and burning flesh. Spain caused the last twitch of Europe's dying conscience."[6]

Looking back on his own part as a Comintern agent rallying for-

[5] *Ibid.*, p. 615.

[6] Arthur Koestler, *The Invisible Writing*, p. 326.

eign support for the Republic, Koestler says, "We know now that our truth was a half-truth, our fight a battle in the mist, and that those who suffered and died in the war were pawns in a complicated game between the two totalitarian pretenders for world domination,"[7] but there was little of this recognition among the supporters of either side at the time. Claud Cockburn, who reported from Spain for the London *Daily Worker,* writes admiringly of the privately "cynical or just tough" attitude which the Russian publicist Mikhail Koltzov revealed when not speaking for publication,[8] but lack of passionate conviction was the last charge that could be made against the vast majority of those who became involved in the war, either in Spain or abroad.

The Spanish Civil War accelerated the leftward movement of many British intellectuals who had been leaning increasingly in that direction since 1931.[9] For the British Left—and this group included the most moderate Fabians, "Christian Socialists," and various dissenting Marxists as well as Communists—the fight for the Spanish Republic represented a positive hope, not merely a courageous resistance to reactionary aggression. Philip Toynbee, who was an undergraduate Communist at Oxford in 1936, later wrote:

> It is easy to see now that the Spanish Civil War was, from the very beginning, the tragic, drawn-out death agony of a political epoch. Once the Generals had made their revolt, they would eventually win it: once they had won it, a world war would be fought *against* fascist aggression, but not *for* anything we had hoped for in 1936. And even at the time there was some sense that this was the last chance for the politics of Attempting the Good, as opposed to the subsequent politics of Avoiding the Worse. The political optimists were never more united in England, or more enthusiastic.[10]

But pro-Loyalists in Britain were by no means all from the Left. Many of the committees and organizations that proliferated in England, such as the Committee for War Relief for Republican Spain, the Spanish Milk Fund, the Committee of Inquiry into Foreign In-

[7] *Ibid.*, p. 325.
[8] Claud Cockburn, *In Time of Trouble: An Autobiography*, p. 245.
[9] See Chapter III.
[10] Philip Toynbee, *Friends Apart: A Memoir of Esmond Romilly and Jasper Ridley in the Thirties*, p. 90.

tervention in the Spanish War, the Friends of Spain, and the Spanish Medical Aid Committees, had been created and were largely controlled by Communists under the direction of Willy Münzenberg, head of the West European Agitprop, of whom Koestler wrote, "Willy produced Committees as a conjurer produces rabbits out of a hat; his genius consisted in a unique combination of the conjurer's wiles with the crusader's dedication."[11] But the governing boards and sponsors of these organizations, as well as those who worked for them and financed them, were drawn from eminent people of the Center and even the Right, as well as from the Left. Eleanor Rathbone, an Independent M.P., the Liberals Richard Acland, Wilfred Roberts, and Sir Walter Layton, and the Conservatives Richard Boothby and Katherine, Duchess of Atholl (who, naturally enough, early acquired the sobriquet "the Red Duchess")[12] were all active and vocal in the Republican cause.[13]

It is fruitless to speculate on whether these moderates and conservatives were "duped" by the Communists. They were certainly not unaware that many of their allies were Party members; far from concealing membership in the Communist Party during the thirties, a fair number of people, like John Strachey, called themselves Communists when they actually were not members.[14] In this sense, no one was deceived. Perhaps some of the non-Communists would have cooperated less enthusiastically with the Communists if they had been better informed on the workings of communism in action, in Russia or in Spain; but perhaps they would have considered such information of doubtful relevance to the Spanish War in any case. They did not desire, and would no doubt have strenuously resisted, social revolution of the sort their leftist friends, Communist and non-

[11] Koestler, *Invisible Writing*, p. 314. Münzenberg, who is credited with much of the success of Communist propaganda in the thirties, had broken with the Comintern by 1938 and was murdered in France in 1941, probably, says Koestler, by Stalinist agents.

[12] The Duchess ruined her political career by her efforts on behalf of the Loyalists. In 1938 she resigned her Conservative seat in protest against Non-Intervention and stood for Parliament as an Independent Conservative. She lost (Thomas, *Spanish Civil War*, p. 393).

[13] Neal Wood, *Communism and British Intellectuals*, p. 54.

[14] There were also, of course, people who did conceal their Party membership for tactical reasons. The Nobel Laureate Professor J. B. S. Haldane and his wife were among these (Thomas, *Spanish Civil War*, p. 389).

Communist, hoped for, but they were strongly opposed to fascism, and they saw the Nationalist Movimiento as Fascist. If, in supporting the Spanish Republic, they were in fact aiding the cause of Stalin, so was Stalin aiding the cause of antifascism. In 1936–1939, as perhaps at other times, it was easier to achieve unity against something than for something, and in the struggle against Hitler and Mussolini, the enemies of fascism were not disposed to quibble over details that seemed at the time to be of secondary importance. As Koestler had remarked, "It seems almost impossible to mobilize public emotions for an ideological two-front war."[15]

Britain's "nearest equivalent of a popular front"[16] was the Left Book Club, founded early in 1936 by the publisher Victor Gollancz, a former Liberal turned Christian Socialist working within the Labour party. Early in the thirties there had been a great upsurge of interest in the possibility of reconciling Christianity and socialism.[17] Among the more articulate of those to whom socialism meant Christianity in action was Conrad Noel, the "Red Vicar" of Thaxted, who preached the social gospel of a "militant revolutionist" Christ and flew the red flag and the Sinn Fein banner next to the Cross of St. George. Also active was the Cambridge biochemist Dr. Joseph Needham, who declared that the professed atheism of Communists really embodied a "sense of the holy" and that Christians should work for a socialist kingdom based on true brotherhood and the rule of man. Dr. John Lewis described the "new Christ" as "an insurgent proletariat, the uprisen people of God," and J. Middleton Murry deplored Stalinism but hoped for a "human" British communism, an amalgam of Marxism and the social gospel. John MacMurray of the University of London also disliked Russian Communism but considered socialism an offspring of Christianity which offered great hope for the future.[18] Perhaps the most flamboyant of the Christian Socialists was Hewlett Johnson, the "Red Dean" of Canterbury. Johnson differed from his fellows in that, far from sharing their reservations about Stalinism, he quickly developed into as enthusiastic a

[15] Koestler, *Invisible Writing*, p. 365.

[16] Wood, *Communism and British Intellectuals*, p. 61. See also Stuart Samuels, "The Left Book Club," *Journal of Contemporary History*, I, No. 2 (1966), 65–86.

[17] See John Lewis, *Christianity and the Social Revolution.*

[18] Wood, *Communism and British Intellectuals*, pp. 66–69.

devotee of the Party line as any Communist Party member and did not noticeably waver during the years that held disillusion for so many other leftists.

Gollancz personally embodied many of the conflicts that plagued the British Left and that will be considered in more detail in Chapter III. His purpose in founding the Left Book Club was, as stated in the prospectus, "to help in the terribly urgent struggle *for* world peace and *against* Fascism, by giving, to all who are willing to take part in that struggle, such knowledge as will immensely increase their efficiency."[19] Convinced that while communism is "a *pessima corruptio optimi* . . . an (abominable) Christian heresy, Nazi-Fascism is a glorification of evil," he decided that a popular front could act to prevent fascism and war, which he tended to equate. He kept "a semi-assumption at the back of my mind, that, if prevention didn't 'come off', then we must fight," but he refused quite to face the fact that resistance to fascism could mean war and must certainly mean rearmament. "The best that could be said of it," he later wrote of this mental confusion, "is that it wasn't an ignoble muddle."[20]

The conflict of pacifism and antifascism was present in many non-Communist leftists (the Communists had a profound scorn for pacifists, though they were willing to use them when necessary); it was in 1937 that the Oxford Union resolved not to fight for King and Country; and this conflict helps explain the unwillingness of the Labour party, for instance, to take as strong steps against Non-Intervention as it might have done. Gollancz himself was unable to share the militancy of some of his friends:

> I supported the Republicans, of course: I tried to pump up enthusiasm—within myself, I mean—for the International Brigade: but my heart was cold. There was nothing in me, not a trace, of the "Thank God we can now have a smack at 'em" sort of feeling that elated so many antifascists in those days. I saw the dead and dying too vividly.[21]

If Gollancz's heart was cold, the general tone of the Left Book Club was not. His fellow editors, John Strachey and Harold Laski, were fiery enough in their advocacy of the Loyalist cause and in their warm sympathy with their Communist comrades. The Club's activ-

[19] Victor Gollancz, *More for Timothy: Vol. II of an Autobiography*, p. 356.
[20] *Ibid.*, p. 355.
[21] *Ibid.*, p. 357.

ities began with the choice of a book of the month, picked for its usefulness in the battle against war and fascism, and the monthly publication of a bulletin for members which was shortly rechristened *Left News*. But as the Club expanded its membership (there were some sixty thousand members in April, 1939) it also expanded its activities. There were twelve hundred study groups connected with the Club, not to mention rallies, meetings, lectures, weekend and vacation schools, and special professional sections for doctors, scientists, poets, and others. The Poets Group published its own magazine, *Poetry and the People*.[22] The Club and its concomitant activities reached a very broad segment of the British public and can be presumed to have had considerable influence on opinion. And from the outbreak of the Spanish War, the considerable resources of the Left Book Club were devoted very largely to promotion of the Republican cause.

The extent of Communist influence within the Club, as within many areas of British life at the time, is hard to assess. Strachey never missed an opportunity to affirm his Communist convictions, and Laski, though an early critic of Russian Communism, grew increasingly ambiguous in his statements on the relative value of parliamentary and revolutionary means for social change. Gollancz later wrote that he was "for fifteen months during the Spanish War as close to the Communists as one hair to another and . . . for every minute of those months I was billions of light years away from them—as I have been all my life."[23] The Scientists, Poets, and Writers Groups were all dominated by Communists, and many regular writers for *Left News* (Ivor Montagu and Edgell Rickword, for example) were Communists. Yet less than half the book selections were by Communists, and the proportion of Communists in the membership was estimated in 1940 as about one-sixth.[24] Since stated Communist policy during the Popular Front period was virtually indistinguishable from general liberal opinion, it is hard to find specific instances of a Communist line being followed, and, as we shall see later, broad agreement with Communist policies did not preclude severe criticism of Russian policies by British leftists.[25]

[22] Wood, *Communism and British Intellectuals*, p. 62.

[23] Gollancz, *More for Timothy*, p. 357.

[24] Wood, *Communism and British Intellectuals*, p. 63.

[25] Severe difference of opinion within the Club did not come until after

Gollancz has written in retrospect that he feels the Club sometimes produced more propaganda than education, generally through sins of omission in regard to publishing views or information that conflicted with Popular Front dogmata: its attitude toward truths of this sort he characterizes by applying Clough's lines, "Thou shalt not kill, but needst not strive/ Officiously to keep alive." He concludes, however, that with all its failings and excesses, the Club did perform a real service in informing the British public: "*Within the limits of the non-pacifist view*, the Left Book Club—Popular Front tactic was the only possible one. If support had been strong enough it would probably have prevented the war: nothing else could have done so. And it very nearly *was* strong enough."[26] Although a complete pacifist since the nineteen-fifties, Gollancz is convinced that pacifist tactics could not have stopped Hitler under the circumstances then obtaining.

"Very nearly" is the operative phrase, for both the Spanish War and World War II. Proponents of the Republic achieved a great deal of popular support, if we can judge by public opinion polls. In a January, 1937, poll asking whether the Nationalist government at Burgos should be recognized as the legal government of Spain, 86 per cent of those polled said no; in two polls taken during 1938, although 36 per cent refused to express a preference, there were 57 per cent declaring for the Loyalists as against only 7 per cent for the Nationalists; and even at the beginning of 1939, when a Franco victory was almost certain, 72 per cent called themselves pro-Republican, compared with 19 per cent neutral and 9 per cent pro-Nationalist.[27] Of Britons who felt strongly enough about the war to fight in it, Hugh Thomas was able to discover "not more than a dozen" who fought for Franco, of whom most were "at least half Irish" (he dis-

---

the Spanish War was over. Gollancz and Laski supported the war against the Axis from the beginning, but Strachey managed to keep his faith in Russia through the Nazi-Soviet Pact and followed the new Communist "peace" line until the invasion of the Low Countries. The Club continued through the war and was dissolved in 1945, when the Labour party election victory made it, in Gollancz's view, no longer necessary (Wood, *Communism and British Intellectuals*, p. 63).

[26] Gollancz, *More for Timothy*, p. 357.

[27] Thomas, *Spanish Civil War*, p. 574, citing an unpublished Ph.D. dissertation, "The Spanish Civil War," by H. J. Parry of the University of California.

counted the O'Duffy crusaders).[28] The British contingent of the International Brigades (which included a large number of Scots and Irish) totaled 2,762, of whom 1,762 were wounded and 543 killed; of these, not more than half were Communists.[29] There were also an uncertain number of British subjects who served, like George Orwell, in forces other than the Brigades, and a great many who performed noncombatant services, from radio broadcasting in Spain (like David Gascoyne) to medical work, often under combat conditions (like Auden, Wogan Philips, and Julian Bell). And of course there were others who also went to Spain but who kept well behind the lines and confined themselves largely to acquiring conversational ammunition for use on their return to England. The British pro-Loyalists were able to do much for the Republic in the way of nonmilitary aid such as food, clothing, medical assistance, even some funds for disabled International veterans or their widows and orphans. Those who fought in Spain earned much honor for their courage and devotion, and a remarkable number of the finest minds in Britain gave of their best talents in rallying public support; but the great effort failed in its major objective of changing the Non-Intervention policy.

From the distance of thirty years it seems at first surprising that the Republican cause, which most historians now agree was the cause of Western democracy as well[30] and which had such a dazzling array of proponents and such wide popularity, not only in England but in France and the United States, should have failed to win the support of the British government and, since they followed the British lead, the other democracies. But the impression of overwhelming intellectual and popular Republican sentiment in England (as elsewhere) is misleading; the pro-Loyalists as a group wrote the best books and poems about Spain, and their eminence then and later makes it easy to overestimate the extent of their influence during the

[28] Thomas, *Spanish Civil War,* p. 635. On the O'Duffy crusade, see Appendix.

[29] Wood, *Communism and British Intellectuals*, p. 56.

[30] Claude Bowers, U. S. Ambassador to Spain and a fervent pro-Republican, had the dubious satisfaction on his return to Washington at the end of the Spanish War of being told by President Roosevelt that the embargo policy Bowers had fought so hard did appear to have been wrong after all. Bowers' *My Mission to Spain* is a useful account of the war from the point of view of a frustrated diplomat.

war. The degree of leftist domination within the intelligentsia during the so-called Red Decade has been heavily overstated,[31] and even though a majority of Britons may have considered themselves pro-Republican, there is a vast difference between entertaining a preference for one side over another in a foreign war and being willing to risk general war on its behalf. There is every indication that government reluctance to offend the Fascist powers was, if not precisely approved, at least accepted as prudent by a great many Englishmen who were at the same time generous contributors to Spanish Medical Aid and similar organizations.

Despite the opposing claims of pro-Nationalist Englishmen, the media of public opinion in Britain were not monopolized by Loyalist apologists. The *News Chronicle, Daily Herald, Manchester Guardian, Daily Express* and *Daily Mirror* were Republican in their sympathies, but the *Morning Post, Daily Mail, Daily Sketch,* and *Observer* were pro-Nationalist, and the *Times* and the *Daily Telegraph,* which attempted neutrality, supported Non-Intervention.[32] A Right Book Club was founded to counter the Left Book Club, and Franco did not lack for fervent supporters. On the extreme Right, the British Union of Fascists was no mass movement, but it numbered over twenty thousand members within two years of its founding in 1932, a figure the British Communist Party was not to reach and pass until during and immediately after World War II;[33] and its members were always available to hold rallies or attempt to break up popular front meetings. However, most British pro-Nationalists were no more Fascists than the pro-Loyalists were Communists. By the kind of semantic simplification customary in political debate, the supporters of Franco and of the Republic called their opposite numbers "Reds" and "Fascists" with great freedom and rare accuracy. Much of the time terminology was the surest clue to the political position of writers of polemics, and of supposedly

[31] On the staff of the *New Statesman and Nation*, the type of "left-wing intellectual" journal, David Garnett and Raymond Mortimer were anti-Fascist but hardly leftists, as were their colleagues Brian Howard, Cyril Connolly, and V. S. Pritchett; and W. J. Turner and Vita Sackville-West listed themselves as "neutral" on the Spanish War (Wood, *Communism and British Intellectuals*, pp. 70–71).

[32] Thomas, *Spanish Civil War*, p. 222.

[33] Wood, *Communism and British Intellectuals*, p. 69.

objective reportage as well. "Loyalists" and "Republicans," "Nationalists" and "Insurgents" were the terms generally used by those who were trying not to take sides, but passions ran so high that some later writers do not use even these terms without a liberal sprinkling of inverted commas.

If the common denominator of British pro-Loyalists was antifascism, that of the pro-Nationalists was anticommunism. Virtually all of these latter were alarmed by the revolutionary rhetoric employed by some members of the Spanish government and by the frank and vocal identification of their cause with that of the Loyalists by Socialists and Communists in England and Europe. British Conservatives like R. A. B. Butler and Alan Lennox-Boyd may have felt considerable distaste for Hitler and Mussolini as national leaders, but they tended to accept the dictators' description of themselves as bulwarks against bolshevism and so were willing to see the Franco rising as a stern but necessary measure to save Spain from communism. During the first months of the war Winston Churchill could see no British strategic interest involved and, although no more sympathetic to fascism than the Opposition, was disturbed by the "revolutionary character" of the Republic; his counsel for England was "an absolutely rigid neutrality."[34] By the summer of 1938 he was sufficiently aroused by the Fascist intervention, and particularly by the attacks on British shipping, to shift his support to the Republic, but his influence within the Conservative Party was not then decisive.[35]

The two major themes of Nationalist propaganda were the threat of communism and the alleged suppression of religion by the Republic. There was more evidence for the second than for the first. The dominant leaders of Republican Spain were Catholic but anticlerical, and their efforts to secularize Spanish institutions admitted of antireligious interpretation;[36] the Marxists in Spain, however reformist, were still atheist in principle, and the Anarchists were fanatically, religiously antireligious. The widespread rioting of workers and peasants in the months before the revolt always involved church burnings and attacks on the clergy. Nationalist propagandists were guilty of

[34] Thomas, *Spanish Civil War*, p. 222.
[35] *Ibid.*, p. 531.
[36] See Appendix.

shameless distortion and exaggeration in their publicizing of these events, but the events were indisputable. Particularly for those unaware of the reasons behind this mass hatred of the Church,[37] they seemed to confirm the Insurgents' claim that the Spanish Republic was unable to suppress such violence and, indeed, condoned it as part of a conspiracy to make Spain an atheistic Marxist dictatorship.

Many of the conservative British pro-Nationalists were of the sort who have difficulty distinguishing between an extension of social services and the institution of a Communist state; for them, even the halting and hesitant social reforms attempted by the Republic were evidence of imminent revolution, and they tended to approve the revolt from the beginning. Others, who had taken no previous interest in Spanish affairs and were not particularly concerned about politics anyway, were appalled by the reports of real social revolution and mob violence in the first weeks of the war. The collectivization of lands and expropriation of industries which thrilled British leftists with visions of a new and better world had precisely the opposite effect on British conservatives.

Atrocities on both sides were reported in lurid and sometimes fraudulent detail in the press, complete with genuine and faked photographs, and English readers tended to react according to their political predispositions: one side's atrocity was the other's necessary severity in self-defense or justified reprisal. Many Republican apologists contrasted the spontaneous violence of a long-oppressed people against their persecutors with the cold-blooded murder by foreign mercenaries of men and women guilty of nothing worse than belonging to a trade union. Pro-Nationalists, on the other hand, could cite cases of Spaniards shot for no apparent reason beyond the good quality of their clothes, and at least some of them seem to have felt there was a qualitative difference between mass murder of possibly revolutionary workers and peasants, and mass murder of priests, nuns, and aristocrats. They were also under the impression, fostered by Nationalist propaganda, that the "Reds" were enemies not only of Christianity but of all Western civilization and that they were systematically destroying all works of art that came their way. Actually, although much valuable Church art went up in flames in the conscientious Anarchist efforts to *écraser l'Infame*, the Republican offi-

[37] Thomas, *Spanish Civil War*, p. 384.

cials took great trouble and considerable risk to preserve and protect the art works they were able to hide from both Anarchist burnings and Insurgent bombardment.

Sir Arnold Lunn, previously best known as an expert on skiing and an Olympic Games official, was one of the more fervid and energetic supporters of the Nationalist cause, lecturing and debating on its behalf in the United States as well as in England. Like many others on his side, he was a Catholic, and he considered religion the main issue of the Spanish War. He denied any sympathy for fascism, but he felt the defense of Christianity justified seeking help where it was to be had, even from Hitler, although the Nazis were already persecuting Catholics in Germany. In Lunn's view, the question of democracy versus dictatorship did not exist, since the Communists had already destroyed Spanish democracy before the revolt began, and the issue was simply whether Spain was to have a Communist dictatorship that would throttle religion or a dictatorship in which the Church could survive and wield influence. Franco's alliance with the Fascist dictators and the Spanish Church's approval of it were distasteful but necessary and proper.[38]

British pro-Nationalists were earnest but comparatively few, and the continuation of the Non-Intervention policy so useful to the Nationalists was probably due less to their efforts than to the confusion among the pro-Loyalists as to how far they really wanted the government to go toward risking war. It was also due in large part to the sizeable number of British who were genuinely neutral and consequently indifferent as to whether Non-Intervention favored one side over the other. People who took this position, if their motive was more than simple apathy, were likely to be those who believed the propaganda of both sides and saw no advantage in a choice between fascism and communism.

In the fall of 1937, the *Left Review* published the results of a poll of 148 British writers which indicates how the literary world split on

[38] Arnold Lunn, *Come What May: An Autobiography, passim.* Lunn's *Spanish Rehearsal* (1937) recounts his visits to Nationalist Spain as part of a general argument for the Nationalist cause. He does not write like a fanatic, and his rather curious views on the importance of the Communists in the Republic at the beginning of the revolt, like his somewhat easy acceptance of Nationalist versions of various dubious events, may be partly due to his apparently not knowing Spanish.

the Spanish question; few of the writers were content with one-word answers, and *Authors Take Sides* gives a useful cross section of opinion.[39] The leading questions posed at the end of a fiercely anti-Fascist open letter signed by Auden, Aragon, Neruda, Spender, Bergamin, and Heinrich Mann, among others, were: "Are you for, or against, the legal Government and the People of Republican Spain? Are you for, or against, Franco and Fascism?" Statistically, the Republic came out well ahead: there were 127 replies categorized as *For* it, 5 *Against*, and 16 *Neutral?* (the question mark is the *Left Review's*). According to the editors, all replies omitted for lack of space were in the *For* category. Separately printed on the inside front cover was one reply marked *Unclassified*: George Bernard Shaw explained his doubts over whether the Spanish Right or Left was more incompetent and noted that his generally pro-Left sympathies did not extend to the "British Party Parliament system and its continental imitations," but that the capitalist government of Britain was helping Franco by Non-Intervention: "meanwhile I shall not shout about it."

Among the respondents who answered *For* the Republic, the most concise was Samuel Beckett, whose reply reads: "UPTHEREPUBLIC!" A partial list of others in this group would include: Lascelles Abercrombie, George Barker, Kay Boyle, the foreign and political editors of the *News Chronicle* and the editor of the *Manchester Guardian*, George Buchanan, Cyril Connolly, A. E. Coppard, Havelock Ellis, Liam O'Flaherty, Ford Madox Ford, David Garnett, David Gascoyne, Geoffrey Gorer, Lancelot Hogben, Storm Jameson, C. E. M. Joad, Arthur Koestler, John Langdon-Davies, John and Rosamund Lehmann, Erik Linklater, Harold Laski, F. L. Lucas, Rose Macaulay, Louis MacNeice, Francis Meynell, Naomi Mitchison, Ivor Montagu, J. Middleton Murry, Sean O'Casey, Sylvia Pankhurst, V. S. Pritchett, D. N. Pritt, Herbert Read, Stephen Spender, Christina Stead, James Stephens, John Strachey, T. Sturge Moore, H. M. Tomlinson, Sylvia Townsend Warner, Rex Warner, Rebecca West, and

[39] *Authors Take Sides on the Spanish War*, unpaged. The instigator of this poll was one of the Republic's most ardent and loyal British supporters, Nancy Cunard. Some months later, the League of American Writers published a similar survey of American literary opinion, *Writers Take Sides* (Hugh D. Ford, *A Poet's War: British Poets and the Spanish Civil War*). A 1967 *Writers Take Sides* presents opinion on the Viet Nam war.

Leonard Woolf. Many took occasion in their replies to give reasons or qualifications. C. Day Lewis said antifascism was his duty as a writer and as a Communist Party member, and Hugh MacDiarmid, also affirming his Party membership, added that not only he but a majority of Scots were pro-Loyalist and that Scotland would itself be a socialist republic but for the London government, which was also to blame for Franco's successes. Robert Nichols, on the other hand, declared himself for the Republic insofar as it was non-Communist, and Geoffrey Grigson wrote that he was more against fascism than for the Republic. Ethel Mannin expressed her hopes for a triumph of the Anarcho-Syndicalists, and Aldous Huxley, after declaring for the Government "of course," added "especially the Anarchists,"[40] and concluded, "The choice now is between militarism and pacifism. To me, the necessity of pacifism seems absolutely clear." Helen Waddell, although answering *For,* took issue with the reference in the open letter to "unavenged" Fascist crimes: "That the signatories should still, in 1937, be speaking of vengeance is a nightmare: a return to Carthage, or Versailles."

The pacifism apparent in many of the *For* responses also accounted for the refusal of Ruby M. Ayres, Vera Brittain, and Derek Verschoyle to take sides; Miss Brittain affirmed her horror of fascism but felt that as an "uncompromising pacifist" she could not condone forceful resistance to it. Rhys Davies, Charles Morgan, and Vyvyan Holland, also in the *Neutral?* group, expressed equal hatred for all dictatorships and registered objections to the way the questions had

[40] The Spanish Anarchists fascinated and, despite or because of their dedication to violence, attracted foreigners. Cyril Connolly found their extreme individualism rather English, but most visitors saw in their mystical fanaticism, their insistence on personal dignity, and their total freedom from materialist considerations, the essence of Spain. Gerald Brenan quotes (*The Spanish Labyrinth,* p. 251) the English Socialist Edward Conze: "Whilst everywhere the workers' movement is bent on attaining comfort and security, the Spanish Anarchist lives for liberty, virtue, and dignity." When the Anarchists won a town, they did not expropriate the goods of the wealthy: they destroyed them as immoral, they abolished money, and they shot the wicked in a thoroughly righteous spirit. Thomas commented (*Spanish Civil War,* p. 179) that in the early weeks of the war, "if the Anarchists had not spent so much petrol driving future victims to beautiful places to die, and trying to burn churches to the ground," things might have been easier for their armed forces.

been put. More saltily, Sean O'Faolain wrote: "If you want to know, I do think Fascism is lousy. So is Communism, only more so. But there are other ideas in the world besides either of them—thank God (whom neither of you believe in)." He signed his reply, "Yours contemptuously." Although Ezra Pound was later openly to embrace Italian fascism, his answer in 1937 was suitably enough placed in the *Neutral?* category. He described Spain as "an emotional luxury to a gang of sap-headed dilettantes . . . too cowardly to think" and "too lazy" to study the basic problem, "usury," as practiced by the "Banque de France and the stank of England." H. G. Wells's reply was also somewhat sour: he said that he had been for the Republic until it was ruined by the Anarchists and the Franco rising, that the foreign intervention was to be expected and was largely due to the "stupid confusion" of Britain, and that "the real enemy of mankind is not the Fascist but the Ignorant Fool." And Norman Douglas, citing his contempt for humanity in general, excused himself from taking sides, adding, "To hell with sides . . . Everything that ends in 'ism is just b . . . s [*sic*], so far as I'm concerned." T. S. Eliot maintained a higher tone: his entire reply read, "While I am naturally sympathetic, I still feel that it is best that at least a few men of letters should remain isolated, and take no part in these collective activities."

Only five authors declared themselves *Against* the Republic. Edmund Blunden, disclaiming any special competence on Spanish affairs, stated his belief that the revolt was probably for the best and stated his objections to the account of recent German history as given in the open letter. Arthur Machen "beg[ged] to inform that he is, and always has been, entirely for General Franco." Brigadier-General Geoffrey Moss, who had served briefly with the Nationalists, dared the *Review* to print his statement that he had "never seen braver soldiers nor men more filled with high ideals" than in the Franco forces. Eleanor Smith praised Franco's humanitarianism and wrote that "the destruction of so many beautiful objects, and the massacre of so many innocent persons, makes one pity profoundly the ignorant red masses —subsidized by Russia—in Spain." Evelyn Waugh, like other neutrals and pro-Nationalists questioned, doubted the good faith of the writers of the open letter in their stress on the "legality" of the Republic, suggesting that the legality of Hitler's regime did not appear to commend it to them.

The results of the *Left Review* poll probably expressed rather accurately the proportion of writers supporting, to one degree or another, the two sides in the Spanish War. But many of these authors, and others not reached by the questionnaire, had much more to say on the subject than they were able to include in these answers, and it is these opinions, and the literary means employed to express them, that will be considered in further detail in the succeeding chapters.

Chapter II

ON THE RIGHT

The Spanish Nationalists never succeeded in eliciting anything like the enthusiastic sympathy in Great Britain which the Loyalists enjoyed. They managed to win without it, and largely because of British government policies; but since they strenuously sought popular support, it is of some interest to examine why they had so little success in these efforts. Much of the difficulty was no doubt inherent in the cause itself. Insofar as most elements on the Nationalist side were frankly, indeed proudly, counterrevolutionary, they were unlikely to win wide support during the thirties when the cry for a return to the status quo ante was simply without appeal for the great mass of people, who were discontented with the economic depression and widespread unemployment of the present but were deeply disillusioned with the recent past. Successful popular movements of the time were always those which promised a new and better order, as in Germany and Italy. The anticommunism that was very nearly the only attitude shared by all components of the Nationalist Movimiento was too negative in itself to command mass support, at least in the late thirties, although the class for which it was sufficient was influential out of all proportion to its numbers.

The only professedly "progressive" element in the Nationalist forces was the Falange, which was small and relatively insignificant at the outset of the war, although it grew rapidly in numbers and power as Italian and German intervention increased and as the Nationalist generals sought a formula for gaining popular approval in the territories they conquered. The Falange, frankly modeled on the German and Italian Fascist movements, did offer a New Order and, as Brenan noted,[1] proposed more sweeping social changes than did the ever-more-moderate Republic. Like the other forms of fascism, however, it limited its international attractiveness by its very nationalism. Worse, by 1937 the aggressive and oppressive behavior of the major Fascist nations had so far alienated public opinion in the Western democracies that their association with the Nationalist cause did it more harm than good.

Possibly the greatest number of sympathizers with the Nationalists was made up of those who accepted their claim to be defenders of religion against atheist barbarism. The attacks on churches and the clergy before and, most intensively, immediately after the generals' rising, were bad enough in themselves, and Nationalist propaganda assiduously magnified their number and ferocity. Particularly Roman Catholics, but others as well, were horrified and incensed, and a good many, like Sir Arnold Lunn, found it possible to overlook all the other factors in the Spanish War and to see Franco as preeminently a defender of Christian civilization forced by the exigencies of war to employ Fascist support in a cause that was really beyond politics. Yet there were neutrals and even pro-Republicans among Catholics from the beginning, and at least some who supported the revolt at its start defected as the war progressed. The loyalty to the Republic of the devoutly Catholic and conservative Basques was as damaging to the simple "holy war" view of the conflict as it was to the basic Nationalist assumption that the Republic was a thinly disguised Soviet satellite; and the execution of Basque priests by Nationalist forces rather tarnished the image of Franco as defender of the faith. The growing publicity of Hitler's persecution of German Catholics increasingly affected his acceptability as an ally in the cause of freedom of religion. As the war went on, fewer people outside of Spain appear to have continued to look upon the Movimiento as a positive good, and even the ranks of those who con-

[1] Gerald Brenan, *The Spanish Labyrinth*, p. 316.

sidered it a lesser evil diminished.[2] As with disillusioned pro-Loyalists, withdrawing support from one side did not necessarily entail shifting it to the other, and it is probably safe to say that there were many more people genuinely neutral about the Spanish War in 1939 than there had been in 1936.

Whether or not the Nationalist cause had as much to recommend it as the Loyalist in the first place, there is little disagreement that its propaganda was markedly inferior. While the Republic went out of its way to win the good will of all foreign visitors and particularly of journalists, the Nationalists did their best to exclude from the start or to expel any who were not clearly and emphatically sympathetic to them. Consequently, while the Republic profited by the generally favorable accounts of many foreigners who arrived in Spain uncommitted and were allowed to be sufficiently critical to seem objective, the journalistic reports that were allowed out of Nationalist Spain were so unrelievedly enthusiastic as to inspire considerable skepticism. Works like H. G. Cardozo's *The March of a Nation* and Nigel Tangye's *Red, White and Spain* were received very doubtfully by reviewers who apparently had no pro-Republican bias, while Franz Borkenau's pro-Republican but highly critical *Spanish Cockpit* was accepted with marked respect by reviewers who clearly did not share his sympathies. The broadcasts of the famous Nationalist "Radio General" Queipo de Llano were so excessive in their anti-Semitism that they probably alienated more Englishmen than they

[2] Official Catholic publications in England maintained their support of Franco until the end, and so did most in the United States, with the exception of *Commonweal*, which moved to a neutral position in 1938 at the cost of about a fourth of its subscribers and fierce attacks by the rest of the Catholic press, led by the Jesuit *America*. The anarchistically inclined *Catholic Worker*, not surprisingly, had supported the Republic from the start (Allen Guttmann, *The Wound in the Heart: America and the Spanish Civil War*, pp. 48–50). According to Hugh Thomas (*The Spanish Civil War*, p. 451), a poll of American Catholics showed them six to four in favor of the Republic. In France, the hierarchy supported the Nationalists, but eminent French Catholic literary men were split: Paul Claudel and Charles Maurras were strongly pro-Franco; but François Mauriac wrote on behalf of the Republic, Jacques Maritain defended the Republican Basque priests and asked for neutrality on the part of the Church, and Georges Bernanos's *Les Grands Cimetières sous la Lune*, a horrified protest against Church-supported atrocities in Majorca, did much to diminish French Catholic enthusiasm for the Nationalists (*ibid.*, p. 450).

persuaded, anti-Semitism being a line of argument that never gained wide acceptance in Britain.

The Nationalists of course received the full support of the British Union of Fascists, but this may not have helped them much, since the aping of Continental Fascist uniforms and behavior by Mosley's group impressed many potential sympathizers among conservative Englishmen as tasteless at best. More valuable was the support provided by the editorials, and occasionally by the news columns,[3] of such Conservative newspapers as the *Daily Mail*,[4] the *Morning Post*, the *Daily Sketch*, and the *Observer*. J. L. Garvin of the *Observer* was a dean of pro-Nationalist publicists. The dominant themes in the pro-Nationalist press were the antireligious and revolutionary nature of the Republic and its supposed domination by Russia; in this press "Red" was the customary term applied to all Spanish Republicans. The fact that even the mildest republican or anticlerical elements in Spain had long been referred to as *rojos* (reds) probably helped confuse foreigners. The Nationalists were seen as patriots and gentlemen fighting to save Spain, and perhaps Europe, from an encroaching Red tide. The British who could be expected to respond most enthusiastically to such an appeal were those who were generally pleased with things as they were, or at least doubtful whether change would be for the better. Such conservatives and traditionalists were more likely to be embarrassed than inflamed by extremist propaganda of the Fascist variety, but the Nationalist involvement with fascism nevertheless seemed to them much easier to stomach than the Republican involvement with communism. Since for many of them even the British Labour party seemed dangerously radical, the Nationalist picture of the Spanish Republic as a Moscow puppet was easy to credit.

Those in Britain who sympathized with the Nationalists were perhaps less vocal than the pro-Loyalists, for a reason the Nationalists can hardly have regretted—the early and continuing military successes of the Franco forces. As the pro-Loyalists saw their side fighting one desperate holding action after another, their fervor increased, and as it became clearer that the policies of the British government

[3] British newspapers tended to choose either Loyalist or Nationalist news sources, seldom both; since opposing versions of any given event differed so widely, the effects of such choices were apparent.

[4] Cardozo and Tangye were *Daily Mail* correspondents.

were working to the Nationalist advantage, the pro-Loyalists clamored the louder for changes. The really enthusiastic pro-Nationalists were not satisfied that government policy was on their side, or at least enough on their side; they were angered by what they considered the Communist ability to make the worse appear the better cause, and they worked hard to correct what they considered wide public misunderstanding of the Spanish War. But for those whose sympathy for the Nationalists was only moderate or who saw them as a lesser evil, things seemed to be going well enough, and they felt no great impulse to go into verbal combat.

The ardent pro-Nationalists who did join battle included such eminent Catholic publicists as Sir Arnold Lunn and the historian Arthur Bryant, who used his weekly column in the *Illustrated London News* to try to clarify the issues as he saw them. Also vigorous in his support was the historian Douglas Jerrold, who took public pride in his own part in launching the generals' revolt: he had helped arrange Franco's secret flight by chartered British plane from the Canaries to Morocco on the eve of the rising.[5] Unlike Lunn, who felt it necessary repeatedly to separate his support for Franco from his distaste for fascism as an ideology, Jerrold had praise for British fascism as a reaction of the "unorganized majority" against the "dictatorship" of the British political system. He also went considerably beyond Lunn's admiration of Franco's gentlemanly piety, suspecting that the General might be, indeed, a saint.

Major literary figures who might have been expected to lend their support to the Nationalist cause proved disappointing.[6] T. S. Eliot's by now famous attachment to tradition, royalism, and catholicism (although of the English variety) might have qualified him as a spokesman for the Spanish party that professed the same attachments, but he chose instead, in his reply to the *Left Review* letter, "to remain isolated, and take no part in these collective activities." In context, his expression of "sympathy" might even have applied to the Republican cause, but his other public expressions of opinion during the period indicate a nearly equal distaste for both parties.

In his "Commentary" in the *Criterion* between 1936 and 1939, Eliot

[5] Douglas Jerrold, *Georgian Adventure*, p. 371.

[6] John Harrison's *The Reactionaries* is a recent study of the political ideas of some of the most eminent modern writers: Eliot, Yeats, Pound, Wyndham Lewis, and D. H. Lawrence.

several times deplores the fanatical over-statements on both sides and the lack of objectivity in the press, which he feels operates more to confuse and oversimplify than to clarify the issues. The "real issue of our time," he says, "is between those who believe only in values realizable in time and on earth, and those who believe also in values realized only out of time," but he does not identify the two groups explicitly.[7] Neither of the contesting Spanish camps seems to him a desirable victor, since the very process of winning will assure that it is the secular—not the spiritual—Right, or the Communist—not the humanitarian—Left which will hold power at the end of the war. Therefore, since British interests are not, in his view, involved, there is no point in taking sides, and Non-Intervention is the best policy.[8]

Eliot applauds Jacques Maritain's argument against the Nationalists' effort to picture the Spanish conflict as a "holy war," but he notes that Britain is full of "irresponsible 'anti-fascists'" who seem equally persuaded of the "holiness" of their cause.[9] He takes occasion to criticize the failure of Aldous Huxley, "whose weakness is that he is neither a materialist nor a Christian," to give due weight to the economic causes of war in his arguments for pacifism;[10] and he finds Day Lewis, under the "hypnosis" of the "bogey of fascism," sharing the Popular Front "delusion." He is scornful of the "professed 'realists,' who so far surrender principles as to join in a Popular Front which is meaningless unless it is an extreme Left Front."[11] In his "Last Words" for the final issue of *Criterion*, he justifies his comments on political matters as reflecting his concern over the dangerous lack of "any vital political philosophy, either explicit or implicit," in contemporary English thought and explains that if he has written too much about communism in the past six years it is because the English variety of fascism is of such slight intellectual interest, owing perhaps to its inability to graft itself upon the root of British Toryism as communism so easily grows from "the Liberal root."[12]

Eliot's brief comments on politics during this period show that he was not entirely "isolated," but his impartial criticism of both sides

[7] *Criterion*, XVI, No. 62 (October 1936), 68.
[8] *Criterion*, XVI, No. 63 (January 1937), 289–293.
[9] *Criterion*, XVIII, No. 70 (October 1938), 58–62.
[10] *Criterion*, XVI, No. 64 (April 1937), 473.
[11] *Ibid.*, p. 474.
[12] *Criterion*, XVIII, No. 71 (January 1939), 272.

is consistent with his stated refusal to take part in "these collective activities." If, as seems likely, Franco's Spain came closer than Negrín's to Eliot's idea of a Christian society, he did not publicly say so.

If the Spanish War had begun a few years earlier, the Nationalist cause might have received support from W. B. Yeats. When the Army Comrades Association, popularly known as the Blue Shirts, was formed in April of 1933 as a kind of "National Guard" to give "disciplined service to the country," Yeats was among what Joseph Hone calls "the more conservative and orderly sections of the Irish population" who saw in this home-grown Fascist movement hope for an end to the ignorance, fanaticism, and demagoguery of Irish democracy.[13] What Yeats desired was

> a government which would seek unity of culture not less than economic unity, welding for the purpose museum, school and learned institution. The Government and party which should undertake this work would need marching men. Force would be required (the logic of fanaticism, whether in a woman or a movement being drawn from a premise protected by ignorance and therefore irrefutable), and it would promise not this or that measure but a way of life, a discipline.[14]

In 1933 Yeats invited the Blue Shirt leader General O'Duffy to his house and promised him some "marching songs." As first written, these "Three Songs to the Same Tune" were eminently suited to the purpose, but the poet's enthusiasm for the Blue Shirts fast subsided as they gave increasing evidence of ignorance, fanaticism, and demagoguery at least equal to those of the other Irish parties. In the same 1935 volume that contains the marching songs in their first version, Yeats categorized O'Duffy with De Valera and Cosgrave as sharing in the "lie/ Bred out of the contagion of the throng," in contrast to Parnell: "Their school a throng, his master solitude."[15] He was shortly to rewrite the songs, "increasing their fantasy, their extravagance, so that no party could sing them."[16]

Most of the changes in the original version of the songs are in the

[13] Joseph Hone, *W. B. Yeats 1865–1939*, p. 466.

[14] *Ibid.*, quoting Yeats's comments on the three marching songs.

[15] "At Parnell's Funeral," *A Full Moon in August* (1935), in *Collected Poems of W. B. Yeats* (Definitive Edition, with the Author's Final Revisions), pp. 275–276.

[16] Hone, *W. B. Yeats*, p. 467.

refrains. For example, in the song beginning "Grandfather sang it under the gallows," the verses are unchanged, but the militant refrain,

> *Those fanatics all that we do would undo;*
> *Down the fanatic, down the clown;*
> *Down, down, hammer them down,*
> *Down to the tune of O'Donnell Abu.*

has been replaced with the "fantastic"

> *Robbers had taken his old tambourine,*
> *But he took down the moon*
> *And rattled out a tune;*
> *Robbers had taken his old tambourine.*

The song beginning "Justify all those renowned generations" becomes "Remember all those renowned generations," and the gentler verb is used throughout, although the verses are otherwise unchanged. Here too the refrain is not revised but rewritten, "*'Drown all the dogs,' said the fierce young woman*" giving place to the melancholy

> *Be still, be still, what can be said?*
> *My father sang that song,*
> *But time amends all wrong,*
> *And all that's finished, let it fade.*

The third song, "The soldier takes pride in saluting his Captain," most clearly extols the virtues of a state in which the populace proudly serves its natural leaders, and the rather extensive revisions in the verses leave the sense as it was in the original, but the tune is different. The earlier version is thoroughly appropriate for a Fascist marching song:

> When nations are empty up there at the top,
> When order has weakened or faction is strong,
> Time for us all to pick out a good tune,
> Take to the roads and go marching along.
>
> . . . .
>
> O marching wind, O a blast of the wind,
> Marching, marching along.
> March, march, lift up the song:

The revised version is more ambiguous:

> What if there's nothing up there at the top?
> Where are the captains that govern mankind?

What tears down a tree that has nothing within it?
A blast of the wind, O a marching wind,
March wind, and any old tune,
March, march and how does it run?

and the refrain is hardly likely to stir the martial spirit:

What marches down the mountain pass?
No, no, my son, not yet;
That is an airy spot,
And no man knows what treads the grass.[17]

By 1936 Yeats was in no mood to hail the Nationalist crusade to "unify" Spanish culture, and his letters of the period reveal that his interest in the Spanish War was Irish and personal. Although the war was much discussed in his circle, he wrote, "Certainly I never meet anybody who seems to care which side wins in Spain or anywhere else," possibly because the Irish "have had too much politics in the past to care about them now."[18] Yeats himself was distressed by the growing strength in Ireland of the Christian Front movement, which was profiting by the stories of anticlerical atrocities in Spain. He noted with concern the charge of an Irish priest that the blame for "the outraging of nuns in Spain" could be laid directly upon "all the intellectuals since the Renaissance who have opposed the supernatural."[19] Concluding from Opposition efforts in the Dail Eireann to achieve immediate recognition for the Burgos government that "vast numbers of people believe that Franco is a Catholic fighting against paganism," he became "convinced that if the Spanish War goes on, or if [it] ceases and O'Duffy's volunteers return heroes, my 'pagan' institutions, the Theatre, the Academy, will be fighting for their lives against combined Catholic and Gaelic bigotry."[20] Regarding the outcome of the war, the "old Fenian" in Yeats felt a Fascist victory might

[17] The earlier version, "Three Songs to the Same Tune," appears on pp. 276–279 of the *Collected Poems*, and the later "Three Marching Songs," on pp. 324–327. In a note to the poem (p. 326) Yeats suggests "airy" may be a dialectal pronunciation of "eerie."

[18] Letter to Dorothy Wellesley, February 8 [1937], in *The Letters of W. B. Yeats*, ed. Allan Wade, p. 880.

[19] Letter to Dorothy Wellesley, December 9 [1936], *ibid.*, p. 871.

[20] Letter to Ethel Mannin, March 1 [1937], *ibid.*, p. 885. On O'Duffy's volunteers "In Defense of Christianity," see Appendix.

be useful insofar as it might discomfit the British Empire and force the English to be "civil to the Indians." Aside from this consideration, Fascist causes had apparently lost their appeal for him, and he added,

> But this is mere instinct. A thing I would never act on. Then I have a horror of modern politics—I see nothing but the manipulation of popular enthusiasm by false news. . . . I will defend no cause. Get out of the thing, look on with sardonic laughter.[21]

Yeats's final comment on politics was a short lyric of that name:

> How can I, that girl standing there,
> My attention fix
> On Roman or on Russian
> Or on Spanish politics?
> . . . .
> maybe what they say is true
> Of war and war's alarms,
> But O that I were young again
> And held her in my arms![22]

Ezra Pound, unlike Eliot and Yeats, was more than willing to discuss politics during the time of the Spanish War. Although the *Left Review* had, accurately enough, categorized his answer to their questionnaire as "*Neutral?*" Pound had already been praising fascism and Mussolini for some years before Italy's involvement in Spain, and he was to contribute to the pro-Fascist *British Union*, which was founded during the Civil War. By 1936, however, his audience had become too special for his poetic comments on politics and economics to have any noticeable public effect. In any case, Wyndham Lewis and Roy Campbell, who also wrote for the *British Union*, advocated many of Pound's favorite ideas in forms less generally impenetrable than the *Cantos*.

The two most admired Catholic novelists of the time, Evelyn Waugh and Graham Greene, were of no great use to the Nationalist cause. Waugh had written the *Left Review* that if he were Spanish he would be fighting for Franco and that, given a choice between fascism and communism, he would prefer the former although he called "mischievous" the suggestion that such a choice should be re-

[21] Letter to Ethel Mannin, February 11 [1937], *Letters of W. B. Yeats* (ed. Wade), pp. 881–882.

[22] "Politics," *Collected Poems*, p. 337.

quired of an Englishman. This statement of sympathy from a widely read and respected novelist may have been of some value, but Waugh produced nothing specifically designed to help gain British support, and it is most unlikely that he felt any great enthusiasm for the Movimiento, if we can judge by his novels that touch on international politics.

Scoop, which appeared in 1938, derived partly from Waugh's experiences as *Daily Mail* correspondent in Abyssinia and his travels in Liberia. "Ishmaelia," the mythical country in which the story is set, combines many of the more absurd characteristics of these two nations, but the actual events of the civil war there described more closely parallel those in Spain. Waugh's reporting from Abyssinia and later from Mexico and his stated political views roused much leftist criticism and earned him the position of, in Robert Graves's phrase, "the outstanding die-hard of the intellectual Right,"[23] but *Scoop*, a hilarious plague on all available political houses, is not calculated to give aid or comfort to any political movement, right or left.

The novel chronicles the adventures of the innocent William Boot as foreign correspondent for the *Daily Beast*. Waugh's chief target, though by no means his only one, is the journalism racket. Having been sent to Ishmaelia in a great muddle of mistaken identity, William soon finds that his newspaper superiors want not facts but exciting stories that will support their editorial policies, and that experienced correspondents confine their efforts to fulfilling this requirement. Ishmaelia is in the midst of a civil war between the Patriots and the Traitors: which side bears which label depends on the newspaper policy. The government is a republic with an admirably liberal constitution that is universally praised and ignored. The nation is in fact ruled by the ubiquitous Jacksons, all descendants of the American Negro founding father, and their given names reflect the liberal character of the republic: Earl Russell Jackson, Garnett and Huxley Jackson, General Gollancz Jackson, Mrs. "Teeny" Athol née Jackson (a bow to the Red Duchess), among others. There are two contending extremist movements. Smiles Soum (a grandson of Samuel Smiles Jackson), backed by Germany, is a leader of the White

[23] Quoted in Frederick J. Stopp, *Evelyn Waugh: Portrait of an Artist*, p. 28. His *Waugh in Abyssinia* had praised the Italians for bringing civilization to the backward natives, and the title of his book on Mexico, *Robbery Under Law*, indicates his attitude toward the socialistically inclined government of that country.

Shirts, who claim that Ishmaelia is really a white nation, although deeply sunburned, and who hope to overthrow the republic and thus save it from International Negro Finance and International Negro Bolshevism. The Young Ishmaelites, backed by Russia, are out to save the republic for democracy, collective security, and dictatorship of the proletariat. The real issue of the war is which foreign power is to control the rich gold deposits in the interior.

Incapable of concocting "news" or expressing himself in cablese, William is something of a butt for the army of journalists who have assembled in the capital city, but it is he who finally scoops them all. When the entire press corps heads off on a calamitous safari to report on rumored action in a nonexistent city in the interior, William is left alone to observe and record the briefly successful coup of the Young Ishmaelites and the providential arrival by parachute of the literal *deus ex machina,* the mysterious "Mr. Baldwin," who reverses the coup and saves Ishmaelia for British financial interests by simply buying the whole government. Once his account has been rewritten to suit the *Beast's* editorial policies, William is a national hero. However, he is able, by the same combination of innocence and luck that has served him so well before, to arrange for the knighthood and long-term contract with which his employer, Lord Copper, had intended to reward him, to be given to the distant relative for whom he had been mistaken in his initial assignment to Ishmaelia; and William himself is free to return to the contented obscurity of his family's country seat.

With a little effort, some sort of political message can be extracted from this very lighthearted farce. "Mr. Baldwin" (he had chosen this his most recent pseudonym because it was British, noncommittal, and easy to remember; there is no mention of the Prime Minister), who so gracefully overcomes the forces of international communism and fascism, is an international financier whose interests happen to coincide nicely with those of the Conservative *Beast* management. He is successful not because of his superior moral or economic or political principles but because he is much the cleverest of all the clever scoundrels. The British public is shown to display a credulity and lack of critical intelligence that perfectly mesh with the cynicism of the journalists, who merely provide what their bosses want, and the editors and publishers, whose sole concerns are, respectively, holding their jobs and selling newspapers—although there is a suggestion that the publishers are also interested in protecting their foreign investments. If, as may be entirely possible, the triumph of William Boot is intended to represent the triumph of what is best in England, then the best in England is summed up in Boot Hall, an extravagantly old-fashioned country house full of dim-witted but intensely English eccentrics straight out of P. G. Wodehouse.

Reading *Scoop*, one is quite unable to believe that Evelyn Waugh's breast was seething, as so many others were, with political passion during all the storm and strife of 1937. Four years later, when he was writing *Put Out More Flags*, he was less inclined to dismiss international affairs as simply stupid nonsense, and he ends on a note of almost sober purposiveness. In recounting the adventures of his favorite cad, Basil Seal, during "that odd, dead period before the Churchillian renaissance, which people called at the time The Great Bore War,"[24] Waugh allows himself some excellent satire on the intellectual left-wingers who were so active in the Spanish Loyalist cause. Basil, who has a penchant for pretty and witless girls, drops in on his latest for occasional snatches of Marxist jargon and comment on the latest dicta of the intellectual heroes of the group, Parsnip and Pimpernell, who, however, depart for America when things begin to look dangerous in England.[25] Basil, who does not appear in *Scoop*, nevertheless appears to have been involved, shadily, in some Abyssinian activities, as well as in gunrunning to Spain—Waugh does not specify for which side but it is safe to assume for both. For a time Basil makes a very good thing of resettling evacuated London children but soon finds his real niche in the Ministry of Information, ferreting out subversives. When he finds there is no profit in snitching on the Communist sympathies of his acquaintance, he performs the rather remarkable feat of making Ambrose Silk appear pro-Nazi. Poor Ambrose, a cosmopolitan homosexual left-wing aesthetical Jew, has almost alone among the survivors of earlier Waugh novels found the Bore War nervous-making, and Basil actually develops qualms enough to help him es-

[24] Evelyn Waugh, *Put Out More Flags*, Dedicatory Letter to Randolph Churchill.

[25] Waugh was particularly scornful of the "chumminess" of the Auden group: "They clung together. They collaborated. It seemed always to take at least two of them to generate any literary work however modest." Quoted by Stopp, *Waugh*, p. 27.

cape the police Basil had set on him, to the safety of a war-long exile in an especially damp section of Ireland. Basil then completes his conversion from caddishness by volunteering for combat duty. What with most of the rest of the Bright Young People already in uniform, it is clearly the end of an era.

Waugh has made no further significant comment on the period of the later thirties. The politics of the time play some part in *Brideshead Revisited*: her tour of duty as an ambulance driver in Spain is crucial in the developing saintliness of the heroine's plain younger sister, but she is a minor character; and the political activities of Rex Mottram in this novel are instanced merely to show his essential hollow opportunism. Waugh seems to consider politics, national or international, a fit subject for demonstrating the folly and stupidity of men but not deeply interesting in itself.

Scott-King's Modern Europe (1947) is somewhat to the purpose here as reflecting Waugh's attitudes on politics and on Spain. Here he tells of the brief and disastrous visit of a dim, middle-aged schoolmaster, not unlike Waugh in some ways, to the nation of Neutralia, which, the author tells us, is "imaginary and composite and represents no existing state." Some reviewers found resemblance in Neutralia to Yugoslavia, where Waugh had served as a commando with the partisans during the war; but the likenesses are much more numerous to Franco's Spain, which Waugh visited in 1945 under circumstances similar to those of Scott-King's visit. He describes Neutralia as a scenic but backward country that has experienced every possible variety of internal trouble, climaxed by a bloody civil war complete with anticlerical atrocities by Reds, of which the official guides are happy to give detailed accounts. Now "a typical modern state," it has a one-party system headed by a Marshal and run by a "vast, ill-paid bureaucracy whose work is tempered and humanized by corruption"; the citizens, "a clever Latin race," snigger behind their leader's back but at least credit him with having kept their nation neutral during World War II.[26] Scott-King's experiences in Neutralia are such that, once safely back in his English public school, he replies to the suggestion that he might better serve his students' needs by offering a course in, say, economic history in place of one of his classics courses:

[26] Evelyn Waugh, *Scott-King's Modern Europe*, p. 5.

"If you approve, headmaster, I will stay as I am here as long as any boy wants to read the classics. I think it would be very wicked indeed to do anything to fit a boy for the modern world."[27]

In 1953 Waugh briefly re-entered the modern world to register a protest against the projected visit to England of Marshal Tito ("our guest of dishonour") and inspired a Low cartoon that shows a group of Catholic priests and laymen, of whom only Waugh and Graham Greene are identified by name, remonstrating: "For shame! Now if it were for some sturdy upholder of democracy—like Franco. . . ."[28] To judge by Waugh's novels, Low may have overestimated the author's enthusiasm for the Spanish *caudillo.*

About Graham Greene, Low was probably quite wrong. Greene was, like Waugh, an Oxonian of genteel background who became converted to Roman Catholicism in young manhood, but almost all he shares in outlook with Waugh is a profound conviction of original sin. Greene made no explicit public statement of his sympathies in the Spanish War, and his passing comments in articles of the period reveal little except, as might be expected of him, a certain contempt for the lofty and sometimes inflated rhetoric the war evoked, as in his reference to "the sweeping statements, the safe marble gestures, the self-importance" of most of the contributors to *Authors Take Sides.*[29] Politically, Greene is reminiscent of the nineteenth-century English radicals in his combination of deep religiosity with a passion for social justice; he is, however, entirely free from their belief in progress. He had flirted, though briefly and unsatisfactorily, with communism as an undergraduate, and his approach to social questions remained generally leftist in the sense that he seemed to have more confidence in the efficacy of "new styles of architecture," social change by radical alteration of social institutions, than in a "change of heart" that would make existing institutions somehow more humane and responsible. His conversion to Catholicism did not mean for him, as it did for many Englishmen, a conversion to conservatism. Rejecting Marxism, he took as his basic text the 1931 encyclical on social reform of Pope Pius XI, the *Quadragesimo anno,* which evenhandedly condemns the

[27] *Ibid.*, p. 89.

[28] Stopp, *Waugh*, p. 41.

[29] Graham Greene, "Alfred Tennyson Intervenes," *Spectator*, CLIX, No. 5711 (December 10, 1937), 1058.

evils of both communism and capitalism, and Greene does the same himself. The villains of *England Made Me* (1935) and *This Gun for Hire* (1936) are big capitalists of a blackness dark enough to besmirch the entire system, and the hero of *Stamboul Train* (or *Orient Express* [1932]) is a Communist. *It's a Battlefield* (1934) could almost stand as a model for Marxist fiction except for the figure of Mr. Surrogate, the wealthy leftist whose proletarian sympathies are confined to the highest levels of abstraction. This type of the professional lover of humanity who has no particular use for individual human beings recurs in Greene.

Marxism posed a genuine problem for Greene. He was as aware as any Marxist of the evils of capitalism and as indignant, and he shared their belief in the necessity of correcting or extirpating its abuses. But to him the Marxist view seemed hopelessly limited and oversimplified and hence falsified by its denial of the existence of God and its consequently inadequate understanding of the nature of man. He could be said to consider Marxism inhumane precisely because of its exclusively humanist approach. For Greene what the Marxists left out was what was most essential, and this omission doomed their best efforts. He wrote most explicitly of his belief in the futility of the Marxist dream in the travel book, *Another Mexico* (or *The Lawless Roads*), which described his visit to Mexico in the spring of 1938, but the novel *The Power and the Glory*, written later on the basis of his Mexican experiences, presents his position more dramatically and effectively.

The central and symbolic figures in *The Power and the Glory* are a priest and a police lieutenant. The lieutenant is an almost wholly admirable character: he is humane, industrious, upright, ascetically dedicated to freeing his people from the poverty and ignorance that he attributes to an outworn and unjust social system propped up by a corrupt and hypocritical Church. His pity and indignation are real and rational. The priest, on the other hand, is a poor specimen, a weak, self-indulgent, mediocre little man who is ridden by guilt for his repeated failures to live up to the responsibilities of his vocation. He is in double flight (as the American title, *The Labyrinthine Ways*, stresses), from the authorities who have forbidden religious observances and from the Hound of Heaven Who is demanding from him a heroism of which he feels himself incapable and unworthy. Yet it is the "whisky priest" who wins in the end, and the moral is almost pedantically clear: despite his human virtues and the reasonableness of his aims, the lieutenant is doomed to ultimate futility because he lacks the divine grace made possible by faith—his "righteousness is as filthy rags"; and this divine grace is sufficient to make a heroic martyr of the seediest material and finally triumph over the emptiness of pure secularism.[30]

Greene has written that the "pattern" of his view of life appeared to him at fourteen through a reading of Marjorie Bowen's *Viper of Milan* and was only later to be explained in religious terms: "perfect evil walking the world where perfect good can never walk again, and only the pendulum ensures that after all in the end justice is done."[31] His critics agree that all his work reveals the conviction that "human nature is not black and white but black and grey,"[32] but they differ sharply as to where Greene lays the blame for this depressing situation. George Woodcock firmly states that "in Greene's writing the evil in man is always less than the evil without, arising from the collective activities of society";[33] and Francis Kunkel replies with equal certainty that "Greene recognizes maladjustments in the social order, of course, and even launches a ripple of social criticism now and then, but he always uses darker and bolder strokes to paint the evil within man than the evil without."[34] It is not necessary to take sides on this question in order to note that a man with Greene's outlook could not in any case be expected to have become an ardent advocate of either Spanish cause: his religion would inhibit wholehearted support of the secularist Republic, but his radicalism would prevent his approving a counterrevolution like Franco's.

The Confidential Agent is Greene's Spanish War novel—or, in his designation, "entertainment." As he has done elsewhere, Greene makes

[30] This novel rather closely carries out, with different ideological assignments, the program suggested by Edward Upward for the "best kind of Communist novel," one in which "the capitalist characters were sympathetic people of good will, and the Communist the embittered and unsympathetic. But the novel would make the point that the unsympathetic Communists are right and the middle-class characters of good will wrong" (Quoted by Stephen Spender, *The God That Failed*, ed. Richard Crossmann, pp. 239–240).

[31] Graham Greene, "The Lost Childhood," in *The Lost Childhood and Other Essays*, p. 17.

[32] *Ibid.*, p. 16.

[33] George Woodcock, *The Writer and Politics*, p. 150.

[34] Francis L. Kunkel, *The Labyrinthine Ways of Graham Greene*, p. 16.

a slight effort to suggest that he is writing about a fictitious conflict: his hero, D., in London to buy coal for his government, goes to a language school that teaches both Spanish and D.'s language; but this is as far as the novelist goes with obfuscation, and critics of the novel unanimously take it as referring to Spain. D. is a professor of literature who is acting as agent for a republic that has (in 1939) been engaged for over two years in a losing battle against reactionary revolt. D., an agnostic, considers himself something of a heretic in regard to the "scientific materialism" of his party, and he knows he is being spied upon by agents of his own government; yet he feels that the government, inept, ridden by distrust, and led by corruptible and self-seeking politicians, is nevertheless worthy of his loyalty. A conversation with the heroine reveals his attitude:

"It's no good taking a moral line—my people commit atrocities like the others. I suppose if I believed in a God, it would be simpler."

"Do you believe," she said, "that *your* leaders are any better than L.'s?"

"No, of course not. But I still prefer the people they lead—even if they lead them all wrong."

"The poor, right or wrong," she scoffed.

"It's no worse, is it, than my country right or wrong? You choose your side once for all—of course it may be the wrong side. Only history can tell that."[35]

Also instructive is D.'s meditation after a conversation with L., the aristocrat who is serving as London agent for the rebels and who tries to persuade D. that as a bourgeois intellectual he is fighting on the wrong side. L. has made the mistake, however, of equating his own loss of a valued art collection with D.'s loss of his wife. D. thinks:

It was worth killing a civilization to prevent the government of human beings from falling into the hands of—he supposed they were called the civilized. What sort of world would that be? A world full of objects labeled "Not to be touched"; no religious faith, but a lot of Gregorian chants and picturesque ceremonies. Miraculous images which bled and waggled their heads on certain days would be preserved for their quaintness: superstition was interesting. There would be excellent libraries, but no new books. He preferred the distrust, the barbarity, the betrayals . . . even chaos.[36]

[35] Graham Greene, *The Confidential Agent: An Entertainment,* p. 81.
[36] *Ibid.*, p. 35.

The Confidential Agent is not a "political novel"; the Spanish War simply provides a situation within which Greene can work out his theme, D.'s discovery of love and trust in a world oppressive with treachery and suspicion. It is dangerous, of course, to ascribe to a novelist the attitudes of his characters, but there are grounds for belief that Greene's feelings about the Spanish War were much like D.'s. Despite his fondness for writing from current headlines, he could have chosen a different background, or he could easily have satisfied his propensity for tales of hunters and the hunted by making his seedy underdog a bourgeois Catholic in danger of his life in revolutionary Barcelona. By thinly disguising his background and making his hero an agnostic, Greene was able to avoid making a direct statement of his (thoroughly qualified) sympathies in the Spanish War, but *The Confidential Agent* stands as strong evidence against Low's assumption that because Greene was Catholic he was pro-Franco.

The two Catholic writers just considered seem to have felt very differently about the Spanish War. Evelyn Waugh, a conservative and a traditionalist, had no doubts as to the side he preferred, but his distrust of political ideology and his contempt for political activity of all sorts kept him from showing—or even, probably, from feeling—much fervor in support of his chosen side. Graham Greene, at once Catholic and a social and political radical, found his sympathies so divided that he chose to make no direct statement, although he was probably far more deeply engaged emotionally than Waugh was. Both, however, shared a conviction, entirely consistent with their religious beliefs, of the fallibility of men and the futility of their aspirations toward an ideal society.

A very different sort of Catholic, like them only in being a convert, was the South African poet, Roy Campbell, who was perhaps the most enthusiastic of all Nationalist advocates addressing themselves to the British public. For Campbell, an ideal society was not only possible, it was in process of realization in Nationalist Spain. Original sin, which broods over Greene's novels and underlies Waugh's gayest satires, had been, in Campbell's eyes, at least for the time being, largely canceled for those Catholics who were taking part in the new crusade to restore Spain and Europe to the paradise the Reformation had lost for them. Other Franco adherents in Britain occasionally felt called upon to defend Nationalist actions, such as the alliance with the Fascist powers, the use of Moorish troops, or the mass executions. Campbell never apologizes, although in *Flowering Rifle* (1939) he explains at great length. He repeats the standard Nationalist explanation of the devastation of Guernica, that it was dynamited from within by Government troops, not destroyed by German bombs; but he adds that if the town had indeed been bombed, the Republicans had committed much worse horrors anyway and the "severity" of the Nationalists was only just. Other pro-Nationalist writers were embarrassed by the shooting of García Lorca; Campbell, despite his admiration for the Spanish poet, defends his murder.

> And what if García Lorca died for this
> Caught bending over that forlorn abyss
> For some mephitic whim his soul had spliced,
> As once he boasted, with the Antichrist?
> This weary Faustian hunger for the void
> An age of intellectuals has destroyed:
> In him another Marsyas sang and died,
> The victim of the God that he defied:
> Was Spain to let an enemy escape
> Vowed to her Foe though in an angel's shape
> And lovely as Lalanda with his cape?[37]

Campbell had been schooled in controversy for years before he joined combat in behalf of Nationalist Spain. He had first come to England at eighteen to attend Oxford University. During the two years of this sojourn he made such influential friends as Eliot, the Sitwells, Augustus John, and —perhaps most important—Wyndham Lewis. Back in Durban, his political journalism proved too liberal for the South African government, and he had to return to England in 1926. He soon found himself engaged in a furious battle with Bloomsbury which was climaxed by his *Georgiad* (1931), a remarkably sustained diatribe in the style of Pope which is almost as often funny as

[37] Roy Campbell, *Flowering Rifle: A Poem from the Battlefield of Spain*, p. 93. In his *Lorca: An Appreciation of his Poetry*, p. 7, Campbell offers a revised view of the poet's death: "It is well established that Lorca had no political tub to thump; that his murder was due to a private grudge; that it was perpetrated under the cover of the general epidemic of killings and that his was but one of tens of thousands of deaths that were due to the settling of personal accounts behind the smokescreen of civil strife."

it is simply abusive. He and his wife had received much hospitality from the Bloomsbury set, and there were many to charge him with ingratitude for portraying his erstwhile hosts as a group of solemn and epicene hypocrites. Campbell later answered the charge by reiterating his description of the British literary establishment as made up of effeminate men dominated by masculine women. His summation of his part in this literary battle casts some light on his attitude toward the Spanish War:

> I consider that throughout this farcical comedy I acted with the greatest chivalry. I always act on a precedent and invariably take one of the paladins of Chivalry for my model—the Cid Campeador, Roland, Oliver, or some other worthy of that sort.[38]

It is to muscular and bloodthirsty Christians like these that Roy Campbell bears a much closer resemblance than he does to such modern English Catholics as Waugh and Greene. Not for him the obsession with sin and guilt: he is exultant in the prospect of reversing four centuries of wrong-headed "progress" and restoring the happy medieval days when the rich were brave and responsible, the poor were industrious and respectful, and heretics were brought to salvation by main force. For his literary models Campbell frequently harks back to the eighteenth century, but his political and religious home is the twelfth.

The Campbells had been living in Spain for some years when the civil war broke out, and the generals' uprising did not surprise them. Campbell thought it long overdue. He later wrote that a few weeks before the insurrection,

> I was disgusted at what I took to be the tame, cringing fatalism of the Nationalists who, after all, formed the majority. They had turned both cheeks so many times that it began to look cowardly rather than Christian. . . . Little did I know what a feast of heroism was in store![39]

In Toledo, the Campbells had incurred leftist hostility by sheltering threatened monks, and it was at least partly a political gesture when, in June of 1936, they decided to abandon their "vacillating" Anglo-Catholicism and "step into the front ranks of the Regular Army of

[38] Roy Campbell, *Light on a Dark Horse: An Autobiography (1901–1935)*, p. 258.

[39] *Ibid.*, p. 346.

Christ."[40] They were confirmed in the Roman Catholic Church by Cardinal Goma himself in a secret nighttime ceremony.

Campbell had chosen his side early, and most of the poems in his *Mithraic Emblems*, which was published in the latter half of 1936, after the war had begun, had actually been written well before the outbreak of hostilities and were therefore prophetic rather than descriptive. Among these is "The Flight," first published early in 1935, which depicts a duel between two airplanes, one white and one red. As the red plane goes down in flames,

> I knew the ecstasy, the fearful throes,
> And the white phoenix from his scarlet sire,
> As silver in the solitude he rose.[41]

The victorious pilot proves to be "the Solar Christ." Throughout this volume, and again in *Flowering Rifle*, Christ is identified with the sun god Mithras, whose being everywhere associated with bulls makes possible a further frequent image of Christ as torero. He also appears as a sheepherder, like those of Campbell's native veldt and of the Castilian plain; not the traditional gentle, barefoot keeper of flocks, but a mounted horseman, booted and spurred and a terror to the wolves. Christ again appears as a militant David, still a shepherd, but in Campbell protecting the strong against the weak:

> Slung at his wrists will hang the phantom stress
> Of David's stone—to weigh that all is right;
> Even to daunt him should the weak unite
> In one Goliath, he'll accept and bless,
> Whose home's the Earth, and Everywhere his bed
> A sheepskin saddle to his seat or head,
> And Here and Now his permanent address.[42]

Mithraic Emblems included four poems written after the civil war began, among them a rousing tribute to the heroes of the siege of the Alcazar, but *Flowering Rifle*, published in 1939, was Campbell's major effort on behalf of Nationalist Spain. This long poem, subtitled "A Poem from the Battlefield of Spain," represents the poet as a Legionary of the Tercio. There is some confusion on this point.

[40] *Ibid.*, p. 317.
[41] Roy Campbell, *Selected Poems*, p. 130.
[42] "The Sling," in *ibid.*, p. 154.

Hugh Thomas states that Campbell "narrowly escap[ed] with his life (and that of his family)" from Toledo and "later became one of the most ardent apologists for the Nationalists, without, however, actually fighting for them."[43] In his autobiography written several years later, Campbell speaks of having "killed bolsheviks in self-defense"[44] and suggests that any fighting he did was only part of escaping from Toledo: "As a non-naturalized British subject and a 'Goy,' I did not wish to burden our Embassy as Messrs. Koestler and Co. have since done, though they received every courtesy and were *flown* to safety whereas I had to fight my way out." [45] Yet he speaks in the poem of "We/ Who are in the Legion," and describes taking part in a cavalry charge. His brief autobiography in the 1942 edition of *Twentieth Century Authors* states that he served with the Franco forces besides acting as correspondent for the London (Catholic) *Tablet*, and that he "was cited for saving the Carmelite archives at Toledo in 1937."[46] The Author's Note to *Flowering Rifle* is dated "Airosas. Toledo. III° Año Triunfal," indicating that he was at least *in* Spain at the time, whether as a Legionary or not.

The Author's Note informs us that he expects an unfriendly reception from the purblind leftist reviewers whose sentimental and self-indulgent humanitarianism "sides automatically with the Dog against the Man, the Jew against the Christian, the black against the white, the servant against the master, the criminal against the judge," and he predicts that this poem will be called "romantic" as were his earlier ones on Spain in *Mithraic Emblems.* In what may be the angriest of several angry reviews, Stephen Spender refuses to apply the word to *Flowering Rifle* on the grounds that the romantic poets had "a disinterested passion for truth, equalled only by their love of freedom and justice," whereas in Campbell "we have the Talking Bronco, the Brute Life armed with abusive words, and most unfortunately, not with Mr. Campbell's Flowering Rifle, but with Flowering Machine Guns, Flowering Henkels [*sic*], Flowering Capronis." Spender grants the poem some good rhapsodic and effective

[43] Thomas, *Spanish Civil War*, p. 231 n.

[44] Campbell, *Light on a Dark Horse*, p. 226.

[45] *Ibid.*, p. 345.

[46] Stanley J. Kunitz and Howard Haycraft, eds., *Twentieth Century Authors*, p. 241.

satirical passages, but these are, he says "stones of a certain lustre buried under ignoble sweepings of every kind of anti-Semitic and atrocity propaganda."[47] As one of Campbell's favorite targets, Spender could be allowed some prejudice, but his judgment on the poem is hard to fault. It is perhaps somewhat less incoherent than he thought it, but there is no question that it is indeed "biassed, unobjective, highly coloured and distorted." It is also repetitious and overlong, but it is of interest for this study both for such poetic value as it has and as the most vivid and widely ranging expression made during the period of the Spanish War of the ideas and attitudes of the more extreme pro-Nationalists.

The central theme of the poem is "the Harvest," the triumphal victory of the Nationalist forces over all the pernicious innovations in Europe since the Reformation, symbolized chiefly by the record crops in Nationalist Spain as contrasted with the starvation in Republican territory. Also constantly reiterated is Campbell's delight in beholding the downfall of yet another of the causes supported by his left-wing literary enemies:

> flawlessly this axiom has been kept
> What Auden chants by Spender shall be wept
>
> . . . .
>
> with such bards to trumpet them to battle
> No wonder British reds stampede like cattle!
>
> . . . .
>
> When Britain and her poets stand for causes
> That aren't foredoomed by foul inhuman crime
> They'll change their present sanctions to applauses
> And own me for the prophet of my time.
> Since the whole trouble with the other chaps is
> Whatever cause they flunky for collapses.[48]

[47] Stephen Spender, review of *Flowering Rifle* in *New Statesman and Nation,* XVII, No. 420 N.S. (March 11, 1939), 370. Campbell's publisher was able to quote in his advertisements at least two favorable notices. Above the suggestion, "Why not read it yourself?" he printed a quotation from Spender's review, followed by a quotation from Edmund Blunden's review, ". . . a wonderful display of passionate and eloquent poetry. . . . Nobody else alive could have struck such a blow in verse," and one from F. Yeats-Brown's review, "*Flowering Rifle* is a great poem and will be read long after the Civil War in Spain is ended."

[48] Campbell, *Flowering Rifle,* pp. 20, 21, 25.

Like others on his side, Campbell has considerable fun with a famously fatuous line from Day Lewis, "Why do we all, seeing a Red, feel small?", and he returns to it with undiminished glee throughout the poem. A typical reference is in his invocation of the "Equestrian Muse of our Castilian Trails," whom he asks to help him tell

> why communists feel small
> And we so perpendicular and tall
> (Like a Cathedral over Comrades' Hall[49]
> . . . .)

Campbell is addressing a British audience, and his attacks upon the leaders of the Spanish Republic are of measurably less virulence (although degree is hard to find in this poem) than his continuing assault upon their British supporters, whom he calls variously "Charlies," "Wowsers," and "Pommies," among other things.[50] These are his old antagonists from Bloomsbury, as well as the newer Auden group, with whom he felt himself in unequal battle, aided only by Wyndham Lewis,

[49] *Ibid.*, p. 17. See Chapter VI.

[50] According to Eric Partridge's *A Dictionary of Slang and Unconventional English* (3d ed.), *s. v.*, "wowser" was, in the thirties, a popular term of abuse with special connotations of spoil-sport puritanism and priggishness, which is about the way Campbell uses it; but he seems to employ the other terms in a very personal way. "Pommy" is listed as an Australian slang term for a newcomer, a "greenhorn," especially from England, but Campbell's meaning seems to be more a portmanteau of "pink Tommy" for the "lock-stepping intellectuals" described as "all in order lined,/ Poking each other from behind/ To face a single muzzle-loading gun [Campbell's]/ Because it gets its nitre from the sun" ("Dedication to Mary Campbell," *Selected Poems*, p. 177). "Charley" or "Charlie" is comparable to the American "Mac" or "Joe" as an all-purpose name in Britain, and some of its many slang uses may have contributed to Campbell's intention: "night watchman" (the commonest nineteenth-century usage, archaic by 1900) or "round-shouldered person" (obsolete by 1920); during World War I, either a soldier's knap-sack or an officer's Chaplin-style mustache. A hundred years earlier, "charlies" (always plural) could refer either to a woman's paps or a man's testicles (useful connotations for referring to homosexuals). In popular British riming slang, there were also "Charley Howard"=coward and "Charley Ronce"=ponce (by extension "=very smart, 'one of the boys' "). "Good-time Charleys" might apply, or, most likely, the reference could be primarily to Charlie Chaplin, symbol of "the little fellow" and much admired by the intellectuals Campbell disliked.

Daring the rage of all who vainly think
Against a Nation to uphold a Stink,
In the fat sty of pederast and Jew
Whose kingdom is the Newsrag and Review,
Who hold by fraud the fort of English letters
Against the final triumph of their betters,
As Spain was held with such in its high places,
Before her Resurrection kicked the traces!

. . . .

And few but Wyndham Lewis and myself
Disdain salaaming for their praise and pelf,
With cleansing bombs to air the stuffy dens
Wherein they pick their noses with their pens.[51]

There is a great deal more similar comment on Campbell's literary contemporaries, but this may suffice to indicate the flavor.

The pink pansies of London literary teas form only a part of the enemy ranks. The trouble with Europe began more or less at the time of the Reformation (Bolshevism is "but the Reformation come to roost/ Four hundred years after its rage was loosed"), or perhaps earlier: the Nationalist God is "Emperor of the *Middle Ages*" because "there's been no 'renaissance' up till now." But "the old world is 'braver' than the 'new'," and God will destroy the godless, "Cough though the scientist or squirm the Jew,/ Or stink, abjectly dead, the poets too."[52]

The "scientist" is the Darwinian, who talks

As if Created Adam but exists
Through kind permission of anatomists,
And life were a condition of the body,
Not vice versa, as the merest noddy,
By reasoning, can swiftly ferret out,
Till reason makes him skeptical of doubt.[53]

Darwin was not a Jew, nor were Jews responsible for the founding of the Church of England and the lies about Spain that

An age of creeping wowsers in disguise,
For centuries have still been forced to spin

[51] Campbell, *Flowering Rifle*, p. 35.
[52] *Ibid.*, p. 64. [53] *Ibid.*, p. 62.

To cover the lewd haunch of Ann Boleyn,
And with smug incense to deodorize
Their pimping to a murderous cuckold's sin—
Which gave us first our famous unemployed
And now would sell our sons to Marx and Freud.[54]

However, the rest of the trouble with the twentieth century can be charged directly to that race which once

Wore on its brows, the diadem still pearled
Of Adam's sweat, the mandate of the world,
Before they left their heritage seraphic
In usury and drugs to make their traffic,
Of Freuds and Marxes, priests of desolation,
To spread their plagues of famine and damnation,
Death to the soul and Hunger to the land,
The slow paralysis of heart and hand.[55]

Campbell's opinions on Jews are roughly comparable to those of Julius Streicher, but it is doubtful whether the Nazi could have risen to the heights of theological ingenuity from which the poet explains Christ's Jewish birth:

That sovereign Serum, bred in Jewish veins
From Jewish poison, that with mortal pains
The Good Physician suffered to procure,
Against their venomed fangs to make us sure,
And bore both Jewish flesh and Jewish hate
To furnish that Celestial Mithridate,
Whose vaccination signed upon our heads
Immunes us from the weakness of the Reds,
In whom the Jew-bite, though it quick their pulse,
In the long run will stifle and convulse,
As we have seen with Moscow and Geneva,
Reduced to impotence by the same fever.[56]

Such flights require a rich poetic fancy.

Campbell is naturally sympathetic toward Hitler's problems with the Jews:

[Marx's] whole knowledge of the earth and sun
Was of a boarding house for exiles run

[54] *Ibid.*, p. 95. [55] *Ibid.*, pp. 84–85. [56] *Ibid.*, p. 81.

With dodging rent as the chief role of man
And being as much a nuisance as one can:
Which is why Hitler gives them [the Jews] leave to quit:
Rather than be with his own broomsticks hit
By his own lodgers, firing all such boarders
Before, instead of after, the disorders.[57]

In the course of the poem Campbell performs the service of elucidating one of the doctrines of anti-Semitism which nonbelievers have generally had difficulty in understanding; that is, how *both* international finance and international communism could be controlled by the same Jews:

The racket of the Invert and the Jew
. . . .
Is through art and science to subdue,
Humiliate, and to a pulp reduce
The Human Spirit for industrial use
Whether by Capital or Communism
It's all the same, despite their seeming schism,
In that for human serfs they both require
Limpness, servility, and lack of fire,
And that's the task of modern art and verse
Whose high-paid priests are certified perverse
From those who race or sex degrades them most [*sic*]
Before they raise them to their envied post.[58]

Although he ranges far in his strictures on international Jewry and communism, modern art of all kinds, Darwinian biology, psychoanalysis, the Church of England, and the League of Nations ("that sheeny club of communists and masons"), and pauses at times to criticize the British Empire and even, surprisingly in view of his attitude toward divorce, to side firmly with the recently abdicated Edward VIII ("A King too generous, direct, and manly/ For fallen England or the likes of Stanley [Baldwin]"), Campbell always returns to the Spanish War itself.

In his account of the origins of the war, he notes that "what was corruptible in all the land/ Was long ago a pawn in Moscow's hand," a hundred years of strife having "winnowed Spain in two distinctive

[57] *Ibid.*, p. 119.
[58] *Ibid.*, p. 109.

clans/ Upon the left, inflammable, the chaff,/ Corn on the right. . . ." The Darwinian, Marxist, Freudian Wowser now faced his "would-be victim" who, "armed chiefly with a sense of Bad and Good/ . . . had retained erect his classic form/ Through all the epidemics of Reform." This true Spaniard has been saved the perils of literacy and "reads less nonsense from his running brooks/ Than waiters, primer-proud, with knowing looks,/ Can mumber out of newspapers and books."[59] Campbell rejects the popular notion that many of Spain's difficulties sprang from widespread illiteracy:

It was the literate lounging class of Spain
That first conceived this rabies of the brain.
The hardest workers, those that read the least,
Could still distinguish Beauty from the Beast,
Experience better serves the most Unread
Who carry no Boloney home to bed.[60]

The Republic, "this all-reforming modern State/ That voted work and eating out of date," was foisted on the real Spain by fraud in the first place, and the elections of 1936, "as if Democracy to slight,/ And show its rusted working to the sight,/ Seated the left, yet counted for the right." Campbell has nothing to say of the period from 1933 to 1935 except to explain why the forces of the Right did not then excise the cancer of communism while they controlled the government:

And if we did not do it long before,
Say, when Gil Robles held the reins of war,
"Thou shalt not kill" was what we waited for:
The binding ban that cannot be untied
Save by the stronger—that on suicide.[61]

The rightist revolt, then, was entirely in self-defense, and begun under terrible handicaps, "half a million"[62] already having been slain by the Red Terror and

[59] *Ibid.*, p. 32. In his autobiography (*Light on a Dark Horse*, p. 318), Campbell describes with disgust watching a Spanish waiter painfully spelling out Plato's *Republic* under the impression that it was a description of the Spanish government.

[60] Campbell, *Flowering Rifle*, p. 41.

[61] *Ibid.*, p. 53.

[62] The total figure for "assassinations" by the Republican side from 1936 to 1939 is given by Thomas (*Spanish Civil War*, p. 613) as "about 66,000."

> Such foreign aid as we were lent,
> The Reds already to the front had sent,
> Out-numbering still, today, by four-to-one,
> And antedating with four months to run:
> Only the mad, Red populace was armed,
> And well the weeded Army had been farmed,
>
> . . . .
>
> With the Red generals in the pride of place
> And ours consigned to exile and disgrace.[63]

The Nationalists' troubles were further compounded by the false propaganda of foreign writers, either bought or purblind:

> Spain was a mirror in a public place
> Where every stranger, seeing his own face,
> Especially if it was botched or sore,
> Believed it for the land that we Restore.[64]

Hemingway's *The Spanish Earth*, for instance, was unrecognizable; and how could Campbell, knowing the country as he does,

> entertain
> The Charlie's Meeting Bates mistook for Spain,
> Whose false experience of the land must yield
> To mine both in the letters as the field[?][65]

Worse than the effort to "set the world against us with its votes/ Whose only crime was to defend our throats," was the flood of foreign supplies and "Red recruits" to attack the true Spaniards and their Moorish friends.

> The hoarse blaspheming of the godless horde
> Against the Cross and Crescent of the Lord,
> The Cross, our Hammer, and the Quarter Moon
> Our Sickle, and Hosanna for our tune![66]

In a man with so little tolerance for heresies of the Jewish and Protestant varieties, Campbell's enthusiasm for his Moslem allies seems at first puzzling. He appears, however, to have considered them pri-

[63] Campbell, *Flowering Rifle*, p. 39.

[64] *Ibid.*, p. 40.

[65] *Ibid.*, p. 43. The reference is to Ralph Bates's novels, *Lean Men* and *The Olive Field*. See Chapter III.

[66] Campbell, *Flowering Rifle*, p. 50.

marily as fellow believers fighting the forces of unbelief. They are also, like the true Spaniards, antidemocratic, and thus glad

> Rather to serve the rightful heirs of man
> Than rule with Charlies on an equal plan
>
> . . . .
>
> Of Liberty and Freedom they've enough
> Who've learned to dread the namby-pamby stuff![67]

Despite the fearful odds, the Nationalists have gone from triumph to triumph, not significantly because of the foreign aid, "proferred, not entreated," but because of their superior courage, intelligence, industry, and idealism, all symbolized by their large food crops[68] and due mainly to their having God on their side. God has in fact been a rightist all along. After all,

> the Good Thief was hammered to the Right
> And bore the nails with valour and delight,
> Unlike the snarling Comrade on the left
> Whose dole and rights all other thoughts bereft
> When he was in the high, Majestic Place,
> Outsoaring Caesar and the suns of space![69]

Even in death the basic difference between Right and Left persists. The bodies of International Brigadiers (the "scum of Europe") are piled high

> To make a huge paella of the plains,
> A dish of rice, with corpses for the grains,
> Whom safe intriguing pedants sent to die
> And sell their scrawny mutton for a lie,
> To perish for an ignominious cause:
> Not as our "dead", in rhyme with Cosmic laws,
> Who die as Queens in childbed, giving birth
> To the resurgent order of the earth.[70]

[67] *Ibid.*, p. 51.

[68] Campbell never mentions the possible connection between the Axis blockade and the contrast between Nationalist plenty and Republican want. The Nationalists in Spain made much of this contrast, on at least one occasion dropping loaves of bread by plane upon Madrid and Barcelona to bring home the point; the Republicans retaliated with an air raid of shirts and socks to demonstrate their superiority in manufactured goods (Thomas, *Spanish Civil War*, p. 567).

[69] Campbell, *Flowering Rifle*, p. 59.

[70] *Ibid.*, p. 52.

This may be one of the passages to which Spender referred as having made him "physically sick." More felicitous is the stirring eulogy of José Antonio Primo de Rivera, the attractive and chivalrous young leader of the Falange, who was executed early in the war for his part in initiating it. Campbell, having declared García Lorca's murder an act of justice "for Spain betrayed," finds it balanced by the death of Don José Antonio,

> Whose epic line (no flourish of the pen)
> Was life and rapture, and whose words were men
>
> . . . .
>
> For in young Primo's grave his slayers stowed
> One fire-brand safe, a whole *mine* to explode,[71]

for his loss inspires all true Spaniards to emulation. The poet envisions the dead Falangist astride a winged horse:

> And for his charger—cloud-careering Spain
> With hide of golden corn and snowy mane,
> Tornadoeing in glory through the sky,
> In steep sierras caracoling high,
> Or in low foothills trotting smooth and far,
> Beneath his sky-blue shirt of morning air
> Braided with scarlet arrows by the Sun,
> A "Falangist" himself, if there is one
>
> . . . .
>
> And happy now a comrade to embrace
> As solar to the land as he to Space.[72]

Some thirty pages before the close of this rambling and repetitious poem, Campbell makes probably the clearest statement of his ideals. He finds that

> style and unity and emulation
> Inform each clean rejuvenated nation,
> Wherever there's a Leader to rebel
> Against the outworn democratic Hell,
> And weld our people under one bright star—
> A Franco, Mussolini, Salazar.[73]

[71] *Ibid.*, p. 94.

[72] *Ibid.*, p. 94. The Falangists wore light blue shirts with an emblem of five red arrows.

[73] *Ibid.*, p. 125.

He repeats his complaint against the pink "modern Southeys" who rule the British literary world while "unbought men" like himself

> Like criminals are shunned throughout the land—
> As for myself I glory in my crime—
> Of English poets first in all my time
> To sock the bleary monster in my rhyme,
> As first in arms to face this Prince of Wowsers
> And drive the bullets through his baggy trousers,
> And now to bring, with his bug-eaten head,
> The tidings that Democracy is dead
> And that where e'er he strives with the New Man
> The Charlie still must be an Also Ran,
> Incompetence and crime still giving place
> When self-less leaders wake the pride of race,
> The grimy proletariat to abolish,
> The "Meeting" and the party to demolish,
> To take away his living with its cause,
> From the poor agitator's grinding jaws
> And strand him, bankrupt of his grouse, to choke
> Among the heedless ears of happy folk—
> A trick which Intellectuals most resent
> Who trade the most in social discontent.[74]

The poem closes on a moonlit tableau of the Legionary addressing his rifle, "flowering," presumably like Tannhauser's staff, because of the Virgin's blessing his cause.

Flowering Rifle makes hard reading for anyone who does not largely share Campbell's attitudes on race, religion, and politics since these make up the real subject of the poem, and the number of such readers must surely be even less now than it was thirty years ago. It is difficult to pay tribute, even where it is clearly merited, to the lyricism of some of the descriptions of the Spanish countryside or the invocations of Christ and the Virgin, when these are so closely interwoven with the savagery of the fanatic crusader. The combination of sincere devotion to a God of love, peace, and mercy, with a ferocious joy in the destruction of His children, has a certain quaint charm in the *Chanson de Roland*, but these echoes of an earlier age are not attractive in a twentieth-century champion of Christian civili-

[74] *Ibid.*, pp. 125–126.

zation. Campbell's imaginative invention, his exuberant vitality, and his passionate conviction seem somehow misplaced.

As a satirist, Campbell is more at home with the meat axe than the scalpel, but he often wields his weapon to good effect. Naturally the critic of satire is hampered by his own bias, but even one who would categorically reject almost the whole of Campbell's ideals and standards would have to grant him credit for exposing certain aspects of the British scene during the period of 1936 to 1939 that may have received less criticism than they deserved. He is skillful with the *tu quoque*: he calls effective attention to the hypocrisy of convinced British imperialists exclaiming over the imperialism of Mussolini; he contrasts the pro-Loyalists' fervent concern for the legality of the Spanish Republic with their rejection of the equal legality of the Third Reich; he makes much of the tortuous efforts of British leftists to justify the totalitarianism of Stalin while decrying that of Hitler or Mussolini. He is on firm ground when he takes sardonic note of the slavish adulation of the working class by gently reared intellectuals whose callouses can all be traced to tennis racquets, golf clubs, and fountain pens and who show no eagerness to develop any other kind. Having been a "worker" himself, as ranch hand, sailor, and stevedore, Campbell had some justification for considering himself better equipped to discuss the nature and aspirations of the proletariat, although his ideal of a working class that knows and happily serves in its "place" does not appear to be widely shared by other members of that class. Campbell also makes some good points about the rather remarkable unanimity of political attitudes on the British Left (although the unanimity was much less than he thought) and about the credulity with which some pro-Loyalists accepted even the most fanciful inventions of Republican propagandists. Yet only the most firmly disciplined Communist Party member can have accepted Republican propaganda with the total faith Campbell gave to his Nationalist sources.

As for his monotonous insistence on "the Invert and the Jew," the prevalence of homosexuality on the British Left (and Right, too, for that matter) is widely substantiated by other, friendlier sources,[75]

[75] Cecil Day Lewis, describing a typical young writer of the thirties, wrote: "The War-environment in which he grew up, combined possibly with a radical weakening of morale in the class from which he springs, tends to drive him to

but its relevance to questions of politics, economics, or even aesthetics has yet to be established. *Flowering Rifle* was written before the events of the next few years were to chasten at least the expression of anti-Semitism, but there is no record of his having since retracted any of his comments on the "Jewish question."

Flowering Rifle is now out of print, and Campbell did not include anything from it in his 1955 *Selected Poems*, but this may have been simply because the poem is too long and does not lend itself to excerpting. His autobiography, published in 1951, gives no indication that he later regretted anything he wrote in 1939. On the contrary, he takes pride in having been anti-Communist before anticommunism became fashionable: "Alone of the British intellectuals [a slight overstatement], I dared to affect a pro-European, anti-Soviet line."[76] He appears to have felt deeply wounded that so many of his former friends considered him a Fascist, though he comforts himself with the reflection that "anyone who was not pro-Red in the Spanish War automatically became a 'fascist'."[77] This is partly true, but *Flowering Rifle* is rather more than "not pro-Red," and if Campbell's critics were intemperate in their judgment of him, he had not set them a very different example.

Campbell volunteered as a private in the British Army when World War II began (a reader of *Flowering Rifle* might almost wonder why), and he served honorably until invalided out as a sergeant. He seemed to consider his service against fascism as having canceled out his earlier services for it, and perhaps it did. In any case, whether *Flowering Rifle* helped persuade any of its contemporary readers of the justice of the Nationalist cause is impossible to know

homosexualism for refuge from responsibilities" (*A Time to Dance, Noah and the Waters, and Other Poems, with an essay, Revolution in Writing*, p. 83). Julian Symons considers the tolerance or even approval of homosexuality during these years part of the general demand for greater freedom in all areas. As editor of *Twentieth Century Verse* he had a large literary acquaintance, and he notes mildly: "It would probably be untrue to say that any writer of heterosexual instincts suffered seriously through this homosexual tendency among the young, but the assessment of writers on the basis of their sexual attractiveness can hardly be anything but damaging to literary standards" (*The Thirties: A Dream Revolved*, p. 32).

[76] Campbell, *Light on a Dark Horse*, p. 226.

[77] *Ibid.*

today, but it did nothing for Roy Campbell's stature as a poet. From the standpoint of his literary career, he might better have confined himself to using his rifle, not writing about it.

A more intellectually respectable proponent of the Nationalist cause was Campbell's friend and, to a degree, mentor, Wyndham Lewis. Like Campbell, Lewis was fiercely combative, fully convinced of the unique rightness of his position on any given subject at any given time, rather happy than not to be in a minority; but unlike his younger friend, Lewis never hesitated to change or even reverse positions in the light of new knowledge and understanding. As "unbought" as Campbell, he was still capable of recognizing when he was wrong, and he repudiated former opinions as unreservedly as he propounded his new ones. It is probably this integrity of character, as much as his independence of intellect and his very remarkable talents as writer and artist,[78] that explains the respect in which he has been held even by those who have rarely been able to agree with him on anything. Hugh Kenner begins his admiring study of Lewis by quoting some of the praise of others—Ezra Pound: "the man who was wrong about everything except the superiority of live mind to dead mind; for which basic verity God bless his holy name"; T. S. Eliot: "the most fascinating personality of our time"—and Kenner himself describes Lewis as "the necessary antidote to everything, from Freud and Lawrence to the cults which have surrounded Eliot and Joyce."[79]

During the period of the Spanish Civil War, Lewis was in deep "occultation" (his word) as a result of his having managed to offend virtually everyone of influence in the British literary world, and he was no more popular in the United States. He had for twenty years systematically "blasted," in his novels and in direct polemics, very nearly every new trend in art or letters from impressionism through Bergsonism and primitivism to literary Marxism—by no means as a conservative deploring change but as a revolutionary without a party. In *Time and Western Man* (1927), he defined and attacked, with exuberant and mordant wit, the "Time-cult" that, he contended, sub-

[78] Walter Sickert called him "the greatest portraitist who ever lived" (quoted by Hugh Kenner, *Wyndham Lewis*, p. xiii), and Joyce immortalized him as the Windy Nous of *Finnegans Wake*.

[79] *Ibid.*, pp. xiii–xv.

sumed almost the whole of serious contemporary art and held disastrous social and political implications. He conceived himself as "The Enemy" (the title of one of his short-lived journals) of the Zeitgeist, which he saw as a vast conspiracy against reason and individuality. In the next decade he was to narrow his range of attack and concentrate on one aspect after another of this conspiracy.

Lewis himself describes his "occultation" as "a purely *political* phenomenon," and says that it began with the publication of his *Paleface* (1929),[80] an attack on the fashionable cult of the superiority in art, sex, and general *savoir vivre* of the dark races that was widely understood as a declaration of white supremacy and hence roundly denounced. This was a misinterpretation, but Lewis' habitual overstatement of whatever case he happened to be making can be held at least partly responsible. Trying to explain some of Lewis' inconsistencies, Kenner notes his tendency to take different tacks in addressing different audiences and urges that it be kept in mind, but he adds, "On the other hand, it must not be forgotten that he has always tended to believe in the exhaustiveness of what he is writing at the moment."[81]

In a study of Shakespeare, *The Lion and the Fox*, and in *The Art of Being Ruled*, both written in the later twenties, Lewis had given vigorous assent to the Machiavellian view of the nature of politics and of man. He stressed the accuracy of Machiavelli's analysis and at least verged on approval of Machiavellian tactics. His suggestion that a strong, not overly scrupulous leader might be a good thing for the intellectually lazy and incompetent mass (or "herd") did not go down well with the majority of British intellectuals, who were already beginning to move, to paraphrase Spender, leftward from liberalism.

From the standpoint of his literary career, Lewis' most disastrous book was *Hitler*, written in 1930. There he presented a generally favorable judgment on Nazi economics, which he later described as much like the Social Credit of "our Major Douglas, who is the economic equivalent of Paul Klee in painting."[82] He was also sympa-

[80] Wyndham Lewis, *Rude Assignment: A Narrative of My Career Up-to-Date*, p. 20.

[81] Kenner, *Wyndham Lewis*, p. 35 n.

[82] Wyndham Lewis, *The Hitler Cult*, p. 26. Social Credit, sometimes called "distributive economics," of which the most striking aspect is the idea of com-

thetic to Nazi criticisms of the Versailles Treaty and of French efforts to dominate Europe, and he then saw some promise in the Nazi movement. In youth, he later wrote, he had been attracted to the notion of a classless society, although more on the lines of Proudhon than of Marx, with "some species of authoritarian control some 'planning' from a creative centre"; but, having already concluded by 1930 that communism was a "racket," he turned to "the *pis-aller* of the traditional Western scene, with its routine half-measures, of which National Socialism was a spectacular specimen."[83] Repelled by what seemed to him the moral corruption of the Berlin of 1930, most apparent in the flagrant homosexuality, he was also favorably impressed by the stern puritanism of the Nazis; and in observing the constant street warfare between the "old proletariat" of the workers and the "new proletariat" of the "penniless rabble," which had been middle-class,[84] he came to see Hitler as a strong, imaginative leader who might bring economic and moral order to Germany. As for the "Jewish question," he did not then consider it an important part of Nazism: "I thought Hitler was only going on about the Jews as Germans always had."[85]

The Nazis did not like Lewis' book, partly because they felt he had scanted their racial doctrines, and they banned it, "though Heaven knows, compared with anything else that was penned about them in those days, it was a song of praise."[86] It was so interpreted in England, where it was taken to prove Lewis' Fascist sympathies and to confirm the charge of racism that *Paleface* had evoked. Lewis had specifically rejected Nazi racist theories in *Hitler*, but presumably those who did not read the book carefully (or at all) assumed that his general approval of Hitler covered these as well. By the end of the decade Lewis felt required to clear himself of anti-Semi-

batting depression by permitting the government to redistribute wealth through paying dividends to all citizens, gained considerable adherence during the thirties in England and Canada, and the Social Credit Party of Alberta is still, thirty years later, an important force. Ezra Pound seemed to consider Social Credit a possible defense against his bête noire, Usury, and Roy Campbell versified in its favor.

[83] *Ibid.*, pp. 21–22.

[84] *Ibid.*, p. 25.

[85] *Ibid.*, p. 17.

[86] *Ibid.*, p. 11.

tism by writing *The Jews: Are They Human?* (his answer was Yes) and of Nazi sympathies by *The Hitler Cult* (1939). In the latter work he offers a revised evaluation of Der Führer:

> With a big palpitating heart upon his homespun sleeve: with a handful of claptrap, and a perfectly good case for the revision of a stupid treaty, he weighed in ten years ago and "saved" what was left of the old and tried, in the midst of a workers' revolution gone wrong. For Herr Hitler is a product of German Communism. . . . He was at best, a "counter-something." . . . but Hitler as a political corrective, and Hitler as Augustus, are two different things.[87]

In his apologia, *Rude Assignment* (1950), Lewis does not specify at what date he lost such illusions as he had had about Nazism, but by the time of the Spanish Civil War he had not reached the point of condemning Hitler in anything like the terms he applied to Stalin. By 1939 he was arguing that "the natural alignment is England, France, and Russia," with American material backing, against Germany and Italy;[88] but as late as 1937 he was describing fascism as no threat at all but a defense against the threat of communism, and his siding with the Fascist-supported Nationalists against the Communist-supported Republic was therefore consistent with his general political attitude.

Yet it is possible to misunderstand Lewis' attitude during the thirties.[89] "I have indulged," he wrote in 1939, "in efforts at 'appeasement' beside which those of Mr. Chamberlain pale in comparison,"[90] but these efforts were primarily motivated not by a preference for fascism over communism but by an urgent desire to avoid war at almost any cost. Although not pacifist for religious reasons, Lewis had served throughout World War I, and he was unable to conceive that anything could be worse than another world war. He was convinced, as he argued in *Left Wings Over Europe* (1936), that the international Communist movement, with the Russian Revolution as its model and the repeated failures of the Left all over Europe

[87] *Ibid.*, pp. 45–46.

[88] *Ibid.*, p. 148.

[89] A plausible interpretation of Lewis' political and racial ideas, considerably less charitable than mine, is given in Geoffrey Wagner's interesting study, *Wyndham Lewis: A Portrait of the Artist as the Enemy.*

[90] Lewis, *The Hitler Cult*, p. viii.

as cautionary examples, had decided that only in the chaos and confusion of a general war could their various revolutionary movements hope for success; consequently, left-wing policy was, he believed, to foment war on any possible pretext.[91] Working from this premise, he had no difficulty in interpreting virtually all expression of anti-fascism—condemnation of Hitler's Jewish policies and German rearmament, the feeble League objections to Japanese and Italian aggression, the widespread support for the Spanish Republic—as hypocrisy masking a cynical conspiracy to bring on a terrible and unjustifiable war. His anxiety and sense of urgency, perhaps compounded by ill-health and personal resentment over the way his books were being attacked or ignored, led him into furious polemics and some unfortunate overstatement. Looking back in 1947, he concluded that his argumentative books of the thirties were "in the main . . . ill-judged, redundant, harmful of course to me personally, and of no value to anyone else," especially in view of the fact, as he now saw it, that appeasement of a "demented military adventurer" was "humane and sensible, but impossible."[92]

The ill feeling Lewis had aroused in British literary circles by *Paleface* and *Hitler* had doubtless been heavily increased by his 1932 novel, *The Apes of God*, a ferocious satire on "the social decay of the insanitary trough between the two great wars"[93] as it showed itself in Bloomsbury. Much of literary London apparently managed to plow through this "dazzling and memorable chaos,"[94] reading it as a *roman à clef* and finding in it a very unflattering reflection. Whether the retaliation upon Lewis was "purely political" as he said, or partly personal, it appears to have existed, although perhaps not to the degree that Lewis felt. In *Rude Assignment*, he tells of his works' being deliberately ignored by literary periodicals and favorable reviews of them refused publication. He recalls that when he sent *The Revenge for Love* to a "friendly" New York publisher, it was returned to him with a brief note suggesting there was no use in sending it

[91] There were leftists who held this view, which has some merit, but the Comintern apparently never adopted it as a policy, and most European and British leftists, in and out of the Communist Party, were as antiwar as Wyndham Lewis. See Chapter III.

[92] Lewis, *Rude Assignment*, p. 209.

[93] *Ibid.*, p. 199.

[94] Kenner, *Wyndham Lewis*, p. 106.

to any other American published.[95] British reviews of his works which appeared during the thirties tended to be brief and unfavorable, but Kenner's statement that Lewis' "books stopped being reviewed at all, and it was arranged that his best novel [*The Revenge for Love*] should suffocate unnoticed in England and go unpublished in the United States for fifteen years"[96] is only partly accurate. *The New Statesman and Nation* and *Time and Tide* gave this novel less attention than it deserved, but they printed reviews, as did Eliot's *Criterion*, and R. A. Scott-James's notice in the *London Mercury* is highly enthusiastic.

Lewis had much to say about the Spanish Civil War. His most extended comment is in *Count Your Dead: They Are Alive,* subtitled "A New War in the Making" (1937), which is in the form of a dialogue between a "wild Irishman" named Ned, whom Lewis identifies as his spokesman, and a Blimp-like clubman named Launcelot Nidwit. Launcelot, a Tory pro-Loyalist who foolishly considers himself a member of the ruling class, struggles futilely to reconcile the Republican propaganda he is fed by the pink British press and the B.B.C. with the "facts" Ned has ascertained from the more reliable Nationalist sources. Finally, just before dying of "an overdose of truth," Launcelot reaches the point of speaking out against the preparations for a general war over nothing, contending that the dead of the next war are still alive and need not die at all if the British public will only face the truth.

Launcelot provides some excellent comedy as he observes that the strongest pro-Communists in Britain, as in France, are real *pukka sahib* types; that the Bolshies seem to be sounder fellows than he had at first thought, now that they are building mansions with servants' quarters in Moscow and are killing Jews like Zinoviev; that Baldwin is really very clever in appearing to play the socialist game by helping their cause in Spain while he is really just dishing the Opposition by stealing their thunder—he could in fact carry thunder-stealing to the point of establishing a Popular Front government without losing the confidence of Tories like Launcelot. Launcelot thinks it a little odd that Hitler, "of all people," should have so riled Baldwin as to make him risk war to destroy Nazism; it "*does* seem a

[95] Lewis, *Rude Assignment*, p. 215.
[96] Kenner, *Wyndham Lewis*, p. 85.

little *disproportionate* somehow. In other times, Mr. Baldwin might even have been suspected of being a little mad,"[97] but of course there must be some reasonable explanation, obscure as it may be to Launcelot.

Speaking as the voice of reason, Ned explains why the international loan capitalists, *of* Britain though not *for* her, who make up the "financial directorate" that controls the British government and the mass media,[98] have aligned themselves with the forces of international communism: they have as much to gain through the centralization of financial power as the Reds have through the centralization of political power; both, having long since abandoned true socialism or economic liberalism, want an International State Capitalism, "a big Americanized mass-state."[99] Baldwin, stupid but honest, really believes that his crypto-socialist policies are temporarily fending off communism, although he unconsciously (in England "nothing is conscious") senses that communism offers the only real solution to British economic problems. Actually, communism is not the only solution: "I will be very naughty, and say that Fascism might be a very good solution indeed. But any solution would be better than Marx."[100]

According to Ned, the British belief that Hitler is a threat to Europe is both dangerous, since likely to bring on an "entirely purposeless" war, and false: actually it is Hitler who is being threatened, who is being told he must become "part of the Franco-Soviet military system" (which is what is really behind the League of Nations front), must borrow from British, French and American banks, and must accept communism or "be prepared for attack."[101] Ned cannot accept Hitler's notions that the Jews are after political power (all they are really after is money) or his theories of Aryan superiority, but otherwise Hitler seems pretty rational, certainly more so than the British government.

As for Spain, says Ned,

[97] Wyndham Lewis, *Count Your Dead: They are Alive: A New War in the Making*, p. 191.
[98] *Ibid.*, p. 29.
[99] *Ibid.*, p. 230.
[100] *Ibid.*, p. 83.
[101] *Ibid.*, p. 77.

General Franco is an ordinary old-fashioned anti-monarchical Spanish *liberal* . . . If no Communist agitators (that is salaried officials of the Imperial Red Government of our friend and ally Russia) had entered Spain, sojourned there, stirred up a Soviet revolution there, then there would have been no Franco, no Alcázar, no bombing of Madrid, no nothing. Just backward old Spanish liberalist democracy, jogging along, on its sleepy, penurious, dignified way. Ever so picturesque, and probably happier than it will ever be again—in spite of the lazy squalor and corruption.[102]

More thorough students of Spanish history do not share Lewis' certainty that without foreign agitation the Spanish poor would have remained content, nor do the "facts" from Nationalist sources with which Ned so triumphantly refutes Republican propaganda always merit his confidence. He is safe enough in ridiculing the Loyalist custom of proclaiming the capture of military objectives well before it has taken place, if it happens at all. On the other hand, he is poorly informed on the power and extent of Russian or Comintern influence in Spain before the Civil War, and his estimates of the numbers and political complexion of the International Brigades are badly off. His account of the sequence of events in 1936, that German and Italian aid was not sent to the Nationalists until December, indicates too exclusive a reliance on Nationalist sources. It is easy to concur in the judgment of R. A. Scott-James that *Count Your Dead*, although interesting, vigorous, and lucid, fails of persuasiveness because it assumes so many "facts" that "we cannot swallow as facts."[103]

What is rather distressing for the admirer of Lewis is the suspicion that he was less than entirely candid in his comments on Germany in this book. It is possible that the events of something over a year, between the writing of this book and of *The Hitler Cult*, were sufficient in themselves to effect the complete turnabout that Lewis made in his evaluations of Nazi policies and intentions;[104] yet it seems

[102] *Ibid.*, p. 196.

[103] "Two Books by Mr. Wyndham Lewis," *London Mercury* XXXVI, No. 212 (June 1937), 201.

[104] He also turned about sharply in regard to the Spanish War. In *The Hitler Cult* of 1939, he wrote (pp. 182–183) that Britain had had two "sane" alternatives in that war, either "to refrain from all action and offer our services at its conclusion to whoever happened to have come out on top" or, better, to have "sunk all the pocket-battleships and 'barred' Spanish waters to Axis shipping for the duration . . ." Supporting Franco and accepting Axis intervention as justified no longer seemed "sane" to him.

likelier that he was less sure of their peaceful and defensive nature than he let himself appear in *Count Your Dead*. As he explained later, he was then convinced that whether war could be avoided depended on good relations between Britain and Germany. That he deliberately overstated his judgment of Hitler's peaceful intentions in this book is at least possible, and although such distortion is expected of politicians and publicists, and may even be approved as serving a useful purpose, it appears ill in a man who made something of a fetish of honesty.

More disturbing is Lewis' use in this book of anti-Semitic appeals. Despite the charges of his detractors, his attitudes on "race" were never exceptionable by the most "liberal" standards. He always took pains to dissociate his praise of Hitler from his disapproval of Nazi racism, and although he has much to say about Jews in such novels as *The Apes of God*, none of his comment even verges on the anti-Semitic. Yet in his effort to win British support for his views on the international situation he made use of devices calculated to profit from the considerable amount of anti-Semitism that existed in England. Launcelot, as a satirical puppet figure, could be expected to mouth some anti-Semitic clichés without suggesting any author sympathy, but when Ned, in his "factual" speeches, invariably refers to the Soviet Ambassador in Madrid, Marcel Rosenberg, as "Don Moses" and to Trotsky by his Jewish name, Bronstein, the reader has grounds for feeling that Lewis is making use of that most popular of all Fascist propaganda lines, the identification of communism with World Jewry.

The most entertaining, and apt, comment on *Count Your Dead* was the review by Malcolm Muggeridge, no rabid pro-Loyalist himself. Having noted Lewis' "unusual feat" in being a non-leftist intellectual, he described reading him as

> like hearing a Hyde Park orator in the distance and supposing from his tremulously earnest voice that he is some passionate evangelist, then approaching nearer and finding that in fact he is asking where Cain got his wife; or like a Montmartre restaurant being used as an officers' mess.[105]

Muggeridge finds Lewis' conspiracy theory about as plausible as the

[105] Malcolm Muggeridge, "Men and Books," *Time and Tide*, XVIII, No. 21 (May 23, 1937), 693.

leftist charges that Baldwin, Eden, and others were conspiring with Hitler, but he closes:

> This is Mr. Wyndham Lewis' fantasy, only differing from Launcelot's in that, being of the Intelligentsia, he made it up himself whereas Launcelot accepted his ready-made. He demolishes Launcelot's . . . fantasy with such zest and affect that it is rather sad seeing him succumb to one of his own, like being told by a famous brain specialist that he is the Nizam of Hyderabad. If only there were Conspiracies of the Left or Right . . . instead of just the play of everlasting appetites trailing behind them hate and exaltation and envy.[106]

Count Your Dead, whether or not it furthered the Nationalist cause in England, is not important in Lewis' career as a writer, but the publication in the same year of the novel, *The Revenge for Love*, was a significant event, however little noticed at the time. Although it did not quite "suffocate unnoticed," this best of Lewis' novels received considerably less attention than any number of poorer works published in 1937, and the reasons for its neglect seem to have been entirely extraliterary. Lewis was able to cite at least one such instance: a young New York Trotskyist (whose interpretation of the novel as an attack on Stalinism Lewis rejected) wrote him that she had submitted a highly favorable notice of *The Revenge for Love* to a leading "liberal" American periodical (unnamed) which had been regularly printing her reviews; after having turned it down twice without giving reasons, the editor finally explained that he would not print the review because "if Percy Hardcaster was *her* idea of a communist it was not his."[107]

Lewis stated later that his writing about a Communist had enraged people as a non-Catholic's writing about a priest would have done, since Catholic writers like Greene and Mauriac were allowed a freedom in such areas which would never be tolerated in non-Catholics.[108] It is more likely that a good many people, prejudiced against him because of his polemical writings, simply did not read the novel, and that many of those who did, not only found Percy Hardcaster different from their ideas of a Communist, but, more important, found

[106] *Ibid.*, p. 694.
[107] Lewis, *Rude Assignment*, p. 216.
[108] *Ibid.*

the middle- and upper-class parlor-pinks of the novel very different indeed from their ideas of themselves.

The Revenge for Love was reissued in England and first published in the United States fifteen years after its initial publication; the interval has made possible a wider and less prejudiced reading of the novel. In the Lewis canon, it marks a happy departure from the dense and strained style into which his theories of the comic and of prose composition had led him during the previous ten years, which, in Kenner's words, "saw the squandering of an unprecedented talent."[109] *The Apes of God* had brilliantly and deplorably exemplified Lewis' "puppet" theory of satire: "The root of the Comic is to be sought in the sensations resulting from the observation of a *thing* behaving like a person."[110] The effect of making every character in this long novel simply a puppet is to increase the normally valuable comic distance far beyond expediency. The reader's emotions are so completely untouched that he is quite unwilling to make the intellectual effort required to work his way through Lewis' tortuosities of style—and effort is indeed required because of the author's determination to exhaust the descriptive and satirical possibilities of every gesture and inflection, however the strained metaphors and epithets may pile up. The prose is not only dense but rich, so rich as to become indigestible after a very few pages. Lewis' style here, which Kenner describes in another connection as "the fabrication of a world, hardly more than word-deep, by a species of verbal impasto,"[111] in combination with his puppet theory of characterization, produces a novel that is often brilliantly witty in individual passages but is almost unreadably dull as a whole.[112]

The Revenge for Love is quite a different matter. "Chastened" is a word that hardly seems applicable to any of Wyndham Lewis' successive styles, but it approximates the fortunate difference between the prose of *The Revenge for Love* and that of *The Apes of God.* Lewis' highhanded way with syntax remains, and so does much of

[109] Kenner, *Wyndham Lewis*, p. 95.

[110] Quoted in *ibid.*, p. 95. Lewis' disapproval of Bergson's influence did not preclude his borrowing Bergson's ideas.

[111] *Ibid.*, p. 92.

[112] Geoffrey Wagner considers *The Apes of God* Lewis' best novel and the best satire of the present century (*Wyndham Lewis,* pp. 247–255).

his wordplay for its own ingenious sake, but in the later novel the verbal texture is an integral part of the very carefully worked general design; it furthers rather than impedes the narrative, and it rarely obtrudes itself. The novel is singularly free from waste motion in language or incident, thus affording a strong contrast to Lewis' tendency in the immediately preceding works to wander afar in pursuit of interesting irrelevancies. There are remnants of the puppet theory very effectively employed in the treatment of most of the minor characters, but the chief protagonists are given enough genuine life to evoke emotions stronger and more complicated than amused contempt. Kenner describes *The Revenge for Love* as "a sort of act of belief in the existence of other people"[113] for Lewis, and it is certainly his most "human" work.

The title under which the novel was written was *False Bottoms*, and the subject is unreality. Nothing is quite what it seems, from the fruit basket with a hidden compartment in the opening pages to the old bootlegger's bus with a false floor in the last. Least of all are political and artistic appearances and professions, and those who make them, to be believed. Although the novel appeared in 1937, it seems to have been completed in 1936, probably before the outbreak of the Spanish War. In any case, the Spanish government of the novel is the right-wing coalition led by Lerroux, which was voted out in February of 1936. The book is thus not specifically about the Civil War but about the moral, intellectual, and political climate of England at the time. Whether it is a full or fair picture of left-wing London is not quite to the point: as creator of his own game, an author holds the entire deck and may stack the cards as he chooses. He need not be judged by the same standards that are applied to nonfiction, and the reader must meet him on his own terms.

Percy Hardcaster, the English Communist who so offended the liberal editor, is introduced waiting fairly patiently in a prison, probably in Barcelona, for the British government to obtain his release. He unwisely gets involved in an attempt to escape during which he is shot. Recuperating from the amputation of his leg, he is smothered with tender loving care by the nuns of the local hospital, but when he is well enough to return to England and become the lion of the

[113] Kenner, *Wyndham Lewis*, p. 121. Kenner suggests (p. 85) that some of Lewis' bad guesses in the thirties sprang from his confessed propensity for seeing not people but principles.

left wing, he makes their flesh creep deliciously with bloodcurdling accounts of his maltreatment by fanatical Jesuits. Percy really did resent the attentions of the oversolicitous nuns—"he spat as much on kind hearts as on coronets"[114]—and "the Jesuit *was* his enemy—as much as anyone in the world. Since Percy was a good-natured man, it was not much."[115] But his atrocity stories are only one of the more diverting parts of his work, "bluff" being "the tactical basis for the latter-day revolutionary personality . . . The *bogus* in the bursting uplift it was that made it intellectually bearable. It made it a game."[116] Hardcaster, a working-class intellectual who genuinely believes that communism is in the best interests of his class and himself, nevertheless is not concerned with differentiating too nicely between "bluff" and truth: he is interested in tactics, and his attitude toward his work is pre-eminently professional and prudent:

> Percy was not a *front-fighter* or anything of that nature, but rather a careerist of the propaganda section. The technique of the general strike, of the *coup d'état,* he had at his finger-tips: but he was a brass-hat in the class war.[117]

Percy Hardcaster has nothing but contempt for the upper-class Communists and fellow travelers who welcome him and hang so reverently on his words, although the sight of his stump tends to reinforce their feeling that they are destined to be "*the brains* of the Revolution" rather than common troops. The only other real professional in the group is Sean O'Hara, a very John-Bullish Irishman with a taste for conspiracy, a talent for spotting spies, and a past that has been heavily shadowed by suspicion of treachery. The rest are enthusiastic amateurs, university-educated literary and artistic types who have taken up Marxism and the proletariat as they have taken up the fake squalor of Bohemia. Eminent among these are the Phippses: Tristram, a talented artist and docile Party liner who has rebelled against his class by choosing to live penuriously by what he can earn from advertising art, but whose communism is as complacent and uncritical as the Conservatism of his clergyman father; and his handsome wife Gillian, who is at the same time more passionately Com-

114 Wyndham Lewis, *The Revenge for Love*, p. 44.
115 *Ibid.*, p. 46.
116 *Ibid.*, p. 46.
117 *Ibid.*, p. 38.

munist and more insistent on reminding everyone of the very high status which she has repudiated on political principle.

The climactic political dialogue of the book occurs when Percy, expecting amused understanding, mentions to Gillian the falsity of his Spanish atrocity stories. Instead of appreciating his professional technique as a propagandist, she is indignant at his cynicism. She points out that his communism is less pure than hers because he is paid for his work,[118] and when he comments wryly that he isn't paid very well, she answers, "Like all your class, you expect to be paid through the nose for everything you do and then you grumble all the time because you aren't paid enough." Angered, Percy gives her a lecture on revolutionary realities: it is not "heroes" who are needed but competent technicians like himself. The lofty rhetoric of "*salon* revolutionaries" is meaningless—they consider communism a "little romance of revolution" but in fact care not at all for the workers whose cause they profess to espouse. These upper-class fakers have their usefulness, nevertheless, particularly in their financial contributions, and professionals like Percy are perfectly willing to accept their help, while entirely indifferent as to whether such dilettantes survive the revolution they are helping to foment. Hearing all this, Gillian experiences the sensation described in Day Lewis' poem, "for when the sham Communist beholds the real Communist, in all his authentic reality, the former must of necessity feel small—as all other counterfeits must feel diminished under similar circumstances. Even without the poet we could imagine that."[119] She recovers sufficiently to have Percy thoroughly beaten up by another of her hangers-on, and later she reflects:

> Those who were *not* of the class for whom all this was being done had to be a sort of saint, as far as she could see, to stomach all they had to stomach—in the way of ingratitude, recrimination, and general brutality. . . . [She feels] a very angry martyr, . . . seething with *noblesse oblige* . . . full of class-hatred of the class it was her hard lot to have to save.[120]

When her husband comes home, Gillian reveals her suspicion that Percy is really an "unconscious fascist," at best a mercenary and hence

[118] See Chapter VI, for C. Day Lewis' expression of a rather similar attitude.

[119] Lewis, *Revenge for Love*, pp. 181–182.

[120] *Ibid.*, p. 200.

a "potential traitor," since, lacking the independent income that makes upper-class Communists truly disinterested, he looks on the revolution as a job and brings "with him all his working-class cynicism, all his under-dog cowardice and disbelief in everything and everybody."[121] Tris, however, is unshaken in his faith, though he begins to doubt his wife's "sense of reality." Before long, the marriage is over and Gillian has moved in with her bully-boy, Jack Cruze.

Jack is an outsider among the genteel and the professional revolutionaries. A kind of counterpart to Percy in appearance and background, he has also risen in the world, and he devotes himself to the pursuit of women and money (in that order) with the same businesslike competence which Percy gives to the revolution; in the pinch he sides with the upper-class Gillian. A cheerful, nonpolitical satyr, he serves the novelist chiefly as a foil, a piece of solid and vulgar reality against which to show the falsity and hypocrisy of the Phippses' circle.

Also outsiders, and destined to be victims, are Victor and Margot Stamp. Victor is a big, handsome, working-class Australian with Clark Gable dimples and a second-rate artistic talent. Kenner suggests that as Percy Hardcaster represents "Lewis the polemicist reduced to an 'injured party'," Vic is "Lewis the artist deprived of his genius."[122] Possibly, but Vic seems more explicitly to represent Lewis' idea of the "natural man" in contrast to the very unnatural poseurs who surround and exploit him. He is, like Jack, nonpolitical: "He did not give a damn, one way or the other, for 'the People'," and he has "the instinctive scepticism of the cannon-fodder, regarding all wars, of class or nation."[123] Unlike Jack, a simple sensualist, Vic has interests outside himself. He does not reflect for long about anything but painting, but his appraisal of his own talents is both honest and accurate, and his derision of Marx as art critic is pointed. He has a strong sense of personal integrity and of responsibility to Margot, but these derive from "the pact of nature," not from any ready-made moral code (they are not legally married). An unsympathetic intellectual acquaintance has characterized him as "the Kipling man—1930 American version," now "in fact, an outlaw, at best in a Big Game Park."[124] He is not intelli-

[121] *Ibid.*, pp. 205–206.
[122] Kenner, *Wyndham Lewis*, p. 135.
[123] Lewis, *Revenge for Love*, pp. 65–66.
[124] *Ibid.*, p. 321.

gent, but his instincts are dependable. Tris Phipps, defending Vic to his friends—although with some disapproval of his unrealism and individualism—compares him to Germany:

> He is very nationalist. His nation is Victor. And he suffers from a permanent sense of injury. . . . He *feels* like a Great Power . . . a rather impoverished, mutilated, but extremely chauvinistic Great Power! . . . he is quite convinced . . . that you are a lot of hypocritical crooks, between whom and himself there can be no common ground of understanding.[125]

Margot Stamp, in some ways the central character of the novel, nicely reverses the pattern of most of the others, who are plausible fakes: she is an implausible natural, compact of artificiality and affectation but absolutely sound at bottom. Her name is an affectation (she was christened Margaret) and so is her speech, which has a vaguely foreign flavor because she has painfully taught herself English instead of her native Cockney. Her interior monologues are strongly reminiscent of a Gertie MacDowell who has read Virginia Woolf as well as Marie Corelli. Vic is her own private movie star, and she has absolute faith in his "genius." Vic is also her cause, and she is utterly indifferent to any other. She is narrow and commonplace and a little vulgarly genteel, but throughout the novel she is consistently right about everything except Vic's genius, and the reader is left wondering if she may not even be partly right about that. When she first appears in the novel, she is musing that the financial troubles she and Vic are experiencing may represent a "revenge for love" by a hostile world that will not tolerate anything as good and natural and real as their love. She thinks in terms of trashy sentiment, but her conclusion is the "message" of the novel.

Margot is easily intimidated but not deceived. She instinctively dislikes the superior Gillian and distrusts Gillian's friends, whose sympathy for the underdog she finds unconvincing and whom she suspects of designs to exploit her own favorite underdog, Vic. She is confused and puzzled by their Marxist patter:

> It all seemed to register *nothing*—or just nonsense. They recited to each other, with the foolish conceit of children, lessons out of textbooks. . . . she was conscious . . . of a prodigious *non sequitur*, at the centre of every-

[125] *Ibid.*, p. 245.

thing . . . of an immense *false bottom* underlying every seemingly solid surface.[126]

She is particularly mistrustful of the urbane and elegant Abershaw, a wealthy clubman and financier whom she discovers with Sean O'Hara, practicing forgery of Vic's name.

Vic, desperate for money, goes to work for Abershaw as a forger of "modern masters." His friend, Tris, more talented and less individual, proves skillful at the work, but Vic, unable to produce a sufficiently convincing Van Gogh to please his employer, angrily quits. Abershaw is annoyed, but he soon finds more work for Vic: he invites him and Percy to run a load of rifles across the Pyrenees to Spain. Percy is to provide the experience and Victor the muscle, with Margot to stay on the French side as a kind of guarantee that Vic will carry out his assignment. She is suspicious, and Percy has to be assured that the entire operation is simply a commercial venture for Abershaw, with no political implications. Vic, however, looks on the venture as merely a way to earn money rather more honestly than by art forgery.

Margot's misgivings are proven right. Just before Vic is due to cross the Franco-Spanish border driving a false-bottomed bootlegger's bus supposedly laden with rifles for Spanish leftists, their French contact shows them a letter over Vic's signature that identifies him as leader of all the Red smuggling activities. Indignant over the forgery, Margot resolves to "put a stop to all this," and Percy is puzzled. Vic, however, takes his wife's opposition as a dare and secretly leaves on the mission. Percy has approved his leaving, thinking him in no danger, but on discovering that another shipment of rifles is being made at the same time by a different route, he begins to suspect that Vic is being used as a decoy and that the attention of the Spanish authorities has been deliberately directed to him. In a rather startling departure from professional prudence, he hurries to Vic's destination to warn him and is himself picked up by the Spanish police who have been waiting. Margot has gone a different way, and she intercepts Vic but is unable to persuade him to turn back until they are well into Spain, where the bus breaks down and Vic discovers that the false bottom contains not rifles but bricks. They start back toward France

[126] *Ibid.*, p. 148.

on foot but, lost in a mountain storm, stumble off a precipice, the final "false bottom." The novel ends with Percy Hardcaster, again in prison, learning of their death. For the benefit of his Spanish captors he denies any complicity in the smuggling, puts on "the mask of THE INJURED PARTY (model for militant agents in distress)," and demands to see the British consul.

But meanwhile a strained and hollow voice, part of a sham-culture outfit, but tender and halting, as if dismayed at the sound of its own bitter words, was talking in his ears, in a reproachful singsong. It was denouncing him out of the past, where alone it was able to articulate; it was singling him out as a man who led people into mortal danger, people who were dear beyond expression to the possessor of the passionate, the artificial, the unreal, yet penetrating voice, and crying to him now to give back, she implored him, the young man, Absalom, whose life he had had in his keeping, and who had somehow, unaccountably, been lost, out of the world and out of Time! He saw a precipice. And the eyes in the mask of THE INJURED PARTY dilated in a spasm of astonished self-pity. And down the front of the mask rolled a sudden tear, which fell upon the dirty floor of the prison.[127]

Victor Stamp is, of course, the cannon fodder, the likable and innocent victim of the whole self-seeking and hypocritical conspiracy formed by the ambiguous financier Abershaw, the treacherous O'Hara, the foolish but dangerous left-wing dilettantes of London, and the professional agitator Hardcaster. He represents the "true stamp" in a world of forgery and deceit, and his only, inadequate champion is Margot. In a conversation with his French smuggler-colleague, Percy had sardonically conceded that Margot did indeed place her husband above the social revolution and could hence be accused of loving him more than any individual should be loved; but he insisted that for her Vic was a fad, not a passion. Yet despite the fog of sentimental illusion through which she sees Vic and herself, Margot alone is able to discern the true from the false; but she can only die with him, not save him. The power of love is insufficient in a world of false bottoms.

As propaganda, *The Revenge for Love* preaches the message of *Count Your Dead*: the natural man, properly devoted only to his

[127] *Ibid.*, pp. 340–341.

work and to his personal relationships, who is supposed to be the object of the solicitude of those hypocrites who wield real power, is actually their pawn and victim. Their real interests are not what they profess: the international financiers are after profit, the Communists are after power for themselves, and the left-wing intellectuals are really concerned only with maintaining a diverting pose that expresses their neurotic rootlessness.

If this novel proposed to offer a balanced and impartial historical picture of the British left wing on the eve of the Spanish War, it could be faulted on several counts. The history of the period simply does not sustain Lewis' conviction that the "all-powerful, *de facto* ruler of Great Britain" was "that vague entity . . . which went by the name of the 'Left Wing' ";[128] and the implication that all middle- and upper-class leftists fit the highly entertaining satirical pattern that Lewis presents, is belied by both the words and the acts of many who belonged in that category. There is abundant substantiation of the accuracy of the portrait of Hardcaster as one kind of Communist, but there appear to have been other kinds as well during this period. However, *The Revenge for Love* is a remarkably successful work of fiction.

Part of Lewis' achievement is in the nice discrimination he shows in allowing precisely suitable degrees of reality to his cast. Percy, Vic, and Margot—and, to a degree, Jack Cruze—are the only "real" people in the book, and only they are presented as other than the puppets who exclusively populate Lewis' earlier fiction. Dealing with human beings is, as Kenner noted, something Lewis had not tried before, and so is the attempt to evoke emotional, rather than purely intellectual, response in his readers. He manages this by the deft blend of satire and sympathy with which he treats his "victims." Vic embodies good, solid, manly virtue, but he is also thickheaded and fatuously "male." The repeated evocation of his resemblance to Clark Gable and of his wife's movie-fan worship of him provides a kind of satirical edge to cut away any excess sentimentality in the reader's reactions. The combination of unswerving wifely devotion and clear moral perception with absurd affectation in Margot is sustained throughout. As for Percy, he is both villain and victim. Because of the demands of

[128] *Ibid.*, p. 338.

his métier he must bear responsibility for the deaths of a man he likes and a woman he grudgingly respects. As a soldier of communism, which Orwell called "the patriotism of the dispossessed," he exemplifies Lewis' views on the effects of politics of all sorts:

There are no *good* politics. All nations are brutes. What is more, they brutalize *us*: we are born nice, but gradually we develop a bad character. This is largely because of the bad example set us by the State.[129]

Commenting on his Trotskyist admirer's description of *The Revenge for Love* as an exposé of Stalinist "indifference to the people," Lewis has denied that "true Stalinists," as opposed to "sham Stalinists," are thus indifferent.[130] A true Stalinist, Percy is a better man than his work allows him to be. He is essentially a comic character, expressing the Marxism of Groucho as much as of Karl in his behavior, but he is a very attractive figure among the unrelievedly contemptible puppets who comprise the rest of the ranks of the conspiracy against love. His service to his chosen profession is "sincere," but the nature of that profession demands of him the same dishonesty and hypocrisy that come so naturally to the shams. In this novel Lewis has focussed his attack on the falsity and deceit that he felt surrounded the civil conflict in Spain, but he could have written much the same novel about other events, before and since the Spanish War. The disedifying spectacle of political events providing opportunity for the self-seeking, corrupting the decent, and destroying the innocent is, unfortunately, still with us.

Lewis later repudiated, in his thorough way, virtually all of the explicit policies he was so fervently advocating in the thirties ("This is not retraction: it is contradiction"[131]). At that time he tended to associate national sovereignty with personal individualism; by 1950 he had announced himself as a "doctrinaire internationalist" and a firm believer in centralized world government. The attitudes of others may not have changed so much since then, but Lewis appeared confident that in time, "when the passions of the present time are no more than feverish memories, people will take *The Revenge for Love* up and read it *as a novel.*"[132]

[129] Lewis, *Rude Assignment*, p. 22.
[130] *Ibid.*, p. 217.
[131] *Ibid.*, p. 211.
[132] *Ibid.*, p. 215.

In summary, the Nationalist cause elicited relatively little literary support in Great Britain because of its own deficiencies, its confused and clumsy propaganda, and its early and continuing success in Spain, which deprived most of its adherents of the sense of desperation that impelled proponents of the losing Republican side to ever greater effort. The most eminent "traditionalists" who might have been expected to lend their support, Eliot and Yeats, publicly expressed no preferences. Pound was vocal but largely unintelligible to the general public. Of the leading Catholic novelists, Waugh was publicly pro-Franco but the most lukewarm of propagandists, and Greene was publicly silent but revealed a probable Republican bias in his only novel inspired by the war. Roy Campbell fought enthusiastically for the cause, with pen as well as with rifle, but *Flowering Rifle* very likely lost as many previously uncommitted readers by its fanatical ferocity as it gained by its burning conviction, and the poem added nothing to Campbell's stature as a poet. Wyndham Lewis' *Count Your Dead* was shortly rendered obsolete, and *The Revenge for Love*, despite its literary merits, is unlikely to have aided materially the Nationalist cause.

Chapter III

ON THE LEFT: ARGUMENT

The English who supported the Spanish Republic with money, propaganda, even their lives, were many, and they represented a wide political spectrum from the Center to the Far Left. "The pull was terrific," wrote John Lehmann, "of an international crusade to the ideals of which all intellectuals (except those of strong Catholic attachment) who had been stirred by the Fascist danger, felt they could, in that hour of apocalypse, whole-heartedly assent."[1] There were large areas of agreement: that the Republic was a legal, democratically elected government being attacked by reactionary forces that were, if not Fascist themselves, the tools of Fascist allies; that fascism represented the most serious present threat to European civilization and must be resisted in its advance; that communism, whether one approved it or not, was not the issue in Spain, as the Right claimed, and neither was religion; that a Fascist victory would endanger British interests by permitting German and Italian control of the Mediterranean and by surrounding Britain's chief ally, France. All were able further to agree that the Non-Intervention agreement had swiftly become a pious hypocrisy and that the British National government should resist the Axis blockade of the Republic, try to get all foreign "volunteers" withdrawn from Spain, and allow

[1] John Lehmann, *The Whispering Gallery: Autobiography I*, pp. 274–275.

the Republic to buy the arms necessary to defend itself. Nearly all approved the war policy decided upon by the Republican government and supported by the Communists in Spain: deferral of extensive social reforms until after victory, development of a conventionally organized regular army in place of the irregular militia forces, strengthening of central authority, cooperation with small capitalists, and reversal of such revolutionary changes as had taken place during the first chaotic weeks of the uprising.

The most immediately striking thing about this list of attitudes and aims is that they were strictly short-run. On the long-run meanings of the Spanish War, there was extensive disagreement within the pro-Loyalist camp. While Liberals and Conservatives saw a Fascist victory as threatening the peace and security of Europe as it was, the Left saw it chiefly as an obstacle to their hopes for changing Europe to something different and better. Thus the Communist Harry Pollitt and the Duchess of Atholl, Sir Stafford Cripps of the Labour party and Winston Churchill were by mid-1938 in broad agreement on what should be British policy in regard to Spain, but their final aims were very different.

The pro-Loyalists considered in the next pages were only a part, although a large part, of the entire body, and they have been chosen for study because their participation in the general anti-Fascist cause drew sufficient attention to earn for the whole period the label of "The Red Decade," and also because they included many of the most talented intellectuals in Great Britain. Simply to call this group "the Left" would be misleading, since the British Left comprised a wide variety of attitudes. If a "leftist" is defined as anyone who generally accepts the major precepts of Marxist historical and economic thought, there is room within the definition for Communists, certain anarchists, social-democrats, and not a few simple liberals; there is also room for absolute pacifists and the most militant revolutionaries. Among those who share the goal of a classless society there is an almost infinite variety of ideas on how this can best be achieved. The section of the pro-Loyalist camp of primary concern here held certain ideas about means in common and can thus be fairly well differentiated from others with similar goals. For convenience of reference, this section, of which the Left Book Club was the center, will here be called the "Orthodox Left"—Orthodox because they were the leftists who looked most respectfully to Moscow and the British Communist Party for guidance during the confusing days of the thirties.

Probably the most enthusiastic and comprehensive, although not the best, statement of principles of the Orthodox Left at the height of its ebullience is the collection of essays edited by C. Day Lewis and published in 1937 as *The Mind in Chains: Socialism and the Cultural Revolution.* The contributors are all Marxist, some of them Communist, but Day Lewis' claim that they "represent the whole range of Left opinion" is something of an overstatement. The serious misgivings that many leftists had about the Soviet Union are nowhere reflected in the volume, and presumably all the contributors subscribed to the basic assumptions stated by Day Lewis in his introduction.

> *The Mind in Chains* could never have been written were it not for the widespread belief of intellectual workers that the mind is really in chains today, that these chains have been forged by a dying social system, that they can and must be broken—and in the Soviet Union have been broken; and that we can only realize our strength by joining forces with the millions of workers who have nothing to lose but their chains and have a world to win.[2]

The essays cover a wide range of subjects and vary widely both in quality and in their degree of admiration for the Soviet Union. Much of their criticism of contemporary British society was convincing at the time and continues to make sense even to readers who fail to share all the authors' premises. Rex Warner's criticism of British education is reasonable; the ascription to commercialism of many defects in the theater and films is still a commonplace; Charles Madge's attacks on the press and radio were well substantiated in the thirties and are not out of date yet; J. D. Bernal's call for greater public interest in science and for making scientific education more widely available has been echoed and largely implemented since. No one is likely to quarrel with the desire of Barbara Nixon, Anthony Blunt, and Alan Bush to see good drama, art, and music encouraged

[2] Cecil Day Lewis, ed., *The Mind in Chains: Socialism and the Cultural Revolution*, p. 17. The title did not go unchallenged by reviewers. William Plomer, no right-winger but much impressed by Gide's book and by the purge trials, entitled his review "New Chains for Old," *London Mercury*, XXXVI, No. 213 (July 1937), 299–300.

in production and disseminated widely. On the other hand, Blunt's prescription for a new art "less sophisticated, but more vital" than the old and his rejection of the movement toward abstraction and subjectivism have had little appeal for working artists even in Communist countries.[3] Nor have many talented musicians outside these countries shown any great desire to join the workers "to build up an art which springs from their struggle against the capitalist forces."[4] Some of Alistair Browne's criticisms of Freudian psychology seem well taken, yet his essay suffers from the premise, based on what evidence he does not say, that mental health, steadily deteriorating in the bourgeois West, was in 1937 steadily improving in the USSR, naturally enough because there the gap between the real and the ideal was so much smaller and guilt feelings and the need for rationalizations consequently so much less.[5]

Many of the essays are flawed by what seems, to the unconverted, vast oversimplification. Alan Bush's description of the pessimism and longing for death which he finds in Bach's music as "incomprehensible" except as a "reflection in the religious sphere of the dissatisfaction with its material conditions of the class to which he belonged"[6] is not wholly convincing. Nor, without haggling over definitions, could many people accept Anthony Blunt's reply to Herbert Read's concern over whether the demands of art should ever be sacrificed to the common good: "If an art is not contributing to the common good, it is bad art, and therefore to talk of *sacrificing* it is incorrect".[7]

What incurred most criticism of *The Mind in Chains* were the identification of socialism with Russian communism and the assumption, implied or stated, that Stalin's Russia was free from all the mental chains to which the contributors were pointing in England. Some of the contributors had anticipated these objections. Rex Warner explained how Russian dictatorship differed from other kinds, noting the "tremendous enthusiasm for culture" there as opposed to "its

[3] Anthony Blunt, "Art Under Capitalism and Socialism," in *Mind in Chains*, pp. 112–122.

[4] Alan Bush, "Music," in *ibid.*, p. 144.

[5] Alistair Browne, "Psychology," in *ibid.*, pp. 178–180.

[6] Bush, "Music," in *ibid.*, p. 129.

[7] Blunt, "Art Under Capitalism and Socialism," in *ibid.*, p. 122.

stagnation and decay in Germany and Italy." Besides, he added, "socialist" dictatorship is necessary to

defeat just those forces of reaction that are most opposed to culture. . . . [It] has no interest in the suppression of reason and of the culture of Europe, simply because socialism is ready to stand before the bar of reason and is the final flower of European culture. . . . the difference between socialism and the "respectable" creeds of liberalism and Christianity is simply this—socialism has the courage to put all the ideals of liberalism and many of the ideals of Christianity into *practice* . . . while the interests of socialism and the claims of reason and morality tend to coincide, with capitalism exactly the reverse is true. Nowadays . . . one need not be a Marxist, one need only be an ordinarily decent person to approve the immediate practical aims of Marxism. . . . If we find people who will not join with us "for socialism," let us at least be sure they are with us "against war" and "against fascism."[8]

T. A. Jackson deals with possible doubts about intellectual freedom in a Marxist society by demonstrating that Marxism "can be adapted less than any philosophy to the ends of dogmatism and persecution." It is clear from the context that he is speaking of Stalin's Russia (he begins by noting the "liberty of conscience" guarantee in the 1936 constitution), and therefore his arguments ring all the more strangely today. Communism, he says, in seeking "universal solidarity and brotherhood" is "more catholic than the Catholics," and in insisting on the "inalienable right of private judgment in spiritual matters" is "more protestant than the Protestants."[9] He is inclined to agree with Marx that, once a rational society has been established and the need for superstitions has passed, religion, "being a reflex phenomenon," will "die a natural death"; but even if it did not, no Communist society would persecute believers.

"revolutionary dictatorship of the proletariat" . . . is . . . no dictatorship at all in the fascist sense, but the highest form of democracy. . . . Marxism recognizes that finality in knowledge is quite unthinkable. . . . [It] is, and must be, ruthless in its resistance to all and every dogmatism. . . . [There-

[8] Rex Warner, "Education," in *ibid.*, pp. 34, 36–37. Warner was shortly to change his mind about the Russian variety of socialism. See Chapter IV.

[9] T. A. Jackson, "Communism, Religion, and Morals," in *ibid.*, p. 225. Jackson was the only contributor to this volume whose background was impeccably working-class.

fore it has] a bond of affinity with every persecuted sect and heresy in the world. . . . Its self-exclusion from dogmatism cuts it off from all possibility of developing into a religion, since to be a religion involves being at some point anti-critical, anti-rational, and dogmatic.[10]

The Mind in Chains includes a "Sketch for a Marxist Interpretation of Literature" by Edward Upward, whose practice of his principles will be considered in Chapter IV. Other persuasive proponents of Marxist literary doctrine during the thirties were Ralph Fox, whose *The Novel and the People* (1935)[11] makes a good case for "socialist realism," and Stephen Spender, whose *The Destructive Element* (1936) owes much to Marx despite the fact that Spender remained incorrigibly liberal throughout the period. Probably the ablest orthodox Marxist critic was the talented and prolific Christopher Caudwell,[12] whose *Illusion and Reality* and *Studies in a Dying Culture* are of continuing intrinsic value. Reviewing the latter, which was published posthumously in 1938, E. M. Forster declared that "as propaganda, the book is surely a mistake" and "will only cause unbelievers to clutch at their pocketbooks and thank their God that Mr. Chamberlain and Herr Hitler excluded the Reds from Munich."[13] Caudwell is certainly, as Forster said, "always fanatical," and there is more faith than reason in his certainty that "somehow" the classless society will evolve from temporary dictatorship; but he raises serious questions about the nature of liberty, which was for the thirties the heart of the matter, and his criticism of older writers' ideas is full of insight, however indifferent he sometimes seems to be toward them as artists.

Caudwell is very convincing in his explanation of the popularity and respectability of George Bernard Shaw as due to Shaw's having succeeded too well in making his revolutionary message palatable: "The sugar he put on his pill prevented it from acting."[14] This was to

[10] *Ibid.*, p. 226.

[11] In this book Fox recommends Georg Dimitrov as an ideal subject for a Marxist novel. He did not himself write that novel (he was killed in Spain), but Elmer Rice's play, *Judgment Day*, with Dimitrov as hero, had a good run in London during 1937.

[12] Caudwell, whose real name was Christopher St. John Sprigg, had written seven detective novels and five books on aviation, in addition to his works on Marxism, by the time he was killed in Spain at the age of twenty-nine.

[13] E. M. Forster, "The Long Run," *New Statesman and Nation*, XVI, No. 407 N.S. (December 10, 1938), 971.

[14] Christopher Caudwell, *Studies in a Dying Culture*, p. 12.

be expected, says Caudwell, since Shaw could easily resist tainted goods in the form of meat or vaccines but not in the form of money; at heart he was fully with the bourgeoisie, as evidenced by his choice for a hero of St. Joan, symbol of the triumph of bourgeois Protestantism and individualism over feudalism. Shaw's vision of the future, according to Caudwell, is not a classless Communist society but, like that of H. G. Wells, "a world ruled by intellectual Samurai guiding the poor muddled workers; a world of Fascism."[15]

Caudwell explains Wells's failures as due to his inability to escape intellectually from his class, that "most unlovely product" of capitalism, the petite bourgeoisie, whose only ideal is to rise to the high bourgeoisie and whose only fear is of falling into the proletariat. The real bourgeois, he adds, pities the proletarian, having been taught to consider him inferior, but the petit bourgeois like Wells hates and fears him. Hence Wells's pessimism in later years: given his reverence for the bourgeoisie, he could only interpret bourgeois failure as human failure.[16] Like Upward, Caudwell is convinced that D. H. Lawrence also "misrepresented reality" because of having identified himself with the bourgeoisie. He "saw the march of events as a bourgeois tragedy, which is true but unimportant; the important thing, which was absolutely closed to him, was that it was also a proletarian renaissance."[17] In making the, to Caudwell, inevitable choice between communism and fascism, Lawrence chose the Fascist way, the "return to old primitive values, to mythology, racialism, nationalism, hero-worship, and *participation mystique*," which is like "the regression of the neurotic to a previous level of adaptation," in which the artist blames not social relations but man's consciousness of them.[18] Caudwell puts Lawrence in a category with Wells, Proust, Huxley, Bertrand Russell, Wasserman, Galsworthy, and Hemingway, as

> men who proclaim the disillusionment of bourgeois culture with itself . . . [but are] not able to wish for anything better or gain any closer grasp of this bourgeois culture whose pursuit of liberty and individualism led men into the mire. . . . [They are] pathetic rather than tragic figures, for they

[15] *Ibid.*, p. 9. George Bernard Shaw was to write in 1945 that the only possible or desirable equality is of income, and that equality of political power is fatal to democracy (*Geneva, Cymbeline Refinished & Good King Charles*, p. 23).

[16] Caudwell, *Studies in a Dying Culture*, pp. 80, 86.

[17] *Ibid.*, p. 71.

[18] *Ibid.*, p. 59.

are helpless, not because of overwhelming circumstances but because of their own illusion.[19]

This "illusion," the "lie at the heart of contemporary culture, the lie which is killing it," is the bourgeois conception of liberty. Caudwell's treatment of the nature of liberty, which obsessed the young intellectuals of the thirties and which they saw as the central issue of the Spanish War, is probably the best that was written during the period. On the surface, Britain appeared, even in 1937, to offer about as much personal liberty, particularly for bourgeois intellectuals, as was to be found anywhere, certainly more than her warmest admirers could find in Soviet Russia. Yet many members of this favored class felt their minds to be "in chains" and looked to Moscow for "true freedom."

Obviously the problem lay in the definition of "liberty." Caudwell calls illusory the traditional bourgeois notion that man is "naturally free," like the animals, but warped and limited by social structures, that "the basic freedom of society [is] to be free from any relation," and that "with each man freely following his desires, the best interests of society . . . would be served."[20] In reality, man "cannot strip himself of his social relations": he can only disguise them as relations to commodities, markets, cash, capital, "things." In Shelley's words, there is under such a system "no other nexus between man and man than naked self-interest, than callous cash-payment." But the relations remain, however disguised, and

man has enslaved himself to forces whose control is now beyond him, because he does not acknowledge their existence. He is at the mercy of the market, the movement of capital, and the slump and boom. He is deluded by himself.[21]

As D. H. Lawrence turned to the "dark races" in his revulsion against a society based on the "cash nexus," so T. E. Lawrence sought "ampler social relations, purged of the pettiness and commercialism of capitalism" among the desert Arabs. But he discovered that he had "freed" the Arabs to "enjoy" the very kind of bourgeois relations he

[19] *Ibid.*, p. 19.

[20] *Ibid.*, p. xxi.

[21] *Ibid.*, p. xxii. The Shelley quotation is from the preface to *Prometheus Unbound*. This passage in Caudwell permits a plausible reading of Auden's rather obscure sonnet, "And the age ended, and the last deliverer died."

had fled. He then found "a stunted version of his ideal" as an enlisted airman and was killed, symbolically enough, by a motorcycle he had not learned to control.[22] T. E. Lawrence exemplified the best kind of "hero" a bourgeois society could produce, but he was a failure because he tried to flee into the past rather than to join himself to the forces of the future. Unlike this "instinctive hero," Lenin represents the "self-conscious hero [who can] lead man towards the self-conscious society" through his recognition of the "causal laws of society" as revealed by Marx.[23]

True freedom comes *through*, not *in spite of*, social relations. The value of Freud's many useful insights is vitiated by his sharing the bourgeois illusion of naturally free instincts repressed or inhibited by society, and by his inability to see that social relations may indeed be liberating; thus he assumes society to be unchangeable and concentrates entirely on individual adjustment to it, "but he cannot even teach us that first truth, that we must change the world in order to change ourselves."[24]

Freedom is, as Engels said, the recognition of necessity. Our world and environment can determine our lives in greater or lesser degree, according to how well we can understand their laws and behave in intelligent relation to them. To the extent that we understand the laws of the sea we can sail, or of the sky we can fly; and "free will consists in this, that man is conscious of the motive that dictates his action."[25] Animals are not more but less free than man, since they must simply adjust to their world, while he can, by understanding its laws, mold his.

What kind of society is needed to provide the conditions to establish liberty? Since bourgeois freedom means freedom for the bourgeois to exploit others, freedom for all is impossible under a bourgeois system. In the process of destroying that system, a dictatorship of the proletariat is required to repulse bourgeois efforts to reestablish themselves in power, and this dictatorship must entail "censorship, ideological acerbity, and all the other devices developed by the bourgeois in the evolution of the coercive State which secures his

[22] *Ibid.*, p. 39.
[23] *Ibid.*, p. 41.
[24] *Ibid.*, p. 192.
[25] *Ibid.*, p. 205.

freedom."[26] But once the revolution has been fully achieved, and the bourgeois have either died out or been absorbed, there is no longer any unfree, compelled class, for the "owners of the means of production, being also the workers of that means, do not need the existence of an expropriated class."[27] This passage, written before Caudwell's enlistment in the International Brigades, explains why he sided with the Communist rather than the Republican elements in the Spanish Government.

A later generation might question, as Forster did, whether the Communists' confidence in their knowledge of the laws of necessity was really justified, and might hesitate to accept Caudwell's answers, but his statement of the question of the nature of liberty is still meaningful; it is a real pity that he did not live to make further contributions to the continuing debate. As he saw it, it was the duty of the intellectual to overcome his natural "selfishness, which is the pattern of bourgeois culture and is revealed in pacifism, Protestantism, and all varieties of salvation obtained by individual action,"[28] and to put his brains and his talents to the uses of the proletarian movement. Caudwell also gave his life in Spain, as did many others. However, the majority of British intellectuals preferred, perhaps fortunately for posterity as well as for themselves, the pen to the machine gun, and throughout the thirties the ideals and principles that Caudwell expounded were to be expressed in every kind of literary form.

In his interesting book *The Thirties,* Julian Symons proposes a useful metaphor to describe what he calls the "Thirties movement." He suggests a Pyramid made up of Audience, Pragmatists, and Artists. The base is the Audience, about a million well-educated, generally middle-class people who "in spite of their shortcomings and their snobberies, believed sincerely that works of art were the fine flowers of a civilization whose proper glory was free speech"[29]—that is, the liberal intelligentsia. Above them, he places some fifty thousand Pragmatists, younger than the Audience and of more varied social origin, including lower-middle- and working-class intellectuals, all eager to change society through their own efforts as doctors, teachers, scien-

[26] *Ibid.,* pp. 201–202.
[27] *Ibid.,* p. 202.
[28] *Ibid.,* p. 69.
[29] Julian Symons, *The Thirties: A Dream Revolved,* p. 36.

tists, economists, and sociologists, and to persuade the thousand or so Artists at the top to leave their ivory towers and join the good fight. In reference to Spain, the Audience was pro-Loyalist but not very active politically; the Pragmatists and many of the Artists tended to be Orthodox, and it was they who set the tone of the "political-artistic movement of the thirties." Symons, calling his metaphor "too simple, but still useful," gives a synoptic view of the decade:

> as the decade goes on [from about 1933] we shall see the Artists taking nourishment from their roots in the Audience, and at the same time adapting themselves to the Audience's habits and standards. The revolutionary shoots will change their character, and develop into buds of middle-class non-conformity. The Pragmatists in the middle, ideally all readers of the *New Statesman*, will boil away like geysers, frothing anger at the Audience for its smug liberalism and at the Artists for their social inadequacy. And still the pyramid, in spite of its dissonant parts and its changing form, will remain stuck together: its coherent gum the threat of Fascism.[30]

The Orthodox leftists were by no means all members of the Communist Party. Some joined the Party, usually for only a short time; others did not join but still called themselves Communists; still others simply found themselves in agreement with Party policy on virtually every issue that arose. John Lehmann, poet and publisher, hence both Artist and Pragmatist, fell into the third category. In *The Whispering Gallery* he gives a concise summary of the beliefs and attitudes of the Orthodox Left. Of middle- and upper-class background generally, they had been educated to become members of the Establishment, but revulsion against the social decay and economic injustice of the postwar period, and fear of a repetition of cruel and futile world war, converted them to socialism of the reformist Labour party variety. The fiasco of the General Strike of 1926 and the collapse of the moderate Left in the 1931 elections led them to question whether gradualism might not be simply a blind alley.

By about 1934, defeat of the liberals and reformists in Germany and the encirclement of the Social-Democratic government in Vienna seemed to point to the conclusion that "if it was in serious danger, capitalism would stop at nothing to turn back the wheels of democratic progress and social justice and establish its puppets in power." The picture of the Fascist leader as tool of the industrialists, which

[30] *Ibid.*, p. 39.

Auden and Isherwood draw in *On the Frontier*, expressed this view.[31] The Orthodox Left assumed that the only way capitalism could hope to solve its economic crisis was by rearmament and that the target for its weapons would be the Soviet Union, which, because of its socialist economy, was free of the pressures that forced capitalists to be imperialistic. Capitalist society, "sick unto death, . . . had called in the thugs as doctors . . . and they were preparing to sweep away all the traditional liberties of Western civilization and use force to destroy the one country that was not in the grip of economic crisis."[32] The supineness before, and occasional active collusion with, fascism by the British government during this period seemed to confirm their worst fears of the fundamental identity of interest between capitalism and fascism.[33]

In retrospect, Lehmann offers some explanation for the disparity between the harshly critical analysis the Orthodox Left devoted to capitalist Britain and their general optimistic credulity in regard to Russia. Much of it was sheer wishful thinking: since, according to their abstract notions of Marxism, Russia *ought* to be a paradise of economic justice in which the necessary dictatorship of the proletariat was rapidly giving way to full democracy, they were inclined to accept any evidence that it *was* and to discount contrary evidence, either to explain away apparent injustices as temporary necessities or to deny their existence. They were encouraged in their illusions by the skillful propaganda of Communists and the clumsy propaganda of anti-Communists: even with the limited information available, the run of anti-Communist fantasies about Russia was so patently absurd as to call into question the more serious and responsible criticisms that were also being made. A great many Englishmen visited Russia during the early thirties, but they saw what they were looking for, and those who read their reports believed or disbelieved according to

[31] See Chapter V.

[32] Lehmann, *Whispering Gallery*, pp. 216–217.

[33] Leftist suspicion of the Government was so great that almost up until World War II broke out many leftists were far from certain whether Britain would be fighting against or beside the Fascist powers. In mid-1938, Kingsley Martin was advising lovers of peace to work for economic change, resist the conscription and regimentation entailed in war preparations, and resist the war itself if Britain should, as it might, move from being a "reluctant accomplice" to an "active partner of fascism" ("The Peace Movement," *New Statesman and Nation* XV, No. 380 N.S. [June 4, 1938], 947).

their preconceptions. The storm raised on the Left by André Gide's quite mild and sorrowful criticisms of Soviet conformism, complacency, and ignorance of the world, and of the limitations on free expression within the Soviet Union,[34] indicates how heavily left-wing emotion was invested in believing that the motherland of the Revolution was happily free of the horrors they could see so clearly in other countries. Finally, for many leftists, communism seemed the only alternative to fascism.[35] Toward the end of the decade, Englishmen began to look to the Scandinavian countries and New Deal America as possible models for a reformed capitalism that might be more humane, just, and efficient than the existing system and that could be achieved without revolution; but to the Orthodox Left in the mid-thirties British capitalism seemed already well on the road to fascism.

In a very real sense, the period of the thirties was a time of "cold war," although the term had not yet been coined, and the Spanish War, not unlike the Korean War fifteen years later, served to focus and exacerbate public debate. Parallels should not be drawn too closely, but this passage from George Orwell's 1939 novel, *Coming Up for Air*, might strike familiarly upon the ears of a later generation. The hero is musing as he half-listens to a lecture by a "well-known anti-fascist" under the sponsorship of his local Left Book Club.

> A queer trade, anti-fascism. The fellow, I suppose, makes his living by writing books against Hitler. But what did he do before Hitler came along? And what'll he do if Hitler disappears? . . . He's trying to work up hatred in the audience, but that's nothing to the hatred he feels himself. Every slogan's gospel truth to him. . . . Does he have a private life? Or does he only go around from platform to platform, working up hatred? Perhaps even his dreams are slogans. . . . Let's all get together and have a good hate. . . . Let's all grab a spanner and get together, and perhaps if we smash in enough faces they won't smash ours. Gang up, choose your Leader. Hitler's black and Stalin's white. But it might just as well be the other way about, because in the little chap's mind both Hitler and Stalin are the same. Both mean spanners and smashed faces. . . . [In our fear of fascism we

[34] Gide's criticisms were particularly infuriating to the Russians in view of the way they had feted him despite their horror over his just-published *Corydon*. Lehmann, who was in Russia during Gide's visit, had been amused by the spectacle of the puritanical Communists paying homage to an admitted sodomite (*Whispering Gallery*, p. 291).

[35] *Ibid.*, p. 218.

seem to become Fascist ourselves.] So terrified of the future that we're jumping straight into it like a rabbit diving down a boa-constrictor's throat.[36]

Unorthodox though he was, Orwell had proved his antifascism on the Aragon front—in fact, from 1936 to his death, he devoted himself entirely to fighting fascism in all its guises—but he was disgusted by the "romantic warmongering muck" of the home-front anti-Fascists. For him, the worst aspect of the Spanish War was

the immediate reappearance in left-wing circles of the mental atmosphere of the Great War. The very people who for twenty years had sniggered over their own superiority to war hysteria were the ones who rushed straight back into the mental slum of 1915. . . . spy-hunting, orthodoxy-sniffing, . . . the retailing of atrocity stories.[37]

At the heart of Orwell's criticism of the Orthodox Left was his feeling that its most articulate spokesmen, largely because of their sheltered upbringing, thought too much in abstract terms, with only the dimmest sense of what these abstractions meant in actuality.[38] He took strong exception to Auden's "Spain 1937" with its reference to "necessary murder."

Mr. Auden's brand of amoralism is only possible if you are the kind of person who is always somewhere else when the trigger is pulled. So much of left-wing thought is a kind of playing with fire by people who don't know that fire is hot.[39]

It was not that Orwell did not himself believe that murder might at times be necessary, but that he questioned the right of a protected young bourgeois like Auden, "to whom murder is at most a word,"

[36] George Orwell, *Coming Up for Air*, pp. 172, 175–177.

[37] George Orwell, "Inside the Whale" (1940), in *A Collection of Essays by George Orwell*, p. 245.

[38] In "Politics and the English Language," (*Essays*, [1950]), Orwell extended this charge to political discussion in general.

[39] Symons borrows the "playing with fire" image approvingly. Auden, however, properly objected to Orwell's criticism of him as "densely unjust." His attitude was in fact precisely like Orwell's, that murder is always murder and must not be called anything else, but may "*if* there is such a thing as a just war . . . be necessary for the sake of justice" (Letter to M. K. Spears, May 11, 1963, quoted in Monroe K. Spears's *The Poetry of W. H. Auden: The Disenchanted Island*, p. 157, n. 10).

to speak on the subject. Similarly, he found it hard to take seriously the pronouncements of such leftists on the wisdom of proletarian dictatorship: "They can swallow totalitarianism *because* they have no experience of anything but liberalism."[40] Certainly the cheerful enthusiasm with which some intellectuals of the period, by all indications humane and sensitive people, speak of "liquidating" classes and "eliminating" counterrevolutionary elements seems to substantiate the belief that much of the "realism" on which the salon revolutionaries prided themselves consisted chiefly of a refusal to examine the referents of their abstractions.

The Orthodox Left had its comic side, and its bitter enemies were not the only ones to see it. Probably as entertaining and damaging a portrait of a certain kind of upper-class Red as was produced during the period was drawn by Cyril Connolly, who was in substantial agreement with the Orthodox Left on many points. Connolly writes under the pretext of reviewing a book, "*From Oscar to Stalin, A Progress.* By Christian de Clavering," which he hails as "the authentic voice of a generation." The book begins with a page of "fashionable quotations all in German. The middle part by Kafka, the fringe by Rilke and Hölderlin. The rest by Marx. Impeccable!" The author offers arch reminiscences of life at Eton and Oxford and the "amusing" parties of the international set of the twenties, dropping names like rain and revealing his part in forming the life and thought of everyone from the Prince of Wales to Ernest Hemingway. His Waugh-like youth cut short by the Depression, he found a new vision.

> Stephen, Wystan, Cecil, and Christopher. Madge? Bates? Dutt? Those blunt monosyllables spoke a new kind of language to me. . . . It was new. It was vigorous. It was real. It was chic! . . . From that moment I've never looked back. It's been pylons all the way.[41]

Changing his name to the more proletarian Chris Clay, de Clavering joined the workers' movement and achieved his highest moment when, marching in his first antiwar demonstration, he discovered that marching with him were the very sprigs of European nobility he had known in his party-going days: "I couldn't speak. Old friends had met, travelling a stony road, coming to the same hard conclusions,

[40] Orwell, "Inside the Whale," *Essays,* p. 243.

[41] Cyril Connolly, "Where Engels Fears to Tread" (1937), *The Condemned Playground (Essays: 1927–1944),* p. 150.

and together." With an apology for having omitted such minor occurrences as his conversion to Catholicism, Clay ends his book with a warning to reviewers:

> A line is being drawn. . . . One day you're going to see something rather hostile. . . . a machine gun. POINTED AT YOU. And behind it, with his hand on the trigger, Comrade—no, COMMISSAR—Chris Clay. Did you write such an such an article? Yes (No). It doesn't matter which. Tatatat. . . . and that I think could be meditated by the Fascist Connolly.[42]

It would be unjust and inaccurate to take Chris Clay (or Gillian and Tris Phipps) as typical of middle- and upper-class converts to communism. Probably no one should be called typical, but Esmond Romilly serves as an instructive figure as he is depicted in the memoirs of his friend Philip Toynbee and of his wife Jessica Mitford. Romilly had gained precocious fame at fifteen by running away from school to launch a single-handed press war against English public schools in particular and the Establishment in general. At eighteen he joined the International Brigades, impelled partly by Marxist principle and partly by simple adventurousness. Toynbee writes that he and Romilly were both, at the time, strongly under the spell of "romantic warmongering muck." Like many other emancipated young intellectuals of the period, they harbored beneath their socialist hatred of war a strong tendency to visualize themselves performing acts of glory on the battlefield, a tendency not surprising in boys who had grown up reading Kipling and Henty. The Spanish War offered the opportunity to experience the adventure of war, the great test for manliness, in the cause of preserving a revolution and preventing a general conflict. Romilly lost his illusions as quickly as any other soldier in action, and when he returned to England a few months later to recuperate from wounds received at Boadilla, he had only "caustic disgust" for the "hearty heroics" of the British Communists, and he was "funny, but indignant, too, against those breathless left-wing ladies . . . whose clamorous calls to arms reminded us of all we had heard about the overpatriotic ladies of the 1914 war."[43] Like Orwell, Romilly had observed in Spain that the degree of "orthodoxy-sniffing" was in direct proportion to the distance from the fighting

[42] *Ibid.*, pp. 152–153.

[43] Philip Toynbee, *Friends Apart: A Memoir of Esmond Romilly and Jasper Ridley in the Thirties*, pp. 21, 93.

front, and although he considered himself a Communist, he refused to join the British Party because of, among other things, its constant internal bickering over doctrine.

Back in England, Romilly met Jessica Mitford, the youngest girl of an aristocratic family famed for its wealth, influence, and eccentricity. Jessica's generation maintained the tradition: one of her sisters married Sir Oswald Mosely with Hitler acting as best man, another became Hitler's favorite symbol of Nordic womanhood, and Jessica became a Communist. As adolescents, she and her Nazi sister Unity Valkyrie divided their old nursery down the middle and decorated half of it with swastikas and the works of Hitler and Houston Chamberlain, the other half with the hammer and sickle and the works of Marx.

Jessica persuaded Romilly to take her back to Spain with him. Since she was a Mitford and he was Winston Churchill's nephew, the Establishment responded by dispatching a destroyer to Bilboa to return the elopers, "a Palmerstonian gesture, . . . a token of that wonderful upper-class solidarity in England which surely can no longer be exhibited with quite such insolent assurance."[44]

Looking back on their flamboyant elopement and on their later Red Bohemian life in London and the United States, Miss Mitford concludes that while there was no denying her husband's genuine hatred of injustice or his devotion to the cause of a social and economic system more just and rational than the one that had produced him, he shared with her and with many others in their group a tendency to look on communism as a way to settle old scores: "Too much security as children, coupled with too much discipline imposed on us from above by force or threat of force, had developed in us a high degree of wickedness, a sort of extension of childhood naughtiness."[45]

Miss Mitford feels that Romilly had outgrown his naughtiness by the time he was killed on an RCAF mission in 1941, and she credits the same upper-class upbringing that made him "wicked" with having also encouraged his more admirable traits, his self-confidence, independence of mind, and sense of responsibility to society. Philip Toynbee's account of his own youthful communism also conveys a strong sense of sheer boyish high jinks underlying the revolutionary

[44] *Ibid.*, p. 99.

[45] Jessica Mitford, *Hons and Rebels*, p. 220.

impulse. He loved the "friendly and bustling organization" of the Party for which he worked as an undergraduate organizer at Oxford in the early thirties, with its "lively atmosphere of purpose and intrigue," and his enthusiasm was hardly affected by his friend Romilly's irreverence.[46] He felt no compunction about faking a limp and passing himself off as a wounded veteran from Spain to add poignancy to his speeches before Popular Front audiences, in spite, or perhaps a little because of, his position as the son of an eminent pursuer of Truth.

Toynbee did not remain a Communist long, but although he left the Party "in greater wisdom and greater sadness," he was not embittered. He thought the Party "indelicate, authoritarian, and possessive," with "much crudity of judgment" and "bluff insensitivity about love affairs and all other human relations"; but while "it was often foolish and it practised dishonesty as a principle, . . . it was not in itself, either a joke or a monstrosity. Few of its members were wild, embittered or silly, and many were genuinely compassionate and self-sacrificing."[47]

There has been much speculation as to why so many young bourgeois intellectuals attached themselves, formally or informally, to a party of which one unconcealed aim, despite temporary expedients like the Popular Front against fascism, was to destroy their class. It is not necessary to seek deep psychological explanations for the wide acceptance of the Marxist interpretation of the unhappy state of things in Europe and Britain during the interwar period: that interpretation is at least as plausible as any other. What is remarkable is the number of bourgeois who went beyond traditional British socialism, with its emphasis on democratic means and personal liberty, to embrace the Communist ideology that justified the tem-

[46] He notes that "good Communists always spoke of Romilly with the shuddering distaste of a nanny referring to the rough street urchin playmate of her charges" (*Friends Apart,* p. 64).

[47] *Ibid.,* p. 61. Arthur Koestler, fresh from the hard school of continental underground communism, found British Communists baffling: "They put decency before dialectics and, even more bewilderingly, they tended to indulge in humour and eccentricity—both of which were dangerous diversions from the class struggle. . . . I came to the tentative conclusion that the majority of English Communists were not revolutionaries but cranks and eccentrics, and that they were certainly closer to the Pickwick Club than to the Comintern" (*The Invisible Writing,* p. 382). Also see discussion of Day Lewis, Chapter VI.

porary abrogation of these long-held values, and to submit, almost joyfully, to a hierarchical higher wisdom on matters of judgment.

A simple explanation, popular with their detractors, is that these bourgeois revolutionaries were moved by neurotic malice: "Leftness is the cause of the wrong 'uns—those who regard themselves as the 'victims of circumstances' in the sense of being victims of themselves."[48] Victor Gollancz, speaking from his years of intimate contact with British Communists in leadership of the Orthodox Left, acknowledged that there were some in the group who were simply projecting their own personal rebellion into political terms, but he did not feel there were many such.

A more widely applicable explanation was offered by Virginia Woolf in an essay, "The Leaning Tower," which raised considerable discussion. Her metaphor was of a young intellectual living in a tower built upon his parents' "station" and "gold," from the top of which he can see clearly the changes in society, the appearance of revolution, the shadow of war. Precisely because of the breadth and clarity of perspective afforded him by this "eminence," he develops feelings of guilt for his unearned advantages and hatred for the "tower," the society that has raised him to this point of view.[49] Louis MacNeice, writing in agreement with this view, added that the great influence of Marx lay not in his historical theories but in his emphasis on the need to change bourgeois society, and he quoted what was probably the favorite Marxist text among British intellectuals: "The philosophers have only *interpreted* the world, in various ways; the point, however, is to *change* it."[50]

It was the "realistic" activism of revolutionary Marxism, or "militant socialism" as some preferred to call it, as opposed to what seemed the impotent idealism of more libertarian and moderate socialism,

[48] Harry Kemp, Laura Riding, and others, *The Left Heresy in Literature and Life* (1939), p. 4. This ill-tempered, oversimplified, and dogmatic attack on the bad temper, oversimplification, and dogmatism of the Left contains some telling arguments.

[49] Virginia Woolf, "The Leaning Tower," *Folios of New Writing*, Autumn 1940, pp. 11–33. She thought the literary work that sprang from these feelings was generally bitter, violent, and confused, of value chiefly for the self-analysis to which the youthful rebels felt driven.

[50] Louis MacNeice, "The Tower That Once," *Folios of New Writing*, Spring 1941, p. 39. The quotation is from Karl Marx's *Thesis on Feuerbach*.

that drew many young intellectuals. Day Lewis later wrote that what most attracted him in communism was "the concept that we discover reality by acting upon it, not thinking about it; to one whose grasp on reality seemed so insecure, and who at times craved for action as for a drug, this concept felt like salvation."[51] The win-the-war spirit so central to communism, with its connotations of subordinating individual wishes and scruples for the purpose of expediency in action, had great appeal to young people with a strong sense that the times were out of joint and required more than Hamlet-like decisiveness. There was a widely shared feeling that a little more willingness to employ extraconstitutional force might have saved the liberty-loving Weimar Republic or the admirable Social Democracy of Vienna. The writings of the thirties are full of images of sinking ships and embattled outposts, critical situations in which cooperative and quick mass action precludes individual niceties of conscience or open debate. With the collapse of the moderate British Left in the 1931 elections, there had been wholesale defections from the Labour party: Maxton and Brockway started the splinter Independent Labour party; Sir Stafford Cripps founded the Socialist League; and in one of the more peculiar partnerships of this peculiar period, John Strachey and Oswald Mosley combined to form the New Party, although only to split very soon as Strachey threw in his lot with communism and Mosley went on to establish the British Union of Fascists.

At first glance, it is a little surprising that Mosley was unable to take a larger delegation of intellectuals with him into fascism; on the Continent, displaced and disillusioned intellectuals were about as likely to choose fascism as communism. Yet, although the British Union of Fascists grew faster and larger than the Communist Party during the thirties, it was lamentably short of intellectuals. Neal Wood suggests that the greater appeal of communism for Englishmen lay in the British tradition of liberalism and democracy. Fascism is thoroughly activist, but it "promises nothing but more nihilism and greater activism until the world is consumed by hell fire," while communism "appears to offer . . . appeal to the reasonable and to the humanitarian."[52] Gollancz, profoundly opposed to communism

[51] Cecil Day Lewis, *The Buried Day*, p. 212.

[52] Neal Wood, *Communism and British Intellectuals*, p. 111. Cf. Eliot's comments in *Criterion*, quoted in Chapter II.

though he was, insisted that most of the British intellectuals who embraced that ideology did so "neither in selfishness nor in morbidity, but from concern for the good of mankind," and he praised their altruism and their "attention to conscience." Conceding that since the initial conscientious decision to join the Party entails placing one's conscience at the Party's disposal, thenceforth Communist attention must be to a "second-hand conscience," he still contended that "a second-hand conscience, in spite of everything, is better, a lot better, than no conscience at all."[53]

R. H. S. Crossman, who was, like Gollancz, never tempted by communism himself, also stresses its moral appeal, noting that

> the idea of an active comradeship of struggle—involving personal sacrifice and abolishing differences of class and race—has had a compulsive power in every Western democracy. The attraction of the ordinary political party is what it offers to its members: the attraction of Communism was that it offered nothing and demanded everything, including the surrender of spiritual freedom [which, he wrote earlier, is the most precious sacrifice an intellectual can make].[54]

The emotional investment required on entry into the Communist Party was heavy, but so was the return, at least for a while. Stephen Spender writes of how the intense moral certainty of the convinced Communist with his conscience "anchored—if not petrified—in historical materialism" could make a vacillating fellow traveler "feel small."

> What power there is in a conscience which reproaches us not only for vices and weaknesses but also for virtues, such as pity for the oppressed, if they happen to be the wrong oppressed, or love for a friend, if he is not a good Party member! A conscience which tells us that . . . we can attain a massive, granite-like superiority over our own whole past . . . simply by virtue of converting the whole of our personality into raw material for the use of the Party machine, . . . that liberal scruples, well-meaning though they may be, ignore the ultimate good of all.[55]

[53] Victor Gollancz, *More for Timothy, Vol. II of an Autobiography,* p. 49.

[54] Richard H. S. Crossman, ed., *The God That Failed,* p. 6. This book, which consists of essays by Koestler, Silone, Wright, Gide, Fischer, and Spender on their experience with communism, is extremely useful and revealing.

[55] Spender in *ibid.,* p. 244.

Crossman observes that the first stage for the bourgeois intellectual convert to communism was a humble and apologetic eagerness to prove himself worthy of inclusion in the workers' movement, since he had come only by strenuous intellectual effort to the mental attitude that was the worker's birthright; but it did not take him long, particularly if he visited Russia, to reach a second stage, based on

> the belief (for which Marx, who had an utter contempt for the Slavs, gave plenty of authority) that the West must bring enlightenment to the East, and the middle class to the proletariat. This belief was both the beginning of disillusionment and an excuse for remaining in the Party. Disillusionment, because the main motive for conversion had been despair of Western civilization, which was now found to contain values essential for the redemption of Russian Communism; an excuse, because it could be argued that, if the Western influence were withdrawn, Oriental brutality would turn the defense of freedom into a loathsome tyranny.[56]

If an intellectual's desire to be a Communist had anything masochistic in it, his Party experience was likely to be as bruising as he could have secretly hoped. From its inception in 1920, as Neal Wood points out in his excellent study of *Communism and British Intellectuals,* the C.P.G.B. was suspicious of intellectuals. Lenin had considered intellectuals necessary to the movement, but he relied on the workers to curb their "anarchistic" tendencies, and he equated intellectualism with Menshevism, as opposed to the true Bolshevism of the proletariat.[57] The British Party, largely working class in both members and leaders, tended to consider intellectuals too volatile and individualistic to be trusted, and even those intellectuals who were occasionally allowed on the Executive Commission had little power and were placed there chiefly to gain outside prestige.[58]

There was considerable rank-and-file resentment over the special

[56] Crossman in *ibid.,* p. 8.

[57] Wood, *Communism and British Intellectuals,* p. 18.

[58] *Ibid.,* pp. 25–29. Émile Burns and Joseph Klugmann are the only intellectuals who remained on the commission steadily from 1930 on. Others who enjoyed brief periods on the commission have been the biometrist J. B. S. Haldane (who later split with the Party on the Lysenko issue), the classicist George Thompson, the literary critic Arnold Kettle, the film director and producer Ivor Montagu, the headmaster and Teacher's Union chairman G. C. T. Giles, and the labor historian, typographer, and journalist Allen Hutt.

treatment given certain intellectuals at the time of the Popular Front, when some "intellectually photogenic"[59] figures were encouraged to join the Party but were not subjected to Party discipline. Stephen Spender offers a rather comic example. The Party chairman, Harry Pollitt, had tried to persuade Spender that he should go to Spain and, preferably, get himself killed, to give the Republican cause a Byron. When Spender demurred, Pollitt suggested that he might at least publicly join the Party in a demonstration of anti-Fascist solidarity, and he accepted Spender's terms for entry. The result was that the poet's first and only act as a Communist was to write an article in the *Daily Worker* announcing his having joined but simultaneously attacking Party policy on all points at which he disagreed with it.[60] Party regulars—and these included many intellectuals at the time—who were accustomed to stifle their doubts out of loyalty to Party discipline, did not appreciate this kind of poet-coddling.

Doubts grew increasingly hard to stifle after the first exhilaration over the Spanish people's rising to defend their government and the heroic defense of Madrid at the end of 1936. The first of the Moscow treason trials had occurred before the war broke out, but these were taken at face value by Englishmen of all political persuasions. The Left was distressed at the evidence of betrayal of the Revolution within its motherland (the Right was delighted) but was gratified on the whole that the Soviet Union had been able to apprehend those who were ready to sell out their country: recent history had made it quite clear that Fascists were capable of corrupting even apparently honest and loyal men. The appearance of the "Stalin Constitution" that summer had confirmed leftist hopes that the iron dictatorship, of which they had recognized the necessity during the period of consolidating the Revolution, was now giving way to genuine democracy. Louis Fischer had written happily that "today the Soviet State fears nothing from the inside and less and less from the outside. Therefore the dictatorship yields to democracy."[61]

[59] The phrase is Claud Cockburn's, *In Time of Trouble: An Autobiography* p. 239.

[60] Stephen Spender, *World Within World,* p. 192. Pollitt's suggestion that the poet get killed appears in Hugh Thomas, *The Spanish Civil War*, p. 348; Spender does not mention it in this book or in *The God That Failed.*

[61] Louis Fischer, "Soviet Democracy," *New Statesman and Nation,* XII, No. 284 N.S. (August 1, 1936), 150.

Within a few months, however, as the pace and scope of the Moscow purge increased, so did leftist concern in Britain. The dilemma of belief, as stated by Kingsley Martin, a generally Orthodox non-Communist, was this: if the trials were honest, then one could only deplore the totally false picture of unity and devotion to communism which had theretofore been projected by the Soviet Union, and this cast serious doubt on Soviet veracity in other areas; but if the trials were not honest, then the truth about Russia must be immeasurably worse than one wanted to believe.[62]

The purge trials vastly exacerbated the "orthodoxy-sniffing" and "spy-hunting" that are endemic to any movement based on war psychology: if heroes like Zinoviev and Radek could, by their own admission, betray to fascism the Revolution they had helped to make, then who could be trusted? In Spain, Franco's boast of a "fifth column" inside Madrid and the repeated instances of treachery and sabotage within Republican lines tended to support the emerging vision of the Popular Front as honeycombed with Fascist agents masquerading as Loyalists.[63] The charges against the POUM (Partido Obrero de Unificación Marxista) were certainly no more fantastic than those against the Old Bolsheviks who so freely confessed, and to deny either required a readjustment of attitudes which was simply beyond normal powers. It is not surprising that George Orwell's *Homage to Catalonia,* which is, among other things, a defense of the POUM, caused sorrow and anger upon its publication in 1938. Orwell wrote shortly thereafter that friends had advised him against bringing out the book at that time since it could only damage the Republican cause and give comfort to its enemies. He said that he could respect this view, but "I hold the outmoded opinion that in the long run it does not pay to tell lies."[64] He went on

[62] Kingsley Martin, "The Soviet System," *New Statesman and Nation,* XIV, No. 350 N.S. (November 6, 1937), 758–760.

[63] Gustav Regler's *The Great Crusade* (1940) gives a vivid account of the distrust and doubt within the International Brigades during 1937. Regler was political commissar for Brigade XII. His book is a less exciting novel than Malraux's *L'Espoir* but like it in its fair presentation of the variety of political points of view on the Loyalist side. By the end of the war he had broken with the Communists and fled, like many other German refugees who fought in Spain, to Mexico.

[64] George Orwell, Letter to the Editor, *Time and Tide,* XIX, No. 6 (February 5, 1938), 165. Arthur Koestler, describing his efforts to get expelled from the

to draw attention to the fact that not only the pro-Republican British press, but the pro-Franco press as well, had connived to distort or hide the truth about the suppression of the POUM; this seemed to him evidence that the ruling class, "although professing to lump all 'Reds' together and to be equally hostile to all of them, are in fact perfectly well aware which parties and individuals are and are not dangerous to the structure of Capitalism."[65]

Homage to Catalonia was doubly painful to the Orthodox Left. In the first place, it was a public washing of dirty Popular Front linen at a time when many pro-Loyalists felt such matters might better be, if not exactly suppressed, at least not insisted upon. There had been a similar reaction, but stronger because of the eminence of the writer involved, to André Gide's *Return from the USSR* some months before. Spender tells of attending an international writers' congress in Madrid during the summer of 1937 which, despite its lofty agenda, repeatedly degenerated into angry debate over whether Gide had or had not betrayed everything decent by responding so churlishly to Soviet hospitality. Communists of fully "petrified" conscience could simply denounce both books as lying propaganda; others, while deploring their political "innocence" and "naïveté," were concerned less with whether the criticisms might have merit than with whether they would advance or retard the cause. As a Communist press correspondent told Spender, for a dedicated anti-Fascist, truth "lay in the cause itself and whatever went to promote it."[66] V. S. Pritchett, whose views were fairly Orthodox at the time, wryly commented that Orwell stood as an excellent argument against writers' participating in politics, since they must inevitably choose between following the line of their political group, which is bad for them as writers, or becoming, like Orwell, "an annoyance to the cause they espouse." Describing Orwell as "a typical English anarchist, man of action first and politician later by exasperation and disgust . . . constitutionally 'agin the govern-

---

Party (resignation never occurred to him), tells of offending a Communist audience by quoting Thomas Mann, "In the long run, a harmful truth is better than a useful lie" (*The Invisible Writing*, p. 388).

[65] The main purpose of Orwell's letter was to note how much more easily a writer of Communist views could find a British publisher than could a Trotskyist or other "deviationist" (*ibid.*).

[66] Spender, *World Within World*, p. 222.

ment'," Pritchett concluded that his "kicking against the pricks" of expediency was "attractive . . . but nevertheless perverse."[67]

Besides being an embarrassment to the Republican cause in the simple fact of its publication, *Homage to Catalonia* was the more distressing because it represented a criticism of Orthodox Left ideas on grounds that were very meaningful for the Left. It was easy enough to dismiss attacks from the Right as naïve, fascistic, or both; it was not easy to dismiss the criticism of a man who clearly shared leftist values and who wrote from direct personal experience. In 1936 Orwell resolved to devote himself to the cause of democratic socialism, and from then until his death he was a continual gadfly to the Left. It is not at all surprising, however sad, that his last two, most famous books should have become favorite weapons for the enemies of his ideals. Orwell concentrated his attack on the Left for the simple reason that he considered the Right beyond reason: such hope as he had for the future was vested in the Left, and whom he loved he chastened. His first book as a socialist, *The Road to Wigan Pier*, is in two parts: the first, an extraordinarily vivid account of living conditions among the unemployed miners in Lancashire and Yorkshire, concludes by prescribing socialism as the remedy; the second part argues that the priggishness, freakishness, and eccentricity of socialist intellectuals is likely to prevent any wide working-class acceptance of their leadership. This book, like his later ones, evoked admiration and annoyance in about equal parts.

Homage to Catalonia is also, in a sense, two books: the first, perhaps the best English report on what the Spanish War was like during the first six months of 1937 on the Aragon front and in Barcelona, the second, an angry and convincing attack on Communist policy in Spain and on its supporters in Britain. Orwell had just happened to join the POUM. He had gone to Spain to report on the war, but having very shortly decided to join the Republican forces, he signed up with the most readily available group. He was in basic agreement with the Republican-Communist war policy, and he hoped later to join the Communist-led International Brigades because they seemed to be the most effective fighting units. However, seriously wounded

[67] Review of *Homage to Catalonia* by George Orwell in *New Statesman and Nation*, XV, No. 375 N.S. (April 30, 1938), 734–736.

and returned to hospital in Barcelona, he was released just in time to be caught up in the Communist suppression of the POUM. Barely escaping with his life, he went back to England resolved to defend his fellow militiamen against the lies fabricated about them by the Communists in Spain and credulously disseminated by the press throughout the world.

What infuriated Orwell was the now-familiar Communist (but not only Communist) tactic of dealing with dissent. Instead of refuting the arguments of the POUM that social revolution must be expanded rather than reversed if the war was to be won, the Communists proclaimed that these arguments were a deliberate attempt to sabotage the war effort and proved that the POUM were acting, and had been acting all along, as Fascist agents.[68] Orwell knew better, and while he could condone violence in a good cause he never learned to condone falsehood. The intellectuals of the Orthodox Left likewise were made uncomfortable by the necessity of admitting frankly that they simply preferred not to recognize Communist duplicity and their own credulity in this affair, and they probably wished heartily that Orwell had never written the book.

The general line of Orwell's criticism, from 1937 on, was that the British Left was blindly following the leadership of Stalin and that Stalin's Russia represented not revolution but the betrayal of revolution, that the international Communist movement had become merely the "instrument of Russian foreign policy,"[69] which was aimed not at the overthrow of capitalism but at maintaining the present Russian leadership in power at whatever cost in compromise with capitalism or even fascism. Orwell further contended that Stalin was as illiberal, as oppressive of critical or creative expression, and as totally in control of every area of life as any Fascist dictator. These criticisms hurt

[68] Thomas suggests (*Spanish Civil War*, pp. 454-455) that Yezhov, the NKVD chief, may have planned to stage Moscow-type trials in Spain to purge not only the POUM but all anti-Stalinists. However, the refusal of the POUM leader Andrés Nin, despite the most intense "persuasion," to sign documents confessing his own guilt and implicating others, certainly saved many lives. The government finally cleared the POUM of treason, although it sentenced some members for their part in the Anarchist rising in Barcelona earlier. Vindication came too late for Nin, who had been secretly murdered when the Communists finally despaired of forcing his cooperation.

[69] Orwell, "Inside the Whale," in *Essays*, p. 239.

the British leftists, who longed to maintain their belief in communism as a movement toward liberation and justice, and they hurt the more because they tended to confirm the leftists' own growing suspicions.

The other line of criticism most painful to the Left was that of the pacifists. Here too the critics were reasoning upon grounds the Left respected. The Marxist view of capitalism was that it was not only unjust and oppressive within each country but that its very nature depended upon a constant expansion of markets, which in turn assured that capitalist nations must inevitably engage in wars to protect and expand their financial interests. The Great War was widely seen as an instance of this capitalist proclivity and the Versailles Treaty as a further expression of it. If there was one emotion shared by almost all Englishmen, even those too young to remember 1914–1918, it was fear of another war. Military glory had been about as thoroughly debunked since then as any once-held value has ever been. The line of the Orthodox Left and of many nonleftists was that the danger of a new war lay in the aggressive intentions of the Fascist powers to revise the Versailles Treaty by force and bluster. One of the many difficulties in the political thinking of the period lay in the fact that much British intellectual opinion had long held the treaty to be unjust, unrealistic, and likely to increase the chances of war. It was not in fact contradictory to oppose Hitler's efforts to take what many felt should have been freely given to the Weimar Republic—one can oppose military aggression even in a just cause—but for some Englishmen it was awkward at best. Again, although the Left was anti-imperalist, there were among British anti-Fascists a fair number who were in the curious position of objecting to Mussolini's doing in Abyssinia precisely the kind of thing they had approved, and continued to approve, when done in the name of the British Empire. But the most fundamental conflict within the anti-Fascist camp was on the question of how to do "the job—the only one worth attempting in the world and becoming [by mid-1938] daily more difficult to accomplish— . . . to defeat fascism without war; if it comes to war the battle is lost."[70]

The slogan of the majority of anti-Fascists, including many outside the Orthodox Left, was "Collective Security." This entailed a firm

[70] Martin, "The Peace Movement," p. 947.

stand against Fascist aggression on all fronts, in China and Africa as well as in Spain and Europe,[71] working through the League of Nations and specifically with France where possible, but unilaterally if necessary, employing economic sanctions and perhaps a show of force if it seemed called for, as in the matter of Axis attacks on British shipping to Spain. The basic assumption was that the Fascists were probing for areas of weakness of which they could take advantage, but that they were avoiding irretrievable commitments and could be expected to retreat if faced with strong opposition. There is considerable support from later historians for the belief that if, for instance, France, backed by Britain, had marched into the Rhineland, or if effective sanctions, such as cutting off Mussolini's oil supply, had been imposed at the time of the Abyssinian invasion, neither of these early Fascist successes need have taken place. It has been argued that the French army was much stronger than the German at the time Hitler moved into the Rhineland and that even in 1938, despite the ever-increasing rate of German rearmament, the combined forces of the French and the well-equipped Czechs could very likely have withstood and repelled a German attack, even without the promised aid of Britain and Russia. However, each time the democracies buckled before Fascist threats, the Fascists gained in both confidence and resources. Once Czech arms and industrial power were in Nazi hands, the balance had shifted. It is in this light that Thomas, for example, contends that the ability of the democracies to resist fascism grew less as their willingness increased.

The anti-Fascists who argued for a firm line on Spain felt that the Fascist powers could have been deterred from assuring a Nationalist victory if Non-Intervention had actually been enforced and the Republic allowed to buy arms. As Spender wrote later, they believed Fascist intervention in Spain was within limits and "if the liberal forces could have been more effective, these limits would not have been exceeded and there would have been no [later World] war." In reply to the frequent comment that the intellectuals who had been

[71] There was a rather large body of opinion, chiefly Conservative, that while Hitler should be resisted in his European adventures, Mussolini was less fanatical and might, in view of the long tradition of Anglo-Italian friendship, be wooed away from his German partner. This view, which Chamberlain seems to have shared, underlay much of the National Government's reluctance to condemn in very harsh terms the Italian participation in the Spanish Civil War.

so urgently demanding action until 1939 seemed to have developed a kind of apathy when war finally came, he explains, "The fact was that the anti-fascist battle had been lost [by then]. For it was a battle against totalitarian war, which could have made the war unnecessary."[72] For Spender and those who thought like him, the final defeat of the Spanish Republic and the Nazi conquest of Czechoslovakia in early 1939 meant "collapse of the hope that the intervention of certain groups and even by individuals, could decide the fate of the first half of the twentieth century."[73] It meant the difference between joining the International Brigades and becoming a cog in the vast war machines that were to fight World War II.

The chief difficulty in the collective security policy was that it necessarily entailed a willingness to wage war if its basic assumptions were proved wrong, and many leftists were simply unwilling to face this corollary to their policy. In this "not ignoble muddle,"[74] they were at the same time demanding firmness against fascism and opposing rearmament and conscription in Britain. The efforts of the Left Book Club, chief instrument of the Orthodox Left, were directed "against war and fascism," but there was much reluctance to consider the possibility that the first might be necessary to prevent the second. The absolute pacifist position was free of this inner contradiction, and its consistency made for a formidable stance in argument. The most pervasive and continuing debate in British intellectual journals during the later thirties was between the pacifists and the proponents of "peace through strength," many of whom had grave doubts as to the morality of "strength."

The leading pacifist organization in Britain during these years was the Peace Pledge Union (PPU), established in the fall of 1934 through a public appeal by Canon H. R. L. (Dick) Sheppard for support of this resolution: "We renounce War and never again, directly or indirectly, will we support or sanction another." The PPU, first limited to men but later extended to include women up to a limit of half the membership, gained 80,000 members within a year and stood at 130,000 early in 1937.[75] It cooperated with other national and inter-

[72] Spender, *World Within World*, p. 238.

[73] *Ibid.*, p. 237.

[74] See Chapter I.

[75] Aldous Huxley, *An Encyclopedia of Pacifism*, p. 89. When conscription was instituted, only 1.7 per cent registered as conscientious objectors.

national pacifist groups like the War Resisters International and included an undisclosed number of pacifists working illegally in nations that proscribed such activities. In Britain, the PPU argued against rearmament, conscription, the Air Raid Precautions program, and similar militarist phenomena, and in favor of a world conference before which any nation could bring its complaints, a revision of the Versailles Treaty to remove the territorial and penal clauses, reconstruction of the League, and a national program of training in the methods of nonviolent resistance. The PPU did not take sides officially on Spain, although all its more active and articulate members seem to have been pro-Loyalist, but it was active in humanitarian relief work and in condemnation of atrocities.

The PPU attracted many able publicists, the most persuasive of them being Aldous Huxley. His novel *Eyeless in Gaza,* which consists of snatches of narrative interleaved with essays on war and social change, appeared about the time the Spanish War broke out. In 1937 he abandoned the novel form entirely to produce a full and impressively argued statement of the case for absolute pacifism in *Ends and Means.* The title reveals the gist of his argument. His basic premise, that means determine ends, leads him to conclude that warlike and unjust acts cannot achieve results that are other than warlike and unjust. Hence he argues that violent revolutions or "temporary dictatorships" or even "defensive" wars, however noble the intentions of those who employ them, cannot be appropriate or even possible means for attaining a just, peaceful, free, and classless society.

> Essentially all the new moralities, Communist, Fascist, or merely Nationalist, are singularly alike. All affirm that the end justifies the means; and in all the end is the triumph of a section of the human species over the rest. All preach the subordination of the individual to a ruling oligarchy, deified as "the State." All inculcate the minor virtues, such as temperance, prudence, courage, and the like; but all disparage the higher virtues, charity and intelligence, without which the minor virtues are merely instruments for doing evil with increased efficiency.[76]

On the question of Spain, Huxley had written to the *Left Review* that he supported the Republic "of course, . . . especially the Anarchists." He did not there enlarge on his reasons for sympathizing with this group so widely famed for its violence, but apparently he

[76] Aldous Huxley, *Ends and Means,* p. 283.

was attracted by the Anarchist emphasis on individuality, scorn of materialism, and high evaluation of humanity.[77] To judge by his discussion of social organization, he must also have found the Anarcho-Syndicalist system of decentralized government by actively participating local communities much more consonant with his own ideals than socialist centralization and bureaucracy (like most of his audience at the time, he had no use for capitalism).

But Huxley's sympathy for the Loyalists did not involve any belief that they could hope to achieve the freedom and social justice they were fighting for, even if they succeeded in defeating the rebels. The very process of fighting the war and then of "pacifying" the country would force upon them the same kind of military dictatorship they were resisting.[78] His prescription for "pacifist policy" on civil wars, including the one in Spain, was: "pacification of mutually intolerant groups in time of peace; restraint of the war-makers at the first outbreak of civil strife; then, if that proved impossible without mass-murder, non-cooperation."[79] To the criticism that such a policy, if it had ever been possible in Spain, was certainly futile now, his reply was that the policy of violent resistance was equally incapable of bringing about the desired end and was more wasteful of human life and resources.

[77] The Anarchist leader García Oliver told Cyril Connolly in an interview that Anarchist violence in Spain was not an essential part of anarchism but simply the response to violent oppression, and he declared that Anarchist justice would be humane and rational. In his later tenure of office as Minister of Justice, he appears to have approached these ideals, however unconventionally, if the widely credited story is true that his first act as Minister was to destroy all criminal records so as to begin the new era with a clean slate. He told Connolly, "If I had to sum up Anarchism in a phrase I would say it was the ideal of eliminating the beast in man" ("Barcelona" [1936], reprinted from the *New Statesman and Nation* in Connolly's *The Condemned Playground,* p. 195).

[78] In *Homage to Catalonia,* Orwell makes much the same prophecy as to the outcome of the war.

[79] Huxley, *Ends and Means,* p. 25. He quotes with apparent approval (p. 145) a passage from a War Resisters League pamphlet in which J. W. Hughan claims that if Spain had been ready for pacifism in 1931, a pacifist Republic could have prevented the revolt by immediately freeing the Moors and gaining their friendship, dismissing the old-regime generals and returning the troops to civilian life, and removing Church and landowner fears by requiring from Communists and Anarchists "the renunciation of violence during the period of the Popular Front."

The pacifist argument, by condemning all violence, avoids the difficulty of differentiating between justifiable and unjustifiable violence; yet nonpacifists felt such differentiation had to be made. Even C. E. M. Joad, a pacifist himself, doubted the efficacy of pacifism in 1937: it seemed to him "religious rather than political in its nature" and "aimed at the preservation of individual integrity in the face of war rather than at the prevention of war." He thought it "not a policy, but the negation of a policy," but he conceded that "it can never be right to abandon the advocacy of a long-run method of salvation, merely because circumstances are unfavourable to its short-run application."[80]

Huxley's central point, of course, is that long-run and short-run policies must be basically the same. In 1938 he was to receive rather surprising support for this position from E. M. Forster, who was not an absolute pacifist (he disapproved of being an absolute anything) and had until recently shown great sympathy for the "fight-fire-with-fire" Communists. He had written in 1935 that "no political creed except communism offers an intelligent man any hope"[81] and is supposed to have said at that time that if he were younger and braver he would be a Communist himself. He had changed his mind by the end of 1938.

> Many Communists are finer people than myself—they are braver and less selfish, and some of them have gone into danger although they were cowards, which seems to me finest of all. . . . [But their argument] that we must do evil now so that good may come in the long run . . . seems to me to have nothing in it. Not because I am too nice to do evil, but because I don't believe the Communists know what leads to what. . . . My counsel for 1938–39 is rather: Do good, and possibly good may come of it. Be soft even if you stand to get squashed. Beware of the long run. Seek understanding dispassionately, and not in accordance with a theory. Counsels of despair, no doubt. But there is nothing disgraceful in despair. In 1938–39, the more despair a man can take on board without sinking, the more completely he is alive.[82]

The "political quietism" of Forster, as Symons labels it, was to be

[80] C. E. M. Joad, "What is Happening in the Peace Movement?" *New Statesman and Nation*, XIII, No. 325 N.S. (May 15, 1937), 803–804.

[81] E. M. Forster, *Abinger Harvest*, p. 74.

[82] E. M. Forster, "The Long Run," p. 972. These reflections were prompted by Christopher Caudwell's *Studies in a Dying Culture*.

taken up before the end of the Spanish War by two of the chief intellectual heroes of the Orthodox Left, W. H. Auden and Christopher Isherwood. In the novel *Down There on a Visit,* Isherwood has the character called "Isherwood" say in 1938, "My 'England' is E. M. [Forster]; the anti-heroic hero. . . . He and his books and what they stand for are all that is truly worth saving from Hitler."[83] What Forster stood for was stated in his "Credo," first published in September 1938, and it is worth noting in contrast to the confident and abstract certainties that Auden and Isherwood were expressing a few years before and that much of the Orthodox Left continued to express for another year. Noting that "Faith, to my mind, is a stiffening process, a sort of mental starch, which ought to be applied as sparingly as possible," Forster goes on to suggest that one can, however, believe in some things—in personal relationships, for instance: "I hate the idea of causes, and if I had to choose between betraying my country and betraying my friend, I hope I should have the guts to betray my country." He is ready to give "two cheers for democracy," because it "admits variety" and "permits criticism," but only two: democracy is simply the least hateful contemporary form of government. He rejects the Great Man notion but proclaims the existence of an "aristocracy of the sensitive, the considerate and the plucky" and feels that any possible hope for the future lies in utilizing this aristocracy so that "these private decencies can be transmitted to public affairs."[84]

The kind of concentration on personal relationships and individual salvation to be found in Huxley and Forster was not for most of the Orthodox Left, at least not yet. The general feeling was that pacifism and purity of motive are all very fine but simply irrelevant before the threat of fascism. As Brian Howard put it, "if every anti-Fascist becomes a Huxleyan pacifist, Europe will become an intellectual and spiritual desert, and will be then perhaps finally destroyed in an inter-Fascist war."[85] In the general win-the-war spirit, ultimate questions seemed better set aside for the duration.

[83] Christopher Isherwood, *Down There on a Visit,* p. 177. On Isherwood, see Chapter V.

[84] E. M. Forster, "Credo," *London Mercury,* XXXVIII, No. 227 (September 1938), 397–403.

[85] Brian Howard, "Time, Gentlemen, Please," *New Statesman and Nation,* XIII, No. 309 N.S. (January 23, 1937), 124.

George Orwell also rejected the pacifist position, but on different grounds. "The test for a pacifist," he wrote in 1937, "is, does he differentiate between foreign war and civil war? If he does not, he is simply saying that violence may be used by the rich against the poor but not by the poor against the rich."[86] For Orwell, with his distaste for absolutes, the use of violence was not a matter of principle but of strategy, never "right" but sometimes "necessary." In his view, the Spanish War was "in essence . . . a class war. . . . That was the real issue; all else was froth on the surface,"[87] and he was entirely ready to join "the poor against the rich." He refused to palliate the ugliness of war, but he insisted that in some circumstances, "the only apparent alternatives" are to make cruel and inhuman war, fully aware that you are killing and maiming the innocent along with the guilty, or "to be enslaved by people who are more ready to do those things than you are yourself."[88] A possible war with Germany was, however, another matter. He was convinced that no "foreign war" could occur unless the ruling classes expected to profit by it and that any such war would be represented as self-defense against a maniacal enemy, for example, " 'Fascist' Germany next year or the year after."[89] It seemed to him the duty of honest men to expose such propaganda; hence his attack in *Coming Up for Air* on the professional anti-Fascist.

Despite all criticisms and internal divisions, the Orthodox Left remained fairly united until the Nazi-Soviet Pact in the fall of 1939, although faith in the Communist-oriented leadership had been wavering for over a year, chiefly because of the Moscow trials and Communist behavior in Spain. Claud Cockburn, one of the few Oxonian Communists to retain his faith undisturbed at least up until the time he wrote his autobiography in 1956, wrote scornfully of the "cynicism

[86] George Orwell, "Experientia Docet," *New Statesman and Nation*, XIV, No. 34 N.S. (August 28, 1937), 314.

[87] Orwell, "Looking Back on the Spanish War," *Essays*, p. 208. "The Spanish bourgeoisie saw their chance of crushing the labour movement, and took it, aided by the Nazis and the forces of reaction all over the world" (p. 202).

[88] George Orwell, review of *The Tree of Gernika* by G. L. Steer and *Spanish Testament* by Arthur Koestler in *Time and Tide*, XIX, No. 6 (February 5, 1938), 177.

[89] Orwell, "Experientia Docet," p. 314. When World War II broke out, however, Orwell volunteered for military service and, after being rejected because of his poor health, served as a B.B.C. propagandist.

and despair" into which many leftists fell as the war ground to its unhappy end:

> A lot of European intellectuals left their souls dead on the soil of Spain and never again were able to face the continuing realities of life. . . . many of them never found out what it [the Spanish War] was all about, and, in their disillusionment, ended up by being a nuisance.[90]

For the devout Communist, the Spanish War was presumably "about" the furtherance of Soviet national interests, and so there was nothing in the defeat of Republican Spain to drive him to "cynicism and despair"; but few of the Communist-oriented British writers of the period proved to be that devout, and their later works are full of second thoughts and recantations.[91]

Although critical of the leftists of little faith, Cockburn praised their original decision to stand up for what they thought was right, calling it a "Moment of Truth." The Nazi-Soviet Pact provided an-

[90] Cockburn, *In Time of Trouble,* p. 239. Many survivors of the International Brigades were to lose more than their confidence. Thomas quotes (*Spanish Civil War,* p. 621) from Khrushchev's statement in his denunciation of Stalin that "the cadre of leaders who had gained military experience in Spain . . . was almost completely liquidated." In Hungary, Lazlo Rajk "confessed" to Trotskyist activities in Spain, and after his execution "nearly all veterans of the Spanish Civil War in Eastern European countries were arrested and many were shot" (*ibid.,* p. 622). Things were gentler in England, but Hugh Slater was expelled from the Party for joining T. H. Wintringham, his former superior in the British Brigade, who had left the Party at the time of the Nazi-Soviet Pact to train volunteers for home-guard duty (Victor Gollancz, ed., *The Betrayal of the Left,* with essays by John Strachey, George Orwell, Harold Laski, and the editor, p. 65). Another experienced Brigade commander, Jock Cunningham, was rejected for service in the British Army and became a "casual labourer" (Thomas, *Spanish Civil War,* p. 623).

[91] On the difficulty British Communists had in maintaining both their Party membership and their self-respect, Wood writes that "it might almost be said that the *raison d'être* of the C. P. G. B. is the search for the breaking point of every intellectual in its midst" (*Communism and British Intellectuals,* pp. 219–220); and Crossman claims that "with relentless selectivity the Communist machine has winnowed out the grain and retained only the chaff of Western culture" (*The God That Failed,* p. 11). It is idle to speculate on whether several of the most ardent and brilliant English Communists of 1936 might have become disillusioned later: Ralph Fox, Christopher Caudwell, John Cornford, and David Guest were all killed in Spain.

other Moment of Truth. Many leftists were willing to understand and even defend the Russian signing of the Pact on the grounds of political expediency and self-defense, believing that since the Munich agreement had apparently proved the unwillingness of Britain and France to resist Nazism, Stalin had little choice but to gain time as best he could to prepare for the inevitable German attack. What they could not stomach was the overnight change in the British Party line, from collective security and a popular front against fascism, to "revolutionary defeatism." With lightning speed, Hitler and Mussolini, who had been the foremost enemies of civilization and decency, became no worse than any other capitalist leaders. Communists were enjoined to concentrate their efforts on the "real enemy" at home, rejecting any form of cooperation with the "social fascists" (the Labour party) and "reactionaries" (Liberals and Conservatives) who had lately been their Popular Front brothers in struggle, and to resist rearmament, conscription, home-guard and air-raid precautions, and all other forms of militarization, since a war against fascism would be simply another war for capitalist profit at the expense of the workers. There is some irony in the fact that this new line was very close indeed to that which for the previous four years the Party had castigated as Trotskyist.

The leaders of the Left Book Club—and thus of the Orthodox Left—expressed their reaction, in tones more sorrowful than angry, in *The Betrayal of the Left*.[92] Gollancz, Strachey, and Laski seem reluctant to believe that their erstwhile comrades in antifascism can realize the implications of the new line, which would, if widely followed, undermine the British war effort and assure a Nazi victory. Reaffirming their dissatisfaction with the British system and their distaste for war, they try to remind the Communists of their own recent pronouncements on the evils of fascism and the necessity of defeating it before there can be any hope of real and desirable social change. Fortunately for the course of the war, the new Communist policy had no great effect, since most sympathizers and a great many members simply refused to follow it; but it effectively ended the Popular Front and the entire climate of thought in which the Front had flourished.

[92] George Orwell was something of an outsider in this collection of articles. His contributions are not sorrowful, only angry.

The Popular Front period in England lasted for some four years, reaching its point of highest enthusiasm around the end of 1936, then leveling off and declining until its total collapse in 1939. A very large number of its members were highly talented writers, and their works reflect their rising and then falling ardor for the "militant socialism" they saw embodied in communism.

Chapter IV

ON THE LEFT: FICTION

In the better leftist novels of the thirties which were significantly political in intention,[1] the Spanish Civil War is not itself the subject. The novels of Ralph Bates, like Lewis' *Revenge for Love*, deal with events in Spain shortly before the outbreak of the war; Rex Warner's fantasies, like Greene's *Confidential Agent*, are concerned with mythical countries, however thinly disguised; and George Orwell's *Coming Up for Air* is about England during the Spanish War but contains little direct reference to Spain. British writers produced about the war itself no novels comparable to Malraux's *Man's Hope* or even Gustav Regler's *Great Crusade* and Hemingway's *For Whom the Bell Tolls*. In several minor leftist novels of the period, Spain serves as a convenient and symbolic plot device for bringing about a positive ending. A typical example is Day Lewis' *Starting Point*, which closes with the hero's departure from England to join the International Brigades, thus demonstrating the young bourgeois' decision to lay his life on the line for his revolutionary principles, to abandon words for action. Such novels may have had some propaganda value, but they are not very rewarding for later readers. Certainly the finest novel by an Englishman in which the Spanish War plays a significant part is Malcolm Lowry's *Under the Volcano* (1946), but its not having been

[1] Such important fiction as that of Joyce, Virginia Woolf, Henry Green, Ivy Compton-Burnett, or Elizabeth Bowen is, of course, outside this category.

completed until years after the war was over places it outside the scope of this chapter. The best contemporary British book about the Spanish Civil War was Orwell's *Homage to Catalonia,* which is not a novel.

Nevertheless, the novels to be discussed in the next pages can hardly be fully appreciated outside the context of the Spanish Civil War. The conditions in Spain as depicted by Bates were what the war was about, and the issues dealt with in Warner's allegorical novels and Orwell's realistic one were the issues of that war—social revolution, the threat of fascism, war and pacifism, the conflicting claims of freedom and social justice, the duty of the individual toward his society and toward himself.

Just how a novelist devoted to "militant socialism" ought best to employ his talents to forward the cause was propounded and demonstrated by Edward Upward. In the "Sketch for a Marxist Interpretation of Literature," his contribution to *The Mind in Chains,* Upward deplores the naïveté of critics who judge the literature of all ages according to its degree of agreement with Marxist principles, but he affirms the contribution that these principles make toward a "fuller and more scientific" criticism,[2] and he insists that "no book written *at the present time* can be 'good' unless it is written from a Marxist or near Marxist viewpoint."[3] The test of a "good" book is whether it is "true to life," but not in the sense of photographic naturalism. An entirely "accurate" depiction of the "temporarily existing situation" of England in 1937, plagued with poverty, unemployment, and social injustice, controlled by a decadent and inept class, with general war apparently inevitable and the Communist Party a small and almost powerless minority—such a picture might well be pessimistic. However, pessimism would not be "true," since a full understanding of the dynamic forces at work below the dreary surface would yield confident hope for the future. Pessimism is inconsistent with Marxism.

Upward points out that there are no "eternal verities," but claims that the best books are those which, "sensing the forces of the future beneath the surface of the past or present reality, remain true to reality for the longest period of time."[4] Like Caudwell, Upward be-

[2] Edward Upward, "Sketch for a Marxist Interpretation of Literature," *The Mind in Chains: Socialism and the Cultural Revolution,* ed. Cecil Day Lewis, p. 45.

[3] *Ibid.,* p. 41.

[4] *Ibid.,* pp. 46–47.

lieves that Proust, Joyce, and D. H. Lawrence, although well aware of the "decadence of present-day society," were too limited by their bourgeois point of view to see and applaud "the inevitability of revolution"; consequently, they "misrepresented reality."[5] He warns the aspiring writer that if he clings to the bourgeois point of view he will find himself with an ever more limited and distorted vision of life, until he can write only about "dreams or words or the past, but he will not succeed even in this." He must, for his own good as a writer, change his "practical life, must go over to the progressive side of the conflict, to the side whose practice is destined to be successful."[6] His own talents will determine how well he can write from the progressive point of view, but from any other point of view all his talents will not suffice. Since the change in his "practical life" may divert him into nonliterary activities, could possibly even cost him his life, it may "prevent him, but failing to go over *must* prevent him from writing a good book."[7]

Upward seems to have lived his principles. A highly talented young writer, he produced some fragments and one very promising novel but then became so caught up in the "practical" side of communism that he was unable to continue writing. In his slightly disguised autobiographical novel *Lions and Shadows*, Christopher Isherwood tells of creating with Upward, whom he calls "Chalmers" in the book, a marvelous Gothic fantasy world called "Mortmere" which effectively distracted them both from their undergraduate work at Cambridge but was to produce rather surprising literary consequences. Isherwood later introduced some of his other friends to this private world, and themes, characters, and attitudes from Mortmere show up during the next few years in the works of Auden, Day Lewis, and Rex Warner to the considerable bafflement of readers who do not share the secret. For Upward, and for the others to a lesser extent, Mortmere had another function beyond the playful:

> Chalmers needed [Mortmere] . . . at all costs. . . . He was to spend the next years in desperate and bitter struggle to relate Mortmere to the real world of the jobs and the lodging-houses; to find the formula which would transform our private fancies and amusing freaks and bogies into valid

[5] *Ibid.*, pp. 49, 51.
[6] *Ibid.*, pp. 51–52.
[7] *Ibid.*, p. 53.

symbols of the ills of society and the toils and aspirations of our daily lives. For the formula did, after all, exist. And Chalmers did at last find it, at the end of a long and weary search, not hidden in the mysterious emblems of Dürer or the prophetic utterances of Blake, not in any anagram, or cipher, or medieval Latin inscription, but quite clearly set down, for everyone to read, in the pages of Lenin and Marx.[8]

Upward had found his formula in 1937. John Lehmann, his publisher, in speaking of "The Railway Accident" (a Mortmere fantasy), called it "evidence of an imaginative gift in 'Chalmers' the fate of which one will never cease to mourn, slowly killed in the Iron Maiden of Marxist dogma."[9] Lehmann mourned too soon: after a lapse of a quarter of a century, Upward published in 1962 the first novel of an intended trilogy, entitled *In the Thirties*.[10] He has acknowledged that his long silence was largely due to "the attitude toward imaginative writing which I acquired during my politically active years. . . . I never gave up trying, but I couldn't succeed until I had ceased to subordinate writing to politics."[11]

The conflict, which Upward did not then recognize, between his "imaginative gift" and his Marxist principles is apparent in his 1938 novel, *Journey to the Border*. This is one of the best examples of a genre extraordinarily popular in the thirties, the novel that expresses the "awakening to socialism" (of the Communist variety, usually). Among others who wrote such novels, generally their first, were John Lehmann (*Down River*), Ruthven Todd (*Over the Mountain*), Rex Warner (*The Wild Goose Chase*), and the prolific Cecil Day Lewis, who wrote two (*The Friendly Tree* and *Starting Point*).

Journey to the Border chronicles a day in the life of a young English intellectual who is working, as Upward once did, as tutor for

[8] Christopher Isherwood, *Lions and Shadows*, p. 274. For further discussion of the Mortmere-to-Marxism progress, see below, Chapter VI.

[9] John Lehmann, *The Whispering Gallery: Autobiography I*, p. 244.

[10] *In the Thirties* tells of how and why the hero, a Cambridge-educated schoolmaster with poetic ambitions, becomes a Communist Party member. The "Author's Note" promises a second novel, to be called *The Deviators*, which will "show how and why, without becoming anti-Communist, he leaves the Party" in the late forties; and a third, which will show the hero's recognition "that his primary duty is to try once again to live as a poet."

[11] Letter to Author, February 9, 1964. Upward notes that his final disillusion with communism in 1948 did not leave him hating that system or admiring capitalism.

an hilariously awful newly rich "country" family. The tutor, a near relative of Walter Mitty, has timidly submitted to exploitation, relieving his hatred in ferocious fantasies, but on the day of the novel he experiences a kind of crisis in which his imagination converts a prosaic day at the races into a Kafka-like dream of his employer's world as one of wealth and splendor supported by police spies and disguised Fascists. The climax of his nightmare is a Nazi-style demonstration in honor of the Master of the Fox Hounds. In the course of his fantasies, the tutor is tempted by love in the form of a delightfully domineering upper-class girl and by the speciously persuasive arguments of the proponents of a Lawrentian cult of desire and unreason. In a conversation between his split selves, he comes to see that his fantasies have led him to the "border" between sanity and insanity and that his salvation lies in crossing another border, between dreams and action; then he must cross the final border between the bourgeoisie and the proletariat by "going over to militant socialism." There is, his rational self tells him, "no other way of dealing *successfully* with the real external problems which confront you—and which, incidentally, confront the whole of humanity at the present time."[12] Long aware that, as an intellectual, he is being as thoroughly exploited by capitalism as are the workers, he has heretofore confined himself to trying by fantasy to "build up my experiences into a coherent, a satisfying pattern"; now he sees that such efforts are doomed by external reality. He tells himself that what he most values will necessarily suffer in the coming struggle, but

> in capitalist society there is no future for poetry or for anything worthwhile. There is no future for anything except tyranny and death. . . . Only the workers can save the things you value and love. All that is gentle, generous, lovely, innocent, free, they will fight to save. And in the end they will win. There will be a time of harshness and bitter struggle, but out of it will come flowers; splendour and joy will come back to the world. And life will be better than it has ever been yet in the world's history.[13]

Once across the border, the tutor is able to laugh at his fantasies of Fascists at the race track and to overcome his unreasonable resentment of religion. He sees that Christianity did once offer a fairly satisfactory guide to conduct at a time when means did not exist to

[12] Edward Upward, *Journey to the Border,* p. 215.

[13] *Ibid.,* pp. 221–222.

change external reality, but feels it has become archaic now that there are scientific means "for creating—not a heaven on earth, but a society in which every man and woman would at least have the chance to be normally happy." He has even reached such a point of detachment that he can recognize the "more amiable qualities" of his employer "as well as his offensiveness," can "see him as a human being" and "attribute his vices not to deliberate personal wickedness but to his social origin."[14]

Perhaps it is a gain in tolerance and humanity to stop disliking a man personally because of the way he acts and to consider that he could not well behave otherwise because of his social origin; perhaps it is rather a movement away from personal involvement toward abstraction, away from seeing people as individuals and toward fitting them into intellectual categories. Upward obviously felt his hero's movement was in the right direction. The tutor's gain, however, is the novel's loss. The greater part of this novel is extremely sharp and funny, and the satirical fantasies are as good as any written during the period; but as the hero begins to see the light, the wit and detachment tend to evaporate into solemn preaching, and the novel ends as a rather painful example of the kind of leftist "uplift" George Orwell was to excoriate so fiercely. Upward had seen and depicted his bourgeois characters with fine precision, but at least at this point his experiences of the Workers' Movement was not sufficient to make it seem anything but an abstraction.

Idealization of "the worker" afflicted many bourgeois intellectuals besides Upward, yet it was possible to place one's hopes for the future upon the working class without considering it a separate and superior kind of humanity. George Orwell, who had had much closer contact with the "proles" than most of his intellectual contemporaries, was far from idealizing them, but he insisted that they are

> the most reliable enemy of fascism, simply because [their] class stands to gain most by a decent reconstruction of society. Unlike other classes or categories they can't be permanently bribed. . . . The struggle of the working class is like the growth of a plant. The plant is blind and stupid, but it knows enough to keep pushing upward towards the light, and it will do this in the face of endless discouragement.[15]

[14] *Ibid.*, p. 254.

[15] George Orwell, "Looking Back on the Spanish War," in *A Collection of Essays by George Orwell*, p. 207.

This faith in "the people," which perhaps finally deserted him, makes Orwell's books of the thirties paradoxical in their effect. *Homage to Catalonia* is a chronicle of treachery and defeat, and *Coming Up for Air*, written after Orwell's return from Spain, ends in almost total despondency; yet reading either of these is curiously heartening. Orwell stresses the "emotionally widening experience" of solidarity and brotherhood among those who were doing the actual fighting in Spain, and it is this feeling, "one of the by-products of revolution,"[16] that remains most clearly with the reader of *Homage to Catalonia*. What remains after a reading of *Coming Up for Air* is the character of the hero.

In this novel Orwell clearly wishes to depict a broad cross section of British society during the Spanish Civil War period. His hero, George Bowling, is a fat, middle-aged insurance salesman who has risen, largely thanks to having become a "temporary gentleman" by commission during the Great War, from his lowly origin as the son of a small-town shopkeeper who has died as a casualty of business progress in the form of chain stores. George is married, above himself, to an anxious, penny-pinching offshoot of the genteel-poor Anglo-Indian officer class (the class of Orwell's origin). Most of George's friends are white-collar workers of the lower middle-class, but one of his closest confidants is a retired schoolmaster, graduate of public school and university.

George's view of British society is gloomy. He has had little formal education but has read much in an unorganized way and is highly intelligent and perceptive. Bored with suburban life and convinced that he and those like him, dominated by fear of unemployment and the traps of installment buying, are as much oppressed as the "proles" only less aware of the predicament, George returns to his home town in a futile effort to recapture the sense of individuality and emotional security that he associates with "before the war." The town has of course been transformed in his absence into a reasonable facsimile of the suburb George had fled. At the Left Book Club, his suburb's symbol of Progress, George has been frightened by the anti-Fascist lecture, with its implications of face-smashing.[17] When he seeks comfort from his schoolmaster friend, the symbol of

[16] *Ibid.*, p. 202.
[17] See Chapter III.

Culture, all he receives is the assurance that fascism is "ephemeral" and a reading of the "Ode to a Nightingale." George concludes that the schoolmaster's withdrawal into the past proves he is "dead," though he does not know it.

> And it's a ghastly thing that nearly all the decent people, the people who *don't* want to go around smashing faces in with spanners, are like that. . . . [But the] stream-lined men who think in slogans and talk in bullets aren't dead. . . . Dead men and live gorillas. Doesn't seem to be anything between.[18]

His vision of the future is grim:

> The bad times are coming, and the stream-lined men are coming too. What's coming afterwards I don't know, it hardly even interests me. I only know that if there's anything you care a curse about, better say goodbye to it now, because everything you've ever known is going down, down, into the muck, with the machine-guns rattling all the time.[19]

Yet the final effect of *Coming Up for Air* is not depressing. The epigraph, "He's dead but he won't lie down," could apply to the schoolmaster or to the British society in general, but it could just as well apply to George, and in a more hopeful sense. His humor, resilience, decency, and basic good sense brighten even his blackest moods. He has a nightmare that the sloganeers with spanners are after him, but he is resolved they will not streamline *him*, and the reader is inclined to agree.[20] George is confident of his own power to survive largely because of his very ordinariness and his unwillingness to be a hero. Although George is momentarily too depressed to care, Orwell convinces the reader that as long as men like George survive, there is still hope.

The final optimism of *Coming Up for Air* rests in the indomitable qualities of the "common man" rather than in any sense of the "inevitability of revolution," but the Orthodox Left tended to identify these two concepts. Thus, although Orwell had no use for Marxist

[18] George Orwell, *Coming Up for Air*, pp. 188–189.

[19] *Ibid.*, p. 296.

[20] *Animal Farm* and *1984* seem to indicate that Orwell lost his belief in the basic goodness and sanity of the "average man," yet the very fact of his writing these books seems to argue a hope that people might still be persuaded to resist the progress towards totalitarianism.

literary theory, it is a coincidence that *Coming Up for Air* exemplifies Upward's idea of what a good novel should be, better in fact than Upward's own novel does, since, while Orwell's lacks the satirical brilliance of the earlier parts of *Journey to the Border*, it also misses the banality of Upward's closing section. This may be because Orwell's hero fully embodies the thesis of his novel throughout the entire action, while Upward's novel ends "in the future and in abstractions," to borrow the phrase with which Day Lewis characterized the thinking of his whole circle during the thirties.[21]

Perhaps the two novelists of the thirties whose books most effectively express the leftist point of view during the period of the Spanish War are Ralph Bates, an exemplar of "social realism," and Rex Warner, who uses the less respectable (in Marxist circles) technique of fantasy. Ralph Bates's novels are thoroughly social realist, but it is not necessary to assume that he wrote according to formula. The deep seriousness, human compassion, and belief in the potential for progress seem at least as much characteristics of the man himself as of his literary genre. Unlike many of the leftist writers of the period, Bates was a relatively long-time Communist, and his background was working-class. He started working in a factory at the age of sixteen and he served throughout World War I as a private. He joined the British Communist Party shortly after it was founded, and when he went to Spain in 1923 it was as a Communist organizer. Unlike Percy Hardcaster, whom he resembled in background and appearance, Bates was a "front-fighter." In the twenties he organized a fisherman's union, and when the Civil War broke out he set up scouting parties in the Pyrenees. He helped organize the International Brigades, in which he was a commissar, and, except for a speechmaking tour of the United States, fought throughout the war. In 1939 he broke openly with the Party and fled to Mexico.[22]

Bates's first novel, *Lean Men* (1935), seems, like many first novels, strongly autobiographical. The hero, Francis Charing, is an Englishman of about Bates's age and background, whose major interests are

[21] Cecil Day Lewis, *The Buried Day*, p. 218.

[22] Stanley J. Kunitz and Howard Haycraft, eds., *Twentieth Century Authors*, p. 88. In his *Starting Out in the Thirties*, Alfred Kazin tells of hearing, in New York during 1937, one of Bates's speeches, which "conveyed his writer's enthusiasm at being able to describe violence so well rather more than it did the tragedy of Spain itself" (p. 109).

communism and music (Bates's first book was a well-received biography of Schubert). He has lived and worked in a Catalan fishing village and at the time of the novel, 1931, is sent by the Comintern to organize a Workers Centre in Barcelona. The novel is of largely documentary interest, offering an authoritative and convincing account of the confusion and cross-purposes of the Spanish Left at the beginning of the Republic. Charing is able to work moderately well with the Socialists and Republicans, but the Anarchists, whom he respects for their courage and devotion to their ideals, give him constant trouble because of their irrational and mystical approach to the practical problems of achieving social revolution. He is particularly irritated by antireligious fanaticism; as a pragmatic Communist he considers alienating Catholics a tactical error.[23] The book ends with the crushing by government forces of an ill-timed and badly organized strike and rising into which Charing's people have been drawn against their will. Charing himself is faced with the classic choice between morality and expediency as he must decide whether to assure his escape by shooting a guard in the back or to risk capture and death. He chooses to "stake [his] life upon the barest of margins" and manages to escape with his hands unbloodied and his resolution renewed to continue the "vigil," waiting for the "dawn that must change life." Despite the temporary defeat, he is certain the revolution will come when the time is ripe; meanwhile, "I will believe and I will serve."[24]

Lean Men is not a particularly good novel aside from its historical interest. There is a complicated love-plot that is intended to reinforce the main theme, Charing's effort to reconcile his individual needs and desires with his work as a revolutionary, but that actually achieves only distraction. The conception is sound enough—Charing is to see communism as a kind of parallel to music, love, and friendship, all means for breaking through the "husk of loneliness" surrounding the individual—but the execution is uncertain. Bates's prose, too, is very uneven, sometimes extremely evocative and effec-

[23] An interesting sidelight on this period in Spain is Bates's description, substantiated by historians, of the conflict in Spanish leftists' minds over the enfranchisement of women: in theory they approved, but they feared that the "women's vote" would reflect much more than the men's the influence of the priests and would thus work against leftist hopes.

[24] Ralph Bates, *Lean Men*, p. 554. The epigraph is "Ripeness is all."

tive in descriptions of places and scenes of violent action, but sometimes stilted and awkward. *Lean Men* is particularly deficient in humorous dialogue, although Bates clearly considers Spanish humor an essential part of the national character and wants to convey its special flavor. He is regularly forced, therefore, to rely on stating that his characters make "witty sallies," without offering examples.

The Olive Field (1936), a much better novel, deals with the Asturias rising of 1934.[25] Already evident in this upheaval were the salient issues of the Civil War, and Bates's readers were to apply the novel to later events. In this book, Bates is in firmer control of his medium than he was in *Lean Men*. The humorous passages, still sometimes a little strained, are generally successful, and the love-plot functions as an integral part of the whole design.

The novel begins in Andalucía in 1932, where the lifelong friends, Mudarra[26] and Caró, both Anarchists, are engaging in various subversive activities among the wretchedly poor workers of a large olive grove. They are estranged by Mudarra's seduction of Caró's fiancée, but are reunited two years later in political action in Asturias. Caró has by then, like many other Andalucians, despaired of achieving any improvement in his own backward province and gone to Asturias to work in the mines. Now converted to communism, he finds himself cooperating with the Anarchist leader Mudarra in organizing the revolt of the miners. When the rising is put down, Mudarra is wounded, captured, tortured, and shot, but Caró, reconciled with his wife, escapes with her and Mudarra's child back to Andalucía to continue working for the revolution.

It is a long, full, nineteenth-century sort of novel rich in incident and so crowded with characters that Bates felt he had to append a list identifying them all. This appendix is not really necessary, because Bates has taken time to deal affectionately and at some length with almost all of them, and they are vividly and convincingly differentiated. One of the more remarkable features of the book is Bates's sympathetic treatment of those characters who embody political principles he considers wrong. There is not a "fascist hyena" in the novel. The Andalucian landowner, Don Fabrique, is unwilling to spend

[25] See Appendix.

[26] Professor Gregory Rabassa has suggested that "Mudarra" may intentionally allude to the character of that name, the hero of the medieval *Siete Infantes de Lara*.

any of his dwindling fortune to maintain the olive groves on which the very lives of the villagers depend although he is always ready to pay whatever is needed to purchase a rare old book. He feels no compunction over charging his tenants exorbitantly for the water they must have to survive, and when his efficient major-domo is killed, he simply packs up and leaves the estate. Yet he is presented as sensitive and intelligent, a genuine scholar and a kindly, if melancholy, gentleman. In his combination of personal virtue and social irresponsibility, Don Fabrique makes a much better symbol of the social decay of his class than would the cruel and insensitive beast one might more readily have expected in a Communist novel.

Similarly, the major-domo, who swindles his employer and bullies the tenants, is nevertheless admired by them and by the reader for his skill and for his devotion to the work of the groves. The two major clerical figures, the kind and futile old priest and Father Soriano, his brilliant and tormented young vicar, are also handled as human beings. Moreover, Father Soriano is allowed to make a plausible case for the use of political chicanery to uphold the power of the Church. Bates seems to have had his greatest difficulty in presenting the Anarchist case fairly, since he considered it so infuriatingly wrongheaded, but he solves the problem by evading Anarchist views wherever possible and concentrating on the admirable personal qualities of individual Anarchists.

Of course the Communists are the most persuasive spokesmen, but in choosing a dissolute civil servant as his chief exponent of the orthodox Marxist approach, Bates avoids the trap, into which the social realist so readily falls, of allocating virtues among his characters in strict ratio to the degree of their Marxist-Leninist purity. The novel is full of political talk, but not too much for the reader who has been caught up in the action, and political principles are demonstrated more than they are discussed. Bates is particularly successful in evoking a sense of community in the portions of *The Olive Field* dealing with Andalucía. Toward the end, as he covers the events of the Asturias rising, the author feels impelled at moments to correct what he considers false impressions created by news reports made at the time. These bouts of journalistic exposition are novelistic flaws, but the pace of the action at this stage is sufficient to overcome them, and the novel never degenerates into a political tract.

The Olive Field has its imperfections. As in *Lean Men*, Bates seems determined to include everything, sometimes with a haste that is reflected in careless prose, and neither the humorous nor the erotic passages are as effective as those concerning politics and violence. Still, the final effect is of a deeply earnest, strongly felt tribute to human courage and endurance and faith. The novel is continuously interesting and moving, and, as propaganda in the best sense, it is excellent.

In the course of the war Bates apparently lost the confidence in communism which had sustained him for over fifteen years. One might easily speculate, in view of the strong sense of brotherhood and solidarity among Spanish leftists of different political views which is conveyed in these two novels, that what most disaffected him was the sectarian fanaticism that the Communists increasingly displayed during the war. His first novel after leaving the Party offers some clues to his thinking.

The Fields of Paradise (1940) is set in Mexico, apparently in the late thirties. Another conventional, workmanlike novel, it is as nearly nonpolitical as possible in view of its subject matter, the revolt of a small village against their decadent patron and his Fascist-like bravos. More than in the Spanish novels, Bates is concerned here with the problem of ends and means, and the conflict is more moral than ideological. The attitude of the Church toward social revolution is again an important theme, here happily resolved in the reluctant realization by the intellectual Canon Mendoza that a clergy that identifies itself with its flock rather than with their oppressors need not fear antireligion. Unlike the Spanish novels, in which only hope for another chance redeems defeat, this book ends in qualified success: the peons have the freedom and opportunity to restore their blighted lands to what they once were, "the fields of Paradise," and although their future is certain to be difficult, the prognosis is good. The difference, of course, springs not from the novelist's attitude but from the objective situation: the Mexican revolution had succeeded, and the federal authorities, unlike those in the Spain of 1934, were on the side of the peons.

Insofar as it is political, *The Fields of Paradise* lays its chief stress on caution, moderation, limited expectations, and the avoidance of fanaticism. Bates's relation with communism lacks the violent extremism that characterizes some former Communists. This may be because his commitment was never of the passionate kind in which love can be converted into hatred. A practical Englishman, he seems to have looked upon communism as the best and most practical means for achieving the free and just society he wanted;[27] disenchanted, he left the Communist road without altering his ultimate goals. Reversing the pattern of many of his contemporaries, he began political life as a Communist and then turned to moderate social democracy.

Ralph Bates is an interesting and able, but not a major novelist. Each of the three books discussed here shows an advance in skill over the previous ones, and each deserves a respectful reading, but none of them represents any kind of exciting departure in novel form. Each, too, is a good example of the kind of social realism prescribed by Marxist critics: it presents things as they are, in strong and moving terms, and is informed throughout by hope and confidence in things as they may and, according to Marxist theory, will be. Bates's novels are thus "true to life" in Upward's sense, and his work fulfills Lurçat's condition for art in capitalist countries, "non plus un jeu gratuit; c'est une activité offensive."[28]

The method of fantasy had less respectability in Marxist literary circles than social realism. For the more doctrinaire, it shared much of the opprobrium of abstract painting or atonal music as precious, esoteric, removed from "the people," a flight from revolutionary reality. There were those to argue that the revolutionary spirit, dedicated to breaking up and reforming current molds of society, would most fitly be expressed in art forms that did similar violence to current molds in art: the Surrealists considered themselves Marxists, and Picasso had declared himself a Communist. For the more orthodox, however, all this concern with *form* seemed positively frivolous: if art was to be an effective weapon in the class struggle, the revolutionary *content* must be the supreme consideration, and the more popular, accessible, and (although they did not like the term) conventional its vehicle, the better. Consequently the tendency in Marxist criticism during the Stalin era was ever more conservative in terms

[27] Bates's attitude toward the Party may be partly suggested in the passage in *Lean Men* where Charing is ordered back to Moscow (p. 437). He is unhappy to be in defiance of the Comintern, but he considers his work in Barcelona too important to interrupt, and he ignores the order. The Party, infinitely flexible on tactics, later applauds his action.

[28] Quoted by Anthony Blunt, "Art Under Capitalism and Socialism," in *Mind in Chains*, p. 122.

of aesthetics, and the artist interested in revolutionizing aesthetic forms was increasingly frowned upon as bourgeois, idealistic, formalist, and decadent. In Britain, however, this did not prevent some intellectual Marxists from experimenting with nonrealistic devices, chiefly in the drama, but also in the novel. Among the most successful of these was Rex Warner, whose novels during this period are worth examining as instances of fantasy put to the uses of revolution and whose corpus gives an indication of the evolution of political and social ideas in a sensitive and intelligent man.

Although he decried fantasy as unsuitable to the needs of the moment—except perhaps as one element in a realistic novel—Edward Upward predicted that new literary forms might be expected to evolve in a classless society and that writers might then "perhaps give up Tragedy as the highest literary form; maybe the 'fairy' story —celebrating the triumph of man over dangers and difficulties—will appear on a higher, a scientific level."[29] The idea of a fairy tale based on the "science" of Marxism had apparently been bandied about considerably among the young men generally referred to as the Auden Group, which included Upward and Warner, and it had at least some connection with the Mortmere fantasies. There are likenesses among Auden and Isherwood's play *The Dog Beneath the Skin*, Day Lewis' morality play *Noah and the Waters*, and Warner's novel *The Wild Goose Chase* which seem more than coincidental. It was Day Lewis who advised the publisher John Lehmann to look into Warner's effort "to work out an allegory of contemporary politics in action outside the mind."[30] Impressed, Lehmann printed excerpts from the novel in his *New Writing* and was instrumental in finally getting it published in 1937.

Monroe K. Spears calls *The Wild Goose Chase* "probably the best single work from which to recapture the intellectual and emotional atmosphere of the times."[31] It is also Rex Warner's first, and in some ways his best, treatment of the problem that was to occupy him throughout his career as a novelist: how to remold a sadly unsatisfactory society, muddled, inept, hypocritical, and in constant danger

[29] Upward, "Sketch for a Marxist Interpretation of Literature," in *ibid.*, p. 54.

[30] Lehmann, *Whispering Gallery*, p. 246.

[31] Monroe K. Spears, *The Poetry of W. H. Auden: The Disenchanted Island*, p. 83.

of being changed into something still worse, a Fascist dictatorship, without in the process destroying what is of real and lasting value in that society? In the mid-thirties he felt sure that the answer lay in Communist revolution.

The Wild Goose Chase is a Marxist fairy tale, or rather folk tale, and its theme is the Quest. The most obvious influence, aside from Mortmere, is Kafka, whom Isherwood was to call "the Virgil who will be our guide through the unfolding horrors of the contemporary Inferno."[32] V. S. Pritchett saw also, in the best elements of the novel, traces of Wyndham Lewis (presumably *Childermass*) and, in the worst, of *Dracula* and *Lost Horizon*.[33] In fact Warner borrows very freely from all kinds of sources, including Joyce and the eighteenth-century novel. *The Wild Goose Chase* is a very youthful work: Warner is obviously trying to cram into it virtually everything he knows and believes, and at times he fails in consistency or even coherence. Yet with all its structural flaws and political naïveté—Warner was to find the Marxist scientific myth gravely inadequate within five years—this is a richer and more delightful work than his later, better controlled, sadder, and wiser novels. As Pritchett wrote, Warner "has taken a risk, a leap in the dark, and has sinned," but his book is still much better than a "good novel."[34]

Warner's attempt to touch all contemporary political and social bases calls for rather extended summary. Three brothers set forth from an unlocated but very English village in quest beyond the frontier for the great Wild Goose that is reputed to be their father. They are mid-thirties avatars of the traditional three brothers of folk tale. The oldest and strongest, Rudolph, is a "stout fella" type, a daring athlete, who talks and thinks in clichés and represents the romantic and brave, stupid and inept empire builder, a kind of junior Colonel Blimp. One of the funniest sections of the novel is an excerpt from Rudolph's diary, in which very prosaic and rather humiliating experiences take on the glamor of the carefully modest and understated reminiscences of a daring white adventurer triumphing over nature

[32] Christopher Isherwood, "Man of Honor," *New Republic*, XCVIII, No. 1266 (March 8, 1939), 138.

[33] V. S. Pritchett, "New Novels," *New Statesman and Nation*, XIV, No. 344 N.S. (September 28, 1937), 448.

[34] *Ibid.*

and unfriendly savages. In the course of the novel Rudolph comes to see how very feeble has been his grasp on reality, and he ends appropriately as a blind poet, putting to good use the romantic imagination that made him so absurd as a man of action.

The second brother, the clever one of course, is David, winner of academic competitions, a successful and respected intellectual esthete of dubious sexuality. He is to find happiness for a while in the great City beyond the frontier as he becomes totally emancipated from both morality and reality and is able to pursue sensual pleasure and "pure thought," but eventually this total liberty seems empty and meaningless to him.

The third brother, the simpleton, is George,[35] intelligent but unambitious, good at games but lacking in competitive spirit, popular with women and his lower-class friends but quite indifferent to fame and glory. The townspeople expect little of him, but he is to be the successful one who can gain the assistance of disguised Helpers and by pluck and luck destroy the Dragon, in this case the City government.

George's quest takes him through all areas of English thought. He first comes to the moldy manor of Don Antonio of Castelfiore, who lives in semi-Lucullan splendor according to his interpretation of Epicurus. He is attended by two naked, aging hetaerae whom he has trained from childhood to sing lieder and recite Latin verses by rote. After Don Antonio's mysterious death, George learns that one of the sad old girls is married to the chef, actually the Don's younger brother, disinherited for having married beneath him. The couple have meekly endured the older brother's tyranny because they were early converted to Christian nonresistance by Prependary Garlic, the hypocritical minister from George's home village. Now free, they plan to turn the estate into a community based on Garlician principles. So much for pacifism and, in passing, for estheticism.

Moving on, George encounters the center of resistance to the City, the farm of Don Antonio's other, also disinherited, brother Joe. The conspirators offer a fair cross section of political opposition, from

[35] The name "George," perhaps because of its association with the national saint, seemed to embody solid Englishness for leftists. Eric Blair liked it so much he took it for his own, adding the equally English Orwell, and he also gave it to his common-man hero. The Dog of Auden and Isherwood's play is also named George.

stolid trade-union types and intellectuals with personal grievances to ambitious revolutionaries, but almost all are taken in by the hearty assurances of the jolly Reverend Hamlet that friendliness, good will, and an avoidance of boat-rocking will ultimately solve their difficulties. Hamlet is, George soon learns, in the employ of the Convent, the intellectual Establishment that controls the City. And so much for the clergy.

In the City, George discovers that the police enforce order not by naked force but by ridicule and humiliating practical jokes; they are a very Kafkaesque force. George declines admission to the Convent when he learns that a precondition is an operation to make him bisexual, but he finds that David, who had preceded him in the quest, has happily submitted and is now proud of his position as a minor functionary. David shows him the Anserium, a glass-domed structure that allegedly houses the City's deity, and he is annoyed when George, observing with binoculars the Wild Goose, which seems to hover high and dimly visible near the ceiling, exclaims that it is only a stuffed effigy. David advises George that as he grows more civilized he will learn to overcome his credulity about sense-evidence and will come either to take the word of the Headmaster of the Convent or at least to suspend judgment on the nature of the Wild Goose and focus his attention on the more sophisticated area of semantics. So much for post-Wittgenstein philosophy.[36]

Despite his intransigence, George is given work by the Convent, first as a lecturer in English literature. Totally unprepared for his opening lecture, George feels he has done badly, but he is praised for having kept the students laughing since that is the proper function of a university lecturer. His next assignment is to referee a football match, but his efforts to maintain village standards of fair play prove futile and disastrous for him. The description of the game, in which the final score has been determined in advance and in which ingenious mechanical devices and machine guns are employed to ensure the planned outcome, achieves as well as any passage in the

[36] Of Rex Warner's own experience with the study of philosophy, his friend Day Lewis writes that having begun brilliantly at Oxford in Mods, Warner "read philosophy to such effect that one day he saw the Absolute walk in at his door, and taking the hint, saved his sanity by having a nervous breakdown, leaving Oxford for a year, and returning to read for a quiet Pass in English" (*Buried Day,* p. 166).

novel the nightmarish hilarity that Warner commands at his best.

Denounced by the parasite who has been accompanying him and by his brother David, George appeals the verdict of his trial and is allowed to see the king, or rather, at least two false kings and a third who may be the real one. The first is a youthful, sports-minded, modern monarch full of talk about efficiency and initiative and the pursuit of action, virility, and vitality by a "true aristocracy" made possible by "not quite a slave class, but a mechanical class."[37] The second is a black-toothed little scientist, unconcerned about George's case and totally uncomprehending when asked about the Wild Goose, but very proud of his scientific achievements, of which the most heavily symbolic is a means for preserving dead kings in a semialive state by constant transfusions of the blood of living workers. The third, and perhaps true, king is a sympathetic and dignified Edwardian gentleman from whom George narrowly escapes with his life. He is, of course, the real enemy, the bourgeois.

Fleeing the City to join "the inevitable movement of the mass" to overthrow it, George heads for Joe's farm, but on the way there comes upon a large building on a lake, identified as "The Free State of Lagonda." The President welcomes him and tells him how he established his country, and Warner begins his dismemberment of the liberal position. The President, early dedicated to the "free human spirit of the individual," had encountered opposition from his wealthy family for his championing of lower-class interests; they argued "that, as none of the measures which I had so far proposed was of a really revolutionary nature, little would be gained by adopting or rejecting them. I replied that even in small things I would never betray the cause of Freedom."[38] He persisted and gradually gathered a small group of revolutionary workers outside the City walls. He issued a Manifesto proclaiming his Free State and promulgated a Constitution. The Government of the City, however, ignored him, and the workers began to raise difficulties because they,

> whom I had led to Freedom, began to claim credit themselves for what had been achieved . . . demanded seats in the legislature . . . which I

[37] Rex Warner, *The Wild Goose Chase,* p. 221. Julian Symons identifies this "king" as a portrait of Sir Oswald Mosley (*The Thirties:A Dream Revolved,* p. 154).

[38] Warner, *Wild Goose Chase,* p. 259.

proposed to keep vacant until I had attracted to the Free State persons of my own culture. . . . [They] even questioned my title to the Presidency . . . [and] said that . . . their hours of labor had been as long and unremunerative as ever, and though I spoke to them of the dignity of labour and of their place in history, their limited intelligences seemed unable to attach any meaning to the words which I pronounced.[39]

At this point the City offered to recognize the Free State and provide the President with a motor launch for his lake and a personal attendant in return for his assembling his followers so that they could be bombed. He reluctantly accepted the offer, reasoning that despite their bad behavior the workers still were worthy of being sacrificed for liberty, and he even erected a memorial monument and composed an ode in their honor. Now, as leader of a free nation, he is in a position to welcome all victims of oppression, although so far only stray dogs and cats have availed themselves of the opportunity.

George leaves the Free State, the halfway house on the road to revolution, in disgust, and continuing back to Joe's farm, he assembles a revolutionary army which, after various exciting feats of valor and cunning, takes the City. In complete charge now, George begins by investigating the Convent. He finds it full of recluses in pursuit of pure knowledge, including

a poet who had invented a new language, but could neither pronounce a syllable of it nor attach any meaning to any of its words. There was an artist who spent his time rapidly arranging fir cones on the floor of his cell, and sweeping them together again with his hand when he was for an instant satisfied with their arrangement. A critic had discovered what literature ought to be; but he was unable to write. A philosopher had explained the world of sense; but he was blind and deaf, had lost his sense of touch, and had been, he informed them, since childhood unable to distinguish one odour from another.[40]

George has all these unfortunates sent to be cared for in the country. He takes more drastic action with regard to the highly secret Research Department, which, under the direction of the Professor of Love, has long been engaged in exploring the "calculus of sensa-

[39] *Ibid.*, p. 260.

[40] *Ibid.*, p. 392. As Professor John Unterecker has noted, Warner's model here is not Kafka but Swift in his account of Gulliver's voyage to Laputa and Lagado.

tion" to the accompaniment of the screams of its human guinea pigs.[41] George has the building blown up with all its inhabitants.

George has ordered that the students of the Convent select one sex apiece and stick to it. They submit but murmur of tyranny, and George speaks to them on the subject:

> No one is free, and no one has any right to expect to be free. What valuable thing can a man do by himself? Nothing. . . . Just as a woman who will not submit to a man, just as a soul that stands off from its body is a blighted, weak thing, so is a man who will not lead others or serve others. . . . It is sufficient reason for me utterly to condemn your Government because it adored something stuffed, and killed those who chased the real thing. And if one is not free to do that, what freedom is worth a halfpenny?[42]

The revolution is briefly threatened when the third and only surviving king corrupts George's two chief lieutenants, working on the ambitions of one and the reverence for royalty of the other.[43] But George is unmoved by the king's promise of a "thorough change in the personnel of the various ministries" and he denies "the ultimate futility of any drastic change in the organization of the state."[44] The king escapes, leaving the way clear for what Pritchett accurately called the "spectacular and only too simple" close. George delivers before the workers in the Anserium a moving speech justifying the revolution and exhorting them to build a new and better society. At the climax of his address, the roof of the Anserium blows off, the stuffed Goose disintegrates, and a flock of giant wild geese is seen flying silently above.

George's story has been told by a man from his old village who claims to have had it from an old, half-mad man resembling George who reappeared briefly in the village long after the three brothers had set off on their quest. The narrator reminds us that George considered the revolution only incidental to his quest for the Wild Goose ("I have, with great difficulty, retrieved a mistake, and that is all")

[41] The Research Department was part of what Pritchett called Warner's debt to Bram Stoker; today, in view of some of the revelations about Nazi medical research, it seems more prophetic and less merely "the sadistic underside of Mr. Warner's idealism" (Pritchett, "New Novels," p. 448).

[42] Warner, *Wild Goose Chase*, pp. 412–413.

[43] Leftist intellectuals were shocked and depressed by the enthusiasm shown by the working classes over George V's Jubilee.

[44] Warner, *Wild Goose Chase*, p. 425.

and that, after his success in the City, he had still to undergo "the crossing of the marshes, the final battle with the king, birth in the desert and the strange customs of remote tribes"; but even with the future unclear and much left to do, "he knew that something not unworthy had been achieved already."[45]

What exactly the Wild Goose represents is as mysterious as George's later adventures. Warner invokes it as "a symbol of our Saviour" in a prefatory poem, but it is certainly not Christ. It seems to be very like the "Love" of Auden's early poems, a secular and humanist force by which the individual can achieve full self-realization through action in community with others.

Warner's absolute confidence in revolutionary Marxism as the road to individual and social salvation makes *The Wild Goose Chase* only too patently a fairy story for the unbeliever, but it is the source of much of the book's charm. This exuberant enthusiasm has already markedly diminished in Warner's next novel, *The Professor* (1938), and, despite the absence of clear evidence, it seems plausible that some of his diminution of confidence in communism was due to recent events in Spain and Russia. This work is shorter and tidier than *The Wild Goose Chase* and, except for a few sequences, less interesting. It elicited wider and fainter praise and more moderate attack.

The Professor is also a fantasy, but quite without the wild extravagance of Warner's first novel. The Kafka of *The Castle* is more in evidence than the Kafka of *The Penal Colony*. Subtitled "a prophecy," it proved to be that. The hero is an eminent literary scholar who has been called in to form a government at a time of great crisis as his small, democratic nation, remarkably like Czechoslovakia, faces a large and aggressive neighbor at the border while trying to deal internally with two competing extremist groups, an internationally minded revolutionary party called the Reds and a National Legion that imitates and serves the interests of the Fascist party that controls the neighbor nation. The Professor has worked out, well within the framework of constitutional democracy, a thoroughly just and rational program that will satisfy the legitimate aspirations of the workers without undue hardship for the ruling class and with careful attention to giving the aggressive neighbor no pretext for invasion. The Reds warn him that the National Legion, with the connivance of the

[45] *Ibid.*, p. 454.

police chief, is planning a coup with the help of the Fascist neighbor, and they urge him to crush the Legion, arm the workers, and accept the assistance of the Red underground. The Professor is reluctant to believe the police chief could be a traitor, and in any case, he cannot countenance unconstitutional action. Instead he relies on his ability to persuade the nation to follow the path of reason and justice. The coup is successful, the Fascist troops enter triumphantly, and the Professor, who now realizes that only a Red-directed revolution has any hope of retrieving the nation, is shot "while attempting to escape."

The Professor successfully evokes, in several passages, the "weird, dreamlike" quality that Isherwood praised,[46] but in purging his earlier extravagance, Warner also sacrificed some of his readers' willingness to suspend disbelief, with the result that the caricatures in this second, more nearly "realistic" novel are, paradoxically, harder to accept than those in the first. Carried along by the imaginative verve of *The Wild Goose Chase,* a reader can easily defer analysis of the justice and accuracy of the implied criticisms and prescriptions, but in the shorter and more schematic *The Professor,* he finds opportunity to wonder in mid-narrative whether the author has not stacked his cards too obviously, whether the range of choices presented to the hero is as limited as it appears, whether so sophisticated a hero could be so innocent, whether in fact the only alternative to fascism is Communist dictatorship. In a book of which at least one purpose must have been to urge a Popular Front, this lack of argumentative conviction is unfortunate.

In this novel, Warner is still convinced that the Communists have the best answers to the problems of resisting fascism and building a just society, but his earlier scorn for liberalism has vanished. The liberal Professor is shown as misguided and unbelievably innocent for a man who has supposedly been following political events with attention and intelligence for thirty years and whose ideas about social organization are so close to those of his creator, but his downfall is presented as tragic. He bears no resemblance to the President of the Free State of Lagonda.

The Aerodrome, written during the London blitz (1941) but not published until later, reveals that Warner had by then undergone the

[46] Isherwood, "Man of Honor," p. 138.

revulsion of feeling of many within the Orthodox Left. Orwell claimed that the trouble with these intellectuals was that they had wanted to be anti-Fascist without being antitotalitarian. If this was once true of Warner, *The Aerodrome* shows recognition of this error.

Still employing fantasy, Warner chose for the framework of this novel neither folk tale nor parable but nineteenth-century melodrama. The complicated plot hinges on sensational revelations of long-hidden family relationships. The hero, Roy, is torn between the muddled, irrational, hypocritical village and the mysterious aerodrome nearby, which seems to symbolize discipline, efficiency, purpose, and dedication to the ideal. That ideal, he gradually learns, is "the acquisition of power and by power—freedom."[47]

The aerodrome is commanded by an Air Vice-Marshal who considers the government of the village, and of the nation, "ignorant in spite of its complacency, inefficient, though well-meaning, based on a faith that nobody perfectly understands, and that most people, in all practical affairs, disregard entirely."[48] The aerodrome was established to protect this society, but the intention of the Air Vice-Marshal is to transform it—as George Bowling would say, to streamline it. To this end, he trains his airmen in disciplined devotion to his ideal: they must forswear material treasures and child-getting because these enslave one to the present, the past, and the future, and the Air Force is seeking freedom from time:

> "Reflect, please, that 'parenthood,' 'ownership,' 'locality' are the words of those who stick in the mud of the past to form the fresh deposit of the future. And so is 'marriage.' These words are without wings."[49]

Sexual license is permitted to airmen, and the acceptance of love provided none is given in return. Ruthless repression of dissent is also permitted, in fact, required. The Air Vice-Marshal is a compelling figure, but he is clearly the villain of the novel, and when Warner has him quote Engels, saying the airman's first duty is "to obtain freedom

[47] Rex Warner, *The Aerodrome: A Love Story,* p. 207. The Airman as a symbol recalls W. H. Auden's *The Orators* (1932), in which the Airman could as well represent Fascist as Communist idealism. It is not hard to imagine the Air Vice-Marshal's having written the "Airman's Journal" in his youth.

[48] Warner, *Aerodrome,* p. 196.

[49] *Ibid.,* p. 195.

through the recognition of necessity,"[50] it is clear that Warner's disaffection from communism is complete.

Young Roy is attracted by the aerodrome, the more so because he has painfully experienced the moral laxity, intellectual sloth, and hypocrisy of the village. He is successful enough as an airman to become personal aide to the Air Vice-Marshal, who turns out to be—in the best tradition of melodrama and of the more fashionable Search for the Father mode—his real father. But he is repelled by the cruelty his father permits and promotes, and he is instrumental in his father's final defeat. Roy has not raised his estimation of the village, but he rejects the Air Vice-Marshal's efforts to purge humanity of everything that defies refinement into his own sterile scheme.

The novel is subtitled "A Love Story," and it reflects, like all the more thoughtful works of this period, the conviction that the personal relationship of love is intricately involved in the larger and more impersonal areas of socioeconomic realities. George of *The Wild Goose Chase* had scorned the "overcleanly, deliberate love-making" of the City for "profane love,"[51] and Roy, too, sees love as the best symbol of everything that is too complex, mysterious, earthy, and human to find a way into a system based on "freedom through power." There is even a hint that the Air Vice-Marshal's whole ideology of "the transformation of consciousness and will, the escape from time, the mastery of the self"[52] has derived from the bitterness of early disappointment in love. In any case, Roy denies the Marshal's contention that "these crimes, as you call them, must continue so that the world may be clean";[53] he decides for the short run and humanity. Repeating his father's words at the end of the novel, he adds, "Clean indeed it [the world] was and most intricate, fiercer than tigers, wonderful and infinitely forgiving."[54]

The Aerodrome did not exhaust Warner's interest in the problem of how to cleanse society without purging humanity. After the benign and proletarian George and the scientifically minded Air Vice-Marshal comes a new savior who is straight out of the Old Testament, with a little help from Dostoevsky and possibly from Kierkegaard. In

[50] *Ibid.*, p. 205.
[51] Warner, *Wild Goose Chase,* p. 453.
[52] Warner, *Aerodrome,* p. 206.
[53] *Ibid.*, p. 329.
[54] *Ibid.*, p. 336.

Men of Stones (1950),[55] Warner shows a leader who has come to realize that reason and efficiency are unlikely to stir men's minds and hearts enough to permit him to dominate them for their own good as he feels he must. Now Governor of an island prison, he has established a regime there in which he deliberately behaves like the old Yahweh, omnipotent and, by human standards, unreasonable, inhumane, and immoral, and thus all the more mysterious and "godlike." His dream is to spread, by means of the disciples he is training on the island, his control over the world. He sees himself as sacrificing his own humanity in order to present the world with "escape from freedom," the true happiness that lies in relief from the burdens of will and responsibility and in the comfort of blind faith and trust in "god." The novel is of course a variation on the Grand Inquisitor's story.[56] The Governor's grandiose designs are thwarted, but the degree of hope for a better society is still less here than in Warner's previous two books. Like them, *Men of Stones* is admirable in structure and style and contains sequences as funny as they are sharply pointed, but it is Warner's bleakest work.

At this point, he appears to have abandoned his efforts to treat contemporary problems in terms of fantasy and to have turned, as Upward predicted such unbelievers must, to the past. His more recent novels, *Young Caesar* and *Imperial Caesar*, do not require justification: they offer a persuasive and fascinating portrait of a figure who has had great appeal for writers and who could be expected to at-

[55] Between these two novels, Warner wrote *Why Was I Killed?* (1943), which is not here examined in detail because it is not really a novel but, as the subtitle states, "a dramatic dialogue." The "I" is an unknown soldier killed in World War II who listens in on a kind of symposium considering possible justifications for his death. He is moved by the argument of a "Man from Spain" that for all the hypocrisy and betrayal of recent years, the ideals of the International Brigades were worth dying for, but he wonders whether the "vision of ordered justice" might not "lack something of the colour, intricacy, and delight" of his own dying vision of life; and he is sympathetic to the contention of the pacifist widowed mother that life is too valuable to be sacrificed for any ideal. The implicit conclusion seems to be that "I" was killed so that others might better realize the beauty, "intricacy," and ultimate value of life and their common humanity, and that if this realization became general there might be no more wars.

[56] In an interesting essay, "Dostoevsky and the Collapse of Liberalism," Rex Warner credits Dostoevsky with clearer vision than Marx because of his fuller appreciation of human complexities (*The Cult of Power*, p. 110).

tract the interest of the classical scholar Warner has become. But in the context of his earlier books, his choice of Julius Caesar as a hero prompts speculation. As he presents himself in first-person narrative, Warner's Caesar appears to embody the perfect revolutionary, justified by history. He is the "true hero" as described by Caudwell, "a man who dominates and moulds his environment" by understanding and moving with the wave of the future.[57] Opposed by ignorance and by honest but obsolete principles—"all the arguments based correctly on premises that have since changed"[58]—Caesar does not hesitate to use violence and deceit to gain his ends, although when it is even remotely expedient he gives rein to his natural inclination toward tolerance and candor. Best of all, some two thousand years of history have confirmed his position as a force for progress and order and even freedom. Despairing of any such force in the twentieth century, Warner turns to the past. This is not to condemn him: his books on Caesar are excellent, and, as Forster said, "There is nothing disgraceful in despair." In fact, as Warner was in many ways typical in his enthusiasm for communism in the early thirties, he is also typical of the later attitudes of many of his contemporaries. Only a very positive critic can firmly assert that either the early hope or the later despair was quite without foundation.

[57] Christopher Caudwell, *Studies in a Dying Culture*, p. 22. Caudwell notes that the hero's understanding may be very partial and instinctive, and he quotes Cromwell's "No man rises so high as he who knows not whither he is going."

[58] *Ibid.*, p. 29.

Chapter V

ON THE LEFT: DRAMA

The theater as a vehicle for the propagation of social and political ideas naturally attracted the intensely ideological writers of the thirties, but their hopes of reaching large audiences were disappointed. While in New York the deliberately "controversial" plays of such left-leaning writers as Elmer Rice, Clifford Odets, Lillian Hellmann, Sidney Kingsley, and Irwin Shaw were enjoying successful runs, the London commercial theater tended to concentrate on domestic comedies like Dodie Smith's *Call It a Day*, farces like Terence Rattigan's *French Without Tears*, and nonpolitical melodramas like Patrick Hamilton's *Gaslight*. West End audiences were not averse to serious drama: throughout the period there were revivals of classic British and continental works, some as recent as Karel Capek's *Insect Play*, and several verse dramas drew sizable audiences. Eliot's *Murder in the Cathedral* and *The Rock* were played from time to time, although not in large theaters, and both Christopher Hassall (*Christ's Comet*) and Dorothy Sayers (*The Zeal of Thy House, The Devil to Pay*) won attention and praise for their efforts along the lines Eliot had indicated. But these plays on religious themes were in no sense controversial, and the apparent reluctance of most British playwrights to deal with subjects that might give offense was distressing to some critics of the period. Desmond MacCarthy, no admirer of propagandist drama, complained in mid-1938 of the "dimness" of native British plays in contrast to the vitality of such American imports as *Idiot's Delight* and *Golden Boy* and blamed fear of the Lord Chamberlain's censorship for making "Safety First" the "guiding principle" of the English stage.[1]

There are many complaints during this period about censorship, not only of the stage but of films and the press as well. Graves and Hodge tell of the banning of a Spanish War documentary film, *England Expects,* which included scenes of British ships being bombed, and of two issues of the *March of Time,* one of them at the demand of the German embassy. Since pro-Nazi films were being shown freely at all news theaters, anti-Fascist Englishmen suspected political motivation behind the censorship.[2] It was also government policy to censor American periodicals sold on the newsstands, although British subscribers received their periodicals by mail untouched. As for the press, Graves and Hodge state flatly, "It was not censored; it was coerced" by the government threat to withhold information from those newspapers of which the editorial policies seemed "against the National interest."[3] Government censorship does not appear to have bothered either the Unity or the Group Theatre, both of which specialized in plays directly or satirically attacking government policies and the entire capitalist system. The restraint of most British playwrights during this period seems to have been largely self-imposed, and their motives need not concern us here. Terence Rattigan probably spoke for many others when he said in 1938:

[1] Desmond MacCarthy, "The American Stage," *New Statesman and Nation,* XVI, No. 384 N.S. (July 2, 1938), 14–15.

[2] Robert Graves and Alan Hodge, *The Long Weekend: A Social History of Great Britain, 1918–1939,* p. 418.

[3] *Ibid.,* p. 417. There were other Government activities during the thirties which some Englishmen considered threatening to civil liberties. The Disaffection Act of 1934 permitted police search and arrest of people possessing "seditious" literature; and the Public Order Act of 1936, forbidding political uniforms at public meetings and giving the police broad powers to break up demonstrations, although apparently inspired by Blackshirt activities, alarmed leftists and libertarians as a potentially dangerous weapon. The Left was also suspicious of Lord Trenchard's "gentleman bobby" project to attract middle- and upper-class recruits for the police by giving them special training schools and preferment in promotion over other policemen of less exalted social origin. A *Times* editorial (June 1, 1934) acknowledging and approving this means of keeping the force loyal to the bourgeoisie did nothing to allay leftist fears (Graves and Hodge, *Long Weekend,* pp. 302–303).

The dread of war, of civil strife, of national upheaval is far too real, far too intense in England at the present time to allow its audiences to listen with equanimity to gloomy reminders that our civilization is on the brink of destruction.[4]

Despite general restraint, two plays dealing with controversial political issues were written during the Spanish Civil War although neither adds any particular luster to its author's fame and neither had any detectable propaganda effect at the time. Sean O'Casey's *The Star Turns Red* was not to be produced until after the beginning of World War II, and Bernard Shaw's *Geneva* proved to be nonpartisan in the sense of offending all parties indiscriminately. Nevertheless, these plays, although minor, are the work of major writers, and the comment they provide on contemporary events merits consideration.

Geneva, which was produced late in 1938 and must have been written not long before, to judge by contemporary references, is very much a play of Shaw's "dotage." There are few ideas, situations, or characters in it which he had not dealt with before and better; still, Shaw was incapable of writing a totally uninteresting play, and *Geneva* contains numerous sequences that would do credit to a lesser playwright. The plot, as often in Shaw, is simply a transparent device to set the stage for a lengthy discussion in which the representatives of various points of view are allowed to state them and as soon as all the opinions have been aired and a number of variations played upon them, the conversation is arbitrarily cut off.

Through a combination of unlikely but amusing circumstances, the dictators Battler, Bombardone,[5] and Flanco are called before the bar of the International Court of Justice to answer for their crimes against democracy and humanity. When the debate begins to founder, the hearing breaks up with the announcement that the earth is moving into its next quantum, which will bring about a new Ice Age and the end to all human life. The report is false, but "you have nothing to do but mention the quantum theory, and people will take your voice for the voice of science and believe anything."[6] The disillu-

[4] Quoted in John Gassner, *Masters of the Drama*, p. 628.

[5] Charles Chaplin also used the name "Bombardone" for his Mussolini caricature in the film *The Great Dictator*.

[6] George Bernard Shaw, *Geneva, Cymbeline Refinished, & Good King Charles*, p. 130.

sioned Secretary of the League of Nations is relieved that the report has at least cut short the "farce" of the hearing, but the idealistic young Judge takes comfort in the fact that, for all their bluster and defiance, the dictators did obey the summons of the Court. Since his is the final speech, the play can be understood as mildly hopeful that international public opinion might yet be a force for peace and justice; however, the conclusion is less important than the debate.

In a sense, the play is a dialogue between the Judge and the Secretary as they comment upon the speeches of the other characters, the Judge basing his criticism upon the principles of reason and justice and the Secretary arguing from long and depressing experience with the realities of international politics. Dramatically these two characters function to assure that the audience does not miss any of the hypocrisies and absurdities of the participants in the debate.

In *Geneva* Shaw offers two versions, one born and one made, of his favorite target, the Englishman. Begonia Brown, whose initial blunder has set the plot going, is a feminine version of the natural unspoiled English type. She has risen from a small secretarial post to become a Conservative M. P. and a Dame of the British Empire on the strength of her English virtues, of which she is fully cognizant:

> O, I am not a bit proud; and I'm quite used to being a success. . . . although I was always at the top of my class at school, I never pretended to be clever. . . . At first I was frightened of the girls that went in for being clever and having original ideas and all that sort of crankiness. But I beat them easily in the examinations; and they never got anywhere. That gave me confidence. Wherever I go I always find that lots of people think as I do; . . . If you want to know what real English public opinion is, keep your eye on me.[7]

The British Foreign Secretary, Sir Orpheus Midlander, is hampered by his natural intelligence and urbanity, but he strives to achieve at least the appearance of unimaginative mediocrity that is Begonia's by birth. Praised for his astuteness and ambition, he gracefully demurs:

> Thank you, my dear Judge, thank you. But for Heaven's sake dont call me clever or I shall be defeated at the next election. . . . please understand that I am not an intellectual. A plain Englishman doing my duty to my country according to my poor lights. . . . I happen to be fairly well off; but

[7] *Ibid.*, pp. 53–54.

the money was made by my grandfather. Upon my honor I dont know how I got landed where I am. I am quite an ordinary chap really.[8]

Sir Orpheus states British policy, as seen by Shaw, very clearly:

When you ask me what will happen if British interests are seriously menaced you ask me to ford the stream before we come to it. We never do that in England. But when we come to the stream we ford it or bridge it or dry it up. And when we have done that it is too late to think about it. We have found that we can get on without thinking. . . . I am intensely reluctant to lose my grip of the realities of the moment to sit down and think. It is dangerous. It is unEnglish. It leads to theories, to speculative policies, to dreams and visions. . . . We have no speculative plans. We shall simply stick to our beloved British Empire and undertake any larger cares that Providence may impose on us. . . . We are a simple wellmeaning folk, easily frightened. And when we are frightened we are capable of anything, even of things we hardly care to remember afterwards.[9]

Geneva parades a great many political outlooks besides the British muddle-mystique. There is a walking archaism in the opulent form of a handsome widow who threatens a blood feud unless the League agrees to punish the executioners of her late husband, a Latin American president-dictator. With her vengefulness and her obsession with the requirements of her social position, which combined she calls "honour," with her ferocious religiosity and her susceptibility to flattery, she appears to represent the eternal feminine in politics, or perhaps the eternal irrational.

The spokesman for democracy is a "half-Americanized colonist," a "lower middle-class politician" with a passion for parliamentary procedures and a bland indifference to everything else. Specifically,

[8] *Ibid.*, p. 78. If Graves and Hodge are correct, Shaw was not exaggerating. They write that Tory backbenchers had for some years rejoiced in Labour references to theirs as the "Stupid Party," happily associating stupidity with virtue, as against the sneaky intellectuality of the socialists (Graves and Hodge, *Long Weekend*, p. 320).

[9] Shaw, *Geneva,* pp. 95–96. In the Preface Shaw wrote for this play in 1945, he observes (p. 6) that once Hitler had made the mistake of frightening England, she not only took him on "single-handed without a word to the League of Nations nor to anyone else, but outfought him, outbragged him, outbullied him, outwitted him in every trick and turn of warfare, and finally extinguished him and hanged his accomplices." The cool omission of reference to any of England's allies in this enterprise is fairly typical of Shaw in the period he so aptly termed his dotage.

he is unable to see how the persecution of the Jews can be considered reprehensible if it is by majority consent. "If the people vote for it, there is no violation of democratic principle. It's a bit hard on you, I admit. But it's not a matter of principle."[10]

The character of the Jew, who has brought charges against Battler for his persecution, is sufficient to differentiate *Geneva* from most anti-Fascist plays of the period. He is clever and suave, particularly in his dealings with the Latin widow, whom he manages to take out to dinner despite her religious feelings about "God murderers," and he puts his case against Battler with great force. His final action in the play tends, however, to confirm the judgments made upon his race by the anti-Semites in the cast: his immediate response to the news that the world is coming to an end is to rush for a telephone so he can corner the market and die a millionaire.

The Russian Communist diplomat is presented with considerable respect. The Judge notes that his being a Commissar testifies to his ability, since in the USSR "nothing but ability counts." As the Judge sees it, the Soviet Union has at least tried to bring her political philosophy up to date, with the result that "now her politicians are only about fifty years behind her philosophers and saints whilst the rest of the civilized world is from five hundred to five thousand behind it."[11] However, although he is more rational than the rest of the characters (always excepting the Judge and the Secretary), the Commissar is not less nationalistic or dogmatic, and when he hears of the coming end of the world, his reaction is that of a docile Party man: "I await instructions. The Marxist dialectic does not include the quantum theory. I must consult Moscow."[12]

Shaw's gentle treatment of his Communist spokesman in this play is unlikely to have given any fresh offense to his audiences, which had been hearing him praise Stalin for some time, but his handling of the Fascist dictators of his cast cannot have been very pleasing in December of 1938, when the initial relief over the Munich agreement was already beginning to turn to doubt and revulsion. In his 1945 Preface to the play, Shaw was still calling Stalin one of the "able despots" who "made good by doing things better and much more

[10] *Ibid.*, p. 69.
[11] *Ibid.*, pp. 80, 82.
[12] *Ibid.*, p. 128.

promptly than parliaments," but he wrote then that the "adventurers" Hitler and Mussolini had been "finally scrapped as failures and nuisances."[13] In 1938 he saw Mussolini in a rather different light.

General Flanco de Fortinbras, the smallest of the dictators, fits easily into the military silly-ass stereotype. Described as "*very smart, and quite conventional*" in manner, he is respectful toward the British Foreign Secretary but barely civil to Battler and Bombardone, who are clearly not gentlemen. He admits that their aid has helped him, but no more than "the masterly non-intervention policy of Sir Orpheus Midlander." He states his position with soldierly simplicity:

> I stand simply for government by gentlemen against government by cads. . . . For me there are only two classes, gentlemen and cads: only two faiths, Catholics and heretics. I am determined that the world shall not be ruled by cads nor its children brought up as heretics. . . . In that I have the great body of public opinion behind me. . . . Everybody understands my position: nobody understands the pamphlets, the three volumes of Karl Marx, the theories of the idealists, the ranting of the demagogues: in short, the caddishness of the cads.[14]

Like the Commissar's, his reaction to the news that humanity is to be destroyed is to seek instructions from the proper authority:

> The Church . . . knows the truth as God knows it, and will instruct us accordingly. Anyone who questions its decision will be shot. . . . After absolution, of course.[15]

Flanco's gentlemanliness and humanity do not fail to win the approval of that voice of English public opinion, Begonia, who pronounces him a "perfect gentleman." Bombardone, however, comments: "Flanco is dead; but he does not know it. History would have kicked him out were not History now on its deathbed."

Bombardone's judgments are clearly intended to be taken seriously. Described as "*every inch the Man of Destiny,*" he is cynical and Machiavellian, very much an actor at all times, sublimely confident but basing his sense of superiority not on any mystical hogwash about race or pious cant about Providence but upon a conviction, which Shaw seems to share, of the stupidity, credulity, and general irra-

[13] *Ibid.*, p. 22.
[14] *Ibid.*, pp. 116–117.
[15] *Ibid.*, p. 127.

tionality of men. Where Battler is hysterical and sentimental and cruel, Bombardone is unfailingly coolheaded and clear-eyed. He sees himself as an exemplar of the "law of personal gravitation," by which the ablest rise to the top. When the "democrat" asks, "What about democracy?" he replies:

I am what I am: you are what you are; and in virtue of these two facts I am where I am and you are where you are. . . . Democracy has delivered you from the law of priest and king, of landlord and capitalist, only to bring you under the law of personal gravitation. . . . Plutocracy has cut off the heads of kings and archbishops to make itself supreme and rob the people without interference from king or priest, but the people always follow their born leader. When there is no leader, no king, no priest, nor any body of law established by dead kings and priests, you have mob law, lynching law, gangster law: in short, American democracy. Thank your stars you have never known democracy in England. I have rescued my country from that by my leadership. I am a democratic institution.[16]

Charged with "the murder and destruction of liberty and democracy in Europe," he responds: "One cannot destroy what never existed."[17]

Bombardone respects Battler as a technician of demagogy, but he is bored and annoyed by Battler's racist mysticism and is somewhat apprehensive about his Messianic pretensions. Sir Orpheus also dislikes Battler's racism, particularly his talk of "the most advanced race" as destined to rule the world. He distrusts "advanced" people, who are generally "difficult to work with, and often most disreputable in their private lives"; however, he is willing to agree with the proposition if Battler will withdraw the term "advanced" and substitute "the race best fitted by its character—its normal, solid, everyday character—to govern justly and prosperously."[18]

Bombardone is frankly a charlatan, and the moral criticisms of the Judge and the Secretary are wasted on him because he rejects the values by which they judge him, rejects in fact all values but the satisfaction of his own egotism; but Battler, Sir Orpheus, and the rest are shown as not more moral but only more inclined to deceive themselves as they deceive others. Bombardone is the 1938 version of the honest rogue whom Shaw had been depicting with obvious affection for over forty years, and he is an attractive figure in this play.

[16] *Ibid.*, pp. 91, 93.

[17] *Ibid.*, p. 104.

[18] *Ibid.*, p. 119.

If, as the eloquent speeches of the Judge and the Secretary suggest, *Geneva* was intended to be a plea for a reasonable internationalism, the long cherished dream of a world under law, it does not succeed. The Judge and the Secretary speak for reason and morality and the Communist for common sense, but the total effect of the play is that the world of 1938 is largely immune to reason, morality, or common sense, and that in such a world the best we can hope for is leadership by the kind of efficient and honest charlatan that Shaw saw embodied in Mussolini. The play cannot have been very pleasing to anyone who was really concerned about politics at the time.[19] Conservatives must have resented the picture of British duplicity and hypocrisy, and the terms in which Shaw praises the Fascist dictators are not such as any British rightist would care to associate himself with; but *Geneva* is most offensive from the anti-Fascist point of view.

Desmond MacCarthy, a moderate anti-Fascist, was appalled. He deplored the "feebleness" of the case put against the dictators and observed, accurately, that the Judge's "impartial" condemnation of all the disputants was "equivalent to a general acquittal."[20] According to MacCarthy, Shaw had seen in his old age "the most merciless of all revolutions achieving what, theoretically, was a fulfillment of a political system he approved," and thus he was "forced . . . logically into an inhuman leniency toward similar methods in other Totalitarian States." Old age having "blunted his sympathies," Shaw had come to show a "chirpy indifference to realities" and to mistake "indifference for wisdom." His "secret," MacCarthy concluded, "is that he can no longer feel anything much."[21]

This is a harsh statement, but not, perhaps, unjust. Shaw was by no means alone in his errors of judgment. Respect for Mussolini, contempt for Hitler, the assumption that Stalin's Russia was the most

[19] According to John Gassner (*Masters of the Drama*, p. 616), *Geneva* pleased the government enough for it to plan a Canadian tour of the play during 1939 "as anti-German propaganda." Shaw's comment on the plan took the form of an article on "the mistakes of British diplomacy and the real nature of its vaunted democracy."

[20] Desmond MacCarthy, "A Play of the Moment," *New Statesman and Nation*, XVI, No. 406 N.S. (December 3, 1938), 916. The proposition that all European governments were equally rotten was entertained by some Trotskyists in the late thirties, but even they were inclined to consider some governments more rotten than others.

[21] *Ibid.*, p. 916.

nearly rational and just society yet achieved were illusions that many other intelligent men shared, although few managed to hold all three at once as Shaw did, and each had some basis in truth. But the extraordinary detachment with which Shaw could view the world of 1938 still seems more inhuman than superhuman.

If Shaw's contribution to the great debate of 1936–1939 showed some deficiency of feeling, Sean O'Casey's suffered rather from excess of it. *The Star Turns Red,* apparently written during the Spanish Civil War and inspired by the political passions that the war exacerbated, but not produced until later, is his poorest play, strident in tone, crude in symbolism, and sadly lacking in the irreverent humor that makes *Purple Dust,* written shortly afterward and similarly revolutionary in intention, entertaining despite its diffuseness. *The Star Turns Red* is straight propaganda, about on a level with *Waiting for Lefty* and considerably above *Flowering Rifle* because free of the bloodthirst that permeates that poem; it is transparently "sincere," deeply felt, and well designed to spur to greater efforts those who share the author's beliefs, but unlikely to persuade the unconverted or greatly interest the uncommitted.

The Star Turns Red is a mixture of realism and expressionism, with short scenes in apparently casual progression, considerable use of music, carefully unrealistic sets, and a shift into verse for the expression of lofty sentiments. The symbolic "Star" is the Star of Bethlehem, first shining in silver beside a steeple seen through a window on stage, but turning red when the revolution breaks out. At the end of the play, *"The Red Star glows, and seems to grow bigger as the curtain falls."*[22] The moral is that communism is the new *lux mundi.*

The play is dedicated to "The Men and Women Who Fought through the Great Dublin Lockout in 1913," and "Red Jim" is obviously modeled after Jim Larkin, the hero of 1913. The place is Dublin, but the time is "To-morrow, or the next day" rather than 1913. The action of *The Star Turns Red* occurs on Christmas Eve. A stay-in strike called by Red Jim is about to end in the capitulation of the "moderate" trade-union leaders who have been seduced by the wily "Purple Priest of the politicians." The family about whom the action centers consists of a company-man father and an apolitical mother (a weaker Juno), and their two sons, the Communist Jack

[22] Sean O'Casey, *The Star Turns Red* in *Collected Plays,* II, 354.

and the Saffron Shirt Kian. The Saffron Shirts, like O'Duffy's Blue Shirts, are a jackbooted Fascist gang serving the interests of the Christian Front. The first act is lurid enough: Jack's girl Julia is whipped for defying the S.S. leader and when her father, Michael, resists he is shot. Dying, he gently rejects the ministrations of the kind "Brown Priest of the people" and asks Jack to raise and clench his fist for him: "Lift it up, lift it up in the face of these murdering bastards—the Clenched Fist!"[23]

The next two acts afford various occasions for Red Jim to excoriate his temporizing and corruptible fellow labor leaders, the respectable bourgeois (who are full of Red atrocity stories from Spain), and the domineering and puritanical Purple Priest. The Priest insists that the "happiness of the toiling masses is hidden only in the bosom of the holy Church," but Red Jim says the people have repudiated the Church: "Now we stand up, we turn, and go our own way, the bent back changing to the massed majority of the Clenched Fist!" And he and his Red Guards carry off the slain Michael to the Red March: "Red Star, arise, the wide world over!"[24]

In the final act, revolution breaks out as the Star turns red. The second scene shows dead and wounded workers lying about the Lord Mayor's office where they have barricaded themselves, the dead "*each with a stiffened clenched fist held high.*"[25] A final confrontation occurs during a brief truce as the Purple Priest and Kian debate with the revolutionary leaders and with the Brown Priest, who has crossed the barricades to join the workers. Reprimanded by the Purple Priest, he cites the *Quadragesimo Anno* encyclical and affirms that

> The Star turned red is still the Star
> Of him who came as man's pure prince of peace;
> And so I serve him here.[26]

Red Jim, however, has no use for the Church, even of Pius XI:

> Our saints are those who fall beating a roll on
> the drum of revolution.
> We fight on; we suffer; we die; but we fight on

[23] *Ibid.*, p. 276.

[24] *Ibid.*, p. 326. The melody to which the dead march is sung is the one known in the United States as "Shenandoah."

[25] *Ibid.*, p. 349.

[26] *Ibid.*, p. 351.

Till brave-breasted women and men, terrac'd with
strength,
Shall live and die together, co-equal in all things;
And romping, living children, anointed with joy,
shall be banners and banneroles of this moving
world!
In all that great minds give, we share;
And unto man be all might, majesty, dominion, and
power![27]

The play ends in triumph, although Jack has been killed. Julia raises his clenched fist as soldiers and sailors appear at the windows singing the "Internationale," and the Red Star glows and grows.

Baldly summarizing a play is often unfair; all sorts of subtleties and complexities and ironies may be lost. In *The Star Turns Red*, there are none to lose. This is the more remarkable in a play by Sean O'Casey, whose earlier works such as *The Plough and the Stars* and *Juno and the Paycock*, were so rich in irony as to raise doubts in some critics' minds about where his sympathies really lay. There is no such problem here: all is of poster-like simplicity. Yielding to the temptation to speculate on how the tough-minded and sardonic O'Casey came to write such a solemn and sentimental melodrama, one may suggest that the initial error was in the resolve to produce a general statement. The character of Covey in *The Plough and the Stars* shows that O'Casey was perfectly capable of portraying a Communist as a human being rather than as a repository of all wisdom and virtue, and *Red Roses for Me* (1943), which is also based on the 1913 Lock-out, is free of the crudity of *The Star Turns Red*, but both of these dramas deal with specific, even historical situations. In *The Star Turns Red*, O'Casey is working directly with abstract ideas, and this is an area in which he is very weak. When he takes up communism as an idea, he becomes "Irish" in the very sense that he ridicules the "Irishness" of his compatriots; that is, he is sentimental and bigoted.

Granting that O'Casey's ideal of "communism" as representing human brotherhood, the dignity of the individual, social justice, and freedom of the spirit, may be nobler than the ideals of Irish nationalism or Catholic puritanism, his devotion to it is no less fanatical. He began calling himself a Communist in 1928, wanting no truck with the less militant forms of socialism, and throughout the next thirty

[27] *Ibid.*, p. 352.

years this anarchic individualist was completely Orthodox in identifying the cause of socialism with the Soviet Union. His references to Stalin in his autobiographies are as pious as any Irish nationalist's invocation of Parnell or Irish Catholic's of St. Patrick. He is not merely employing a literary device, effective though hardly original, when he fills *The Star Turns Red* with Marxist parodies of biblical passages: in this play, as in the autobiographies, Russian communism is his faith and Stalin is its prophet. Like any religious bigot, he is fiercer toward heretics than toward unbelievers, and he reserves his bitterest invective for unorthodox Marxists like Koestler and Orwell; the shield of his unquestioning faith renders him impervious to argument whenever the Soviet Union is the subject.

In *Sunset and Evening Star* (1954), O'Casey describes a conversation (presumably in the late thirties: he is not very explicit about dates) with a rather loathsome lady, an embittered ex-Communist, who offers him "the truth" about repression, fear, and poverty in Russia. "Softly" and "quietly," but crushingly, he puts aside her hysterical ravings, adding, "And the more you shout, lady, the less I hear."[28] He then offers a lively disquisition on people with closed minds and ends his chapter with the truth about Truth:

> What is Truth? Man in his individual nature was still asking the question, and man in the mass was answering it. Facts, though true, were not Truth; they were but minor facets of it. Parts, but not the whole. The great achievements of the Soviet Union, . . . the inexhaustible energy, the irresistible enthusiasm of their Socialistic efforts, were facts to Sean; grand facts, setting the people's feet firmly on the way to the whole truth, calling all men to a more secure destiny in which all heads shall be anointed with oil, and all cups shall be filled.[29]

A willingness to overlook or deny lesser, contradictory "facts" because of one's conviction of the "larger truth" of one's faith is common enough in the religious, but it seems oddly inconsistent with O'Casey's devastating irreverence toward the pieties of others and with his principled irreligiosity. In his plays by implication, and very explicitly in his autobiographies, he has stood firmly for reason against prejudice, doubt against faith, experience against dogma. Clearly,

[28] Sean O'Casey, *Sunset and Evening Star*, in vol. II of *Mirror in My House: The Autobiographies of Sean O'Casey*, p. 128.

[29] *Ibid.*, pp. 133–134.

one man's faith is another's reason. Never having been subject to Party discipline, and never having visited Stalin's Russia, he managed to keep his faith intact when other sensitive and intelligent men were losing theirs.[30]

In his better plays, O'Casey's special brand of Marxism serves him well, affording a perspective from which to attack the very real evils of religious, moralistic, and patriotic bigotry; but in *The Star Turns Red,* his own personal piety is the subject, and solemn reverence is not an attitude that gives proper play to his great talents. *The Star Turns Red* is not important in the O'Casey *oeuvre*, and if someone else had written it, it would have no interest today except as a period piece.

Also period pieces, but sometimes more than that, were the productions of the two left-wing experimentalist theatrical groups, the Unity and Group Theatres, which enjoyed some success in London during the late thirties. These two groups exemplified in the theater the same divergence in leftist aesthetics that was apparent in the argument over the relative merits of social realism and fantasy in the novel, and in the different poetic standards represented in Edgell Rickword's *Left Review* and Geoffrey Grigson's *New Verse*.[31]

The Unity Theatre was the more Orthodox and less experimental of the two companies. According to Julian Symons, it had great enthusiasm and little taste for subtlety. The members, all unpaid and mostly amateurs of working-class background, were sustained by the "mystique of Communism" and looked upon art entirely as a weapon in the class struggle.[32] They sought out plays with unequivocal propaganda messages, but they found discouragingly little native material, their only very successful production by a genuine English proletarian being *Where's That Bomb?* by a London cabdriver named Herbert Hodge.[33] *The Star Turns Red* is just their kind of play, but they apparently made no contact with O'Casey. They were able to find the kind of dramas they wanted abroad: Elmer Rice's *Judgment*

[30] For O'Casey, to lose faith in Russia was to lose faith in life. See his attack on George Orwell and similar "Kafka-Koestlerian souls" in *Sunset and Evening Star*, pp. 136–147.

[31] See Chapter VI.

[32] Julian Symons, *The Thirties: A Dream Revolved*, p. 89.

[33] No copies of this play seem to be available. Graves and Hodge describe it as a "crude, sincere morality play" (*Long Weekend*, p. 329).

Day, based on the Reichstag fire trial, and Irwin Shaw's socialist-pacifist *Bury the Dead* enjoyed moderate runs, while a double bill of Brecht's *Señora Carrar's Rifles* and Odets' *Waiting for Lefty* drew audiences much larger than the small core of enthusiasts who regularly attended all performances. Symons describes H. G. Wells "squeaking" his excited assent as the audience joined the cast at the end of the Odets play in the cry to "Strike!"[34]

Unity was not interested in sophisticated complexities nor in experimentation for its own sake: it rejected the Auden-Isherwood collaborations as too "unreal." However, it was receptive to theatrical innovations that might strengthen the propaganda force of a play, as in the close of *Waiting for Lefty,* and it borrowed techniques, such as the "Living Newspaper" format, that were developed across the Atlantic by the New York Group Theater and the Federal Theater Project. It even borrowed Paul Robeson, the American Negro singer and actor who had been lionized by the left wing in the United States. Symons, not himself much in sympathy with the Unity point of view, was favorably impressed by a mass recitation of Ernst Toller's requiem for Karl Liebknecht and Rosa Luxembourg, the leaders of the German Spartacist movement, and by a dramatized version of Jack Lindsay's poem, "Salute the Soviet Union." He pronounced the Unity Theatre's "failures . . . more interesting than West End commercial successes."[35] But Unity was not destined for survival. Its greatest success, a musical revue called *Babes in the Woods: A Pantomime with Political Point,* by Geoffrey Parsons and Berkeley Fase, caught the public fancy with its attack on Neville Chamberlain after the Munich agreement and induced giddy visions of Unity's becoming a permanent professional company, but the war ended all that.[36]

The Group Theatre, which also closed down in 1939, was more experimental, more unorthodox, more sophisticated, and, to judge by contemporary reviews, more precious than Unity. It was also responsible for presenting plays of greater intrinsic interest, and during its brief life bore on its roster some of the most brilliant names in contemporary British life, including Tyrone Guthrie, Henry Moore, and Benjamin Britten. It had been founded in 1932 by Rupert Doone,

[34] Symons, *The Thirties,* p. 87.
[35] *Ibid.,* p. 88.
[36] *Ibid.,* p. 170.

formerly a dancer and choreographer with Diaghilev, and by several of his friends, among whom W. H. Auden was, in this enterprise as in all others he engaged in, a dominating figure.

Doone and Auden were convinced that documentation should be left to the films and character analysis to the novel. What they wanted to achieve in the drama was a new theatrical form close to "modern musical comedy or the pre-medieval folk play," in which artists, musicians, and dancers, as well as poets and actors, could provide an experience in which the audience too could participate.[37] The end in view was, broadly, "parable art" as Auden defined it: "that art which shall teach man to unlearn hatred and learn love."[38] At this stage in his life, Auden tended to identify hatred with capitalism and love with socialism, and the plays he wrote alone and with Christopher Isherwood stress this identification. However, direct and specific propaganda of the sort presented on the Unity stage was alien to the Group approach; hence the Group plays to be considered here will prove to have no direct reference to Spain although all are concerned with the issues of the Spanish War and contain political messages intended and taken as relevant to it. Symons feels that the Group productions never became what they were intended to be, "the act of a whole community," were never in fact more than "a gesture made by middle-class radicals to a middle-class audience."[39] He attributes this failure partly to the self-conscious artiness of the performances, in which the plays were excessively slowed by "deliberate stylization and formality," and more importantly to an essential lack of seriousness in the Group's chief playwrights, a charge to be considered below.

It took the Group three years to manage a London season, but 1935–1936 saw productions of Eliot's *Sweeney Agonistes,* Louis MacNeice's translation of the *Agamemnon,* Auden's *Dance of Death,* and the Auden-Isherwood *The Dog Beneath the Skin.* Later productions included the Auden and Isherwood *The Ascent of F6* (1936) and *On the Frontier* (1938), Spender's *Trial of a Judge* (1938), and MacNeice's *Out of the Picture* (1937). The last does not require close

[37] Rupert Doone quoted in *ibid.*, p. 78.

[38] W. H. Auden, "Psychology and Art Today" (1930), quoted by Monroe K. Spears in *The Poetry of W. H. Auden: The Disenchanted Island,* p. 13.

[39] Symons, *The Thirties,* p. 80.

examination. It demonstrates the poetic skill that never failed MacNeice, but it is extremely imitative of the earlier Auden-Isherwood plays. MacNeice chose to reprint only a few of the incidental lyrics later, and referred to it as a "bad experimental play."[40] The critics generally agreed.

Spender's *Trial of a Judge* was also unsatisfactory to its author, but it is not imitative, and it is interesting as revealing the poet's inner conflicts on political questions, conflicts that also disturbed many of Spender's contemporaries. Spender chose not to imitate the rather striking theatrical innovations of his friends Auden and Isherwood because they seemed to him to lead in a direction not ultimately fruitful for poetic drama. In an article published at about the time his play opened, he offered a thoughtful discussion of what modern poetic drama should be.

He begins with a persuasive argument on the value of verse as a vehicle for social and political comment, observing how well the Elizabethans used it to get around censorship: "The prosaic fact offends where the poetic generalization does not. The poetic drama was a means of striking with one blow at the heart of contemporary problems, but the stroke was oblique."[41] But its obliqueness is not the greatest utility of verse: in their use of verse for the speech of kings and nobles and prose for that of commoners, the Elizabethans were demonstrating not snobbery but an understanding that the affairs of the great, which could not but have far-reaching political implications for the whole people, required the heightening and generalizing resources of poetry. At a time when great political forces are increasingly impinging upon individual lives, Spender feels that verse is the most appropriate medium for serious drama, leaving prose for the kind of naturalistic domestic comedy or melodrama that offers only escape or relaxation.

To Spender, the expressionist drama is a symptom of the need for verse drama to deal with large issues rather than a satisfactory medi-

[40] Quoted by Stanley J. Kunitz and Howard Haycraft in *Twentieth Century Authors*, p. 889. Henry Adler wrote in *Time and Tide*: "It is all very fantastic and inconsequential and clever and irritating. . . . This Method is being overdone, and Mr. MacNeice's play is not even a good example of it" (Review of *Out of the Picture* by Louis MacNeice, XVIII, No. 29 [July 24, 1937], 1018).

[41] Stephen Spender, "Poetry and Expressionism," *New Statesman and Nation*, XV, No. 368 N.S. (March 12, 1938), 407.

um in itself. He praises the efforts of German and Irish expressionists (Kaiser, Toller, Brecht; O'Casey, Johnston) to present important social and political problems on stage, but he considers their verse, "like the whole apparatus of the expressionist stage, a hastily constructed improvisation" without poetic distinction. The Auden-Isherwood plays, of which he noted the expressionist derivation, he also considered overly "improvised." Elsewhere[42] he expressed the opinion that nowhere in their collaborative plays did these two writers reach the level each consistently maintained in his individual efforts. Spender's prescription for modern verse drama is not expressionism but "a calm realism . . . with a wide range of reference to contemporary problems and with an approach which can evade the surface naturalism of the prose drama and the whims of the censor."[43]

Trial of a Judge is an interesting, if not very successful, attempt to follow this prescription. Spender departs from realism in the use of a chorus and of soliloquy, and he calls for some unnaturalistic lighting effects, but the play is free of the tricks and surprises of his friends' experimental dramas; it is no more improvisatory than *Murder in the Cathedral,* which in fact it resembles more closely than *The Dog Beneath the Skin.* It did not startle its audience, but it seems to have bored and confused at least part of it. The Group's choice of the Unity Theatre as a place to perform the play—the Group had no theater of its own—was probably unwise. As Symons points out, the regular Unity audience liked its propaganda hot and simple, and "few things interested them less than abstract arguments about justice in the mind of a judge."[44] But some of the trouble lay in the play itself. Spender's compressed, elliptical verse, which offers no difficulties on the page, is perhaps a little too "oblique" for the theater; some of the audience apparently had trouble knowing exactly what was going on. Desmond MacCarthy defended the playwright against the charge of obscurity, noting that not all Shakespearian verse yields its full meaning at first hearing, but he, too, found himself somewhat confused, not by the language of the drama but by a sense that the poet

[42] Stephen Spender, "The Poetic Dramas of W. H. Auden and Christopher Isherwood," *New Writing* N.S. 1 (Autumn 1938), p. 107.

[43] Spender, "Poetry and Expressionism," p. 409.

[44] Symons, *The Thirties*, p. 86.

was writing against his own deepest inclinations, to the extent of subverting his own message.[45] It was a valid observation.

The message is clear enough. It is, like Warner's *The Professor* and the later Auden-Isherwood *On the Frontier,* directed toward liberals and pacifists and intended to persuade them that liberalism and pacifism, however noble in theory, are simply inadequate to the demands of the present crisis, that if fascism is not to triumph these idealistic folk must join the militant proletariat and be ready to fight for the just and peaceful society they desire. The immediate propaganda purpose of the play was clearly to mobilize and intensify support for those fighting fascism in Spain and, underground, on the Continent. In the interests of poetic generalization, Spender does not specify his setting, but it is clearly Germany in 1932–1933 or, if his worst fears are realized, England at some near future time. The liberal Judge, having briefly compromised with the forces of fascism and then reversed himself, is ostensibly being tried for treason to the Fascist state; but he is really on trial in his own mind for his initial willingness to acquiesce in injustice for the sake of preserving order and avoiding violence. At the end of the play, he dies in despair, but the Red prisoners who are executed with him are confident of ultimate victory, for

> in this darkness
> We hold the secret hub of an idea
> Whose living sunlit wheel revolves in future
> years outside.[46]

The play ends with the Red Chorus repeating,

> We shall be free
> We shall find peace.[47]

The young Reds of the play seem to be spokesmen for the correct position. Their ideal is certainly noble. One of them presents it glowingly in a rather overlong dying speech:

[45] "Trial of a Judge," *New Statesman and Nation,* XV, No. 370 N.S. (March 26, 1938), 523.

[46] Stephen Spender, *Trial of a Judge: A Tragedy in Five Acts,* p. 93.

[47] *Ibid.,* p. 88.

Do not say
I was unhappy. I built my mind
In the foundation of that world
Which grows against chaos and will be happiness.
My mind's own peace and my material interest
Centred in a philosophy of unfearing crystal
Whose radius is the peace of cities, and
brilliance
Lack of jealousy between men.[48]

His fiancée eulogizes him and his brother, killed earlier:

Our heroes . . .
Are not the seven-pointed indrawn stars
The centres of their crepe and tear-stained
skies,
But those for whom a freed humanity
Was their joint aim, their lives
Spent like two bullets
To achieve that single target.[49]

She and another of the Reds disdain the Judge's personal regret for his part in the Fascist triumph, and they find his willingness to atone with his own life totally inadequate:

THIRD RED. For Christ also
With his great death betrayed
Humanity he might have saved
FIANCÉE. Since when, his Church holds up a
Golden Bowl
In which the innocent fingers wash away
The world's guilt from the purified soul.[50]

The Reds have no sympathy with the motives that led the Judge first to seek a "realistic compromise" with the Fascists:

You are the mask they wear
Who commit injustices and condone murder.
When their actions are most naked
And their knife flashes in an unashamed moon,

[48] *Ibid.*, p. 54.
[49] *Ibid.*, p. 83.
[50] *Ibid.*, p. 62.

They assume your look of justice
And like a parrot you say 'regret, regret.'[51]

In prison, awaiting execution with the Reds, the Judge defends his aversion to the kind of unrestricted warfare they consider necessary for the defeat of fascism and the triumph of justice, but the Reds condemn the Judge's conception of freedom as bourgeois and destined in its effect, whatever his intentions, to further the tyrant's cause:

You in fighting these our enemies
Who kill you to delete your words,
Yet see with their hypocrite mind; you disclaim
The necessary murderous hatred,
And ignore that you and they must die.[52]

He replies with a speech on the relation of means and ends, contending that to adopt the attitudes and methods of one's enemies is to become like them and thus to lose the struggle whatever the apparent issue.

It is significant that this final argument by the Judge is not answered on the plane of ideas. His debate with the Reds is interrupted by the entrance of a group of Fascist bullies with an intellectual Jew whom they mistreat and humiliate. Perhaps the purpose of this sequence was to indicate that the most idealistic and reasonable theories about means and ends are irrelevant before the ugly realities of totalitarian politics. If so, the purpose is not quite achieved, for the arguments of the liberal Judge are the ones that remain most persistently with the reader, as they apparently did with much of the audience. It is notable that the reviewers of both the Right-leaning *Observer* and the Left-leaning *New Statesman and Nation* agreed that in the three-way fascism versus communism versus liberalism debate of the play, it was liberalism that won, seemingly against the intentions of the playwright. Desmond MacCarthy, recalling Spender's 1936 *Forward from Liberalism,* in which he proclaimed the inadequacy of social democracy,[53] suggested that this play, composed over a period of three years, revealed "some increasing emotional under-tow in him during these years, which if it has not sapped his intellectual convictions

[51] *Ibid.*, p. 48.
[52] *Ibid.*, p. 84.
[53] See Chapter VI.

has prevented them from drawing nourishment from his most spontaneous sympathies."[54]

Some uncertainty as to his convictions may have added to Spender's difficulties in adjusting his poetic style to the needs of the theater and thus have contributed to his dissatisfaction with *Trial of a Judge.* However he may have tried to achieve it, Spender was gravely deficient in the "necessary murderous hatred" of truly militant communism, as his poems about the Spanish Civil War abundantly testify.[55]

His more Orthodox friends tended to criticize Spender for a supposed romantic sentimentalism that blunted his artistic weapons, yet a rather similar softness was becoming increasingly apparent in the poet to whom the young leftists looked as leader, W. H. Auden, and it helps explain the ambiguity of the plays he wrote with Christopher Isherwood, the plays for which the Group Theatre is best remembered.

Isherwood has told of his and Auden's intentions in writing these plays. They had abandoned their earlier glorification of the individualistic artist under the influence of events at the turn of the decade of the thirties:

> What was important, we now declared, were the needs and wrongs of the common man. The function of our art was to proclaim them. We wanted to expose abuses and denounce tyrants and exploiters. We wanted to point the way to a happier era of peace and plenty, equality and civil justice. We were utopian socialists. If our critics called us propagandists, we agreed with them proudly. "All Art is propaganda," we replied. "Intentionally or unintentionally, it is bound to express some kind of a philosophy, either reactionary or progressive. The merit we claim for our propaganda is that it is both progressive and intentional."[56]

The "utopian" in this passage is post-Marxist hindsight. In the early thirties the young leftists were convinced of the "scientific" nature of their socialism; it was others who dreamed of pie in the sky—they were the realists. In seeking models for a new form of drama they were naturally drawn to the left-oriented expressionism of the pre-

[54] Desmond MacCarthy, "Trial of a Judge," *New Statesman and Nation,* XV, No. 370 N.S. (March 26, 1938), 524.

[55] See Chapter VI.

[56] Christopher Isherwood, *An Approach to Vedanta,* p. 11.

Hitler German theater and particularly to the professedly objective and scientific Epic Theater of Bertolt Brecht.

Once he had discovered Marx, Brecht developed a set of theories about how the theater could be used as an educative and activating weapon in the class war. Since the function of the drama was to lead audiences to an understanding of reality (as defined by Marx) and of the action necessary to change that reality, he rejected any conception of drama that was based on empathy or illusion; he did not want to subject his audience to an intense emotional experience but rather to remind them at all points that they were being offered rational argument and a practical plan of action. His key principle was "alienation" (*Verfremdung*): certain events or ideas of the play are to be "elevated (alienated) out of the realm of the ordinary, natural, or expected," in order to receive special attention; and the audience is to be "alienated" emotionally from the action of the play, not "invited to throw itself into the fable as though into a river" but encouraged to "pass judgment in the midst" of the events of the play. This is to be done "by means of inscription, interpolations of music and noise, or the technique of the actor," all of which ensure that "the individual events are tied together in such a way that the knots are strikingly noticeable."[57]

Both Auden and Isherwood had lived in Germany, Auden for a year (1928–1929) and Isherwood for several; they knew and admired the German left-wing expressionists, and both did translations from their works.[58] Since their hopes for the drama were much like Brecht's, they naturally borrowed much of his Epic technique for their plays, but it is of some significance that their plays become increasingly less Brechtian as the authors' confidence in communism as a solution to the world's problems ebbs.

[57] Quoted from Brecht's notes to *The Roundheads and the Peakheads* (c. 1935) and his *Little Organon for the Theater* (1948) by Hans Egon Holthusen in "Brecht's Dramatic Theory," *Merkur*, XV (1961), 520–531, trans. J. F. Sammons and reprinted in Peter Demetz, ed., *Brecht: A Collection of Critical Essays*, pp. 107–108.

[58] Auden's association with Brecht was to be closer after both had settled in the United States. They collaborated after the war on an adaptation of *The Duchess of Malfi* (1946), and Auden translated the songs from *The Caucasion Chalk Circle* and the whole of *The Seven Deadly Sins* and *Mahagonny* (Spears, *Poetry of W. H. Auden*, pp. 91–92).

The Dance of Death and *The Dog Beneath the Skin*,[59] both produced in 1935–1936, although *The Dance of Death* had been written in 1933, do not fit chronologically into this study, but they have some relevance as showing the direction from which the later plays developed. Both are Epic in style and unequivocally Orthodox in content, yet neither is very satisfactory as propaganda. Symons suggests that the chief cause of the Group Theater's failure ever to become "more than a fashionable entertainment for the middle-class intelligentsia lay in the inability of Uncle Wiz [Auden's Group nickname] and his collaborator . . . ever to be wholly serious about their play writing." He speaks elsewhere, disapprovingly, of the "flippancy" and "schizophrenia" of the intellectual left wing as a group,[60] and what he says is true; but it can be argued that the basis of the unseriousness was quite a serious matter, that at least in Auden and Isherwood the "flippancy" represented a kind of hedging of their bet on communism as the cure for "this country of ours where nobody is well,"[61] and the "schizophrenia" a sign of inner uncertainty.

It is hard to believe that an artist of Auden's dazzling virtuosity could not have done a better job of arousing enthusiasm for "militant socialism" than he did in *The Dance of Death*, if he had really been trying very hard. The message of the play is somber and Marxist enough: as stated by the Announcer, it is to present "a picture of the decline of a class, of how its members dream of a new life, but secretly desire the old, for there is death inside them."[62] This Death-Wish is embodied in the Dancer, who depicts it in various guises as physical-culturist, as führer, as daredevil mystic, and as capitalist. The bourgeois Chorus and the proletarian Audience comment in lively and jazzy, if poetically undistinguished, verse, and all rattles along merrily until the Dancer collapses. His demise is explained by "Mr. Karl Marx," who enters as the Chorus sings, to the tune of Mendelssohn's Wedding March:

[59] Noting the less experimental quality of the later plays, Symons sees in these first two "really a presage of something new—one can see their influence, together with that of Brecht and of the American musical, in today's Theater Workshop" (*The Thirties*, p. 84).

[60] *Ibid.*, pp. 81, 66.

[61] W. H. Auden, "The Orators," in *Poems*, p. 93.

[62] Auden, "The Dance of Death," in *ibid.*, p. 185.

O Mr. Marx, you've gathered
All the material facts
You know the economic
Reasons for our acts.[63]

Announces Mr. Marx, "The instruments of production have been too much for him. He is liquidated. (*Exeunt to a Dead March*)."[64] It is a funny scene, but making Marx just one more comic character effectively destroys whatever propaganda value the play might have had. Despite its pointed satire of a dying society, *The Dance of Death* comes perilously close to innocent merriment.[65]

The Dog Beneath the Skin is a delightful play, full of ingenious satire and containing several excellent serious poems spoken by the Chorus as "interpolations" in the Epic manner, but like *The Dance of Death*, it fails to balance its attack on the old society with any effectively projected fervor for the new. Since this play shares nothing but ideological premises with *The Star Turns Red*, comparing them as propaganda works would be fruitless; but a comparison with Rex Warner's *Wild Goose Chase* is revealing. The novel and the play are both Marxist fairy tales of partly Mortmere origin; both use the Quest beyond the Frontier as a framework for a tour of contemporary life and thought; both are extravagant in fancy and boisterous in satire; and both intend a serious moral. Yet the very fundamental difference between the then certain and fully committed Warner, and the still skeptical and uncertain Auden and Isherwood is strikingly apparent in the contrast between the sober and sustained, however oversimplified, exaltation of the entire last section of *The Wild Goose Chase*, and the lighthearted gaiety of the last scene of *The Dog Beneath the Skin*, which is most inadequately balanced by the grave choral epilogue and exhortation to the audience.

This final scene contains the whole positive message of the play, which has up until this point consisted of frequently hilarious but

[63] *Ibid.*, p. 218.

[64] *Ibid.*

[65] Spears's reaction to this play is much like mine: "Its chief defect perhaps is that it is too close in style to what it satirizes, too popular and simple, while at the same time too varied and unfocused as satire, so that what starts out as a macabre and powerful concept winds up as good clean fun" (*Poetry of Auden*, p. 94).

thoroughly negative comment on all of the authors' favorite targets. The Dog, having revealed himself as Francis the missing heir, renounces his inheritance and tells the villagers he has "crossed over" to communism. Like Upward's tutor, he has learned through his new faith to rise above personal dislike:

I don't hate you any more. I see how you fit into the whole scheme. You are significant, but not in the way I used to imagine. You are units in an immense army: most of you will die without ever knowing what your leaders are fighting for or even that you are fighting at all. Well, I am going to be a unit in the army of the other side. . . . We are all of us completely unimportant, so it would be very silly to start quarrelling, wouldn't it? Goodbye.[66]

Francis then leaves the stage, accompanied by the hero and a few other politically perceptive villagers, and when the rest of the cast, the pillars of reaction, line up for a group photograph, they are transformed in a flash into appropriate animals, the General a bull, the Vicar a goat, and so on. As the curtain falls, the remaining villagers have been likewise transformed, and "*Gestures and cries become more incoherent, bestial, and fantastic, until at last all are drowned in deafening martial chords.*"[67] The Chorus now addresses the audience, "whose hours of self-hatred and contempt were all your majesty and crisis," and advises them to choose

another country
Where grace may grow outward and be given praise
Beauty and virtue be vivid there,
Where time flows on as chalk stream clear
And lovers by themselves forgiven
The whole dream genuine, the charm mature
Walk in the great and general light
In their delight a part of heaven
Its furniture and choir.
To each his need: from each his power.[68]

[66] W. H. Auden and Christopher Isherwood, *The Dog Beneath the Skin, or Where is Francis?*, p. 174.

[67] *Ibid.*, p. 178.

[68] *Ibid.*, pp. 179–180. In his very useful *The Making of the Auden Canon*, J. W. Beach gives an interesting account of how Auden made over this chorus from an earlier poem of rather different intention (pp. 161–164).

There is no confusion about the moral of the play, but in context it seems almost tacked on. Perhaps just because of the insouciant charm of the comic scenes, the serious lyrics interspersed throughout have served not so much to punctuate the satire in Brechtian manner as to work against it. Brecht is never as simply funny as Auden and Isherwood are in this play, and this may have something to do with the fact that his plays consistently achieve their sardonically grim effect while *The Dog Beneath the Skin* merely vacillates between a kind of precocious undergraduate hilarity and the sober poignance of the chilling Chorus of the Two or "Happy the hare at morning" or the opening and closing invocations of "Love." Spender offered a plausible explanation for the dramatic weakness of the play's ending. Noting that the final scene represents the first mention of the "other side," from the point of view of which the satire has been directed throughout, he suggests that

> whereas the authors know a great deal about the side of the bourgeoisie—from which they consider themselves disinherited—they know far less about the workers' side which they believe themselves to have joined. *The Dog Beneath the Skin* is a picture of a society defeated by an enemy whom the writers have not put into the picture because they do not know what he looks like although they thoroughly support him.[69]

In retrospect, there is some question how thoroughly Auden and Isherwood were committed to the "other side." Within three years, Isherwood was to decide that his period of militancy had been an aberration, a temporary departure from an engrained pacifism. As for Auden, the progress of his political thinking is to be more closely examined in the next chapter, but it can be said here that by 1936 he had already passed the peak of his enthusiasm for communism and that the peak had not been so high as either his imitators or his detractors seemed to consider it. At his most "Marxist" period, Auden was at least equally interested in the explanations of the world offered by Freud, Georg Groddeck, and Homer Lane, none of which blends at all well with Marx's. For many young leftists, the greatest appeal of Marxism was its inclusiveness: within its elaborate structure could be found the answer to virtually any problem from war to sex. This attractive simplification of life and thought never seems to have occurred to Auden or Isherwood, and consequently their fellow-

[69] Spender, "The Poetic Dramas," p. 105.

traveling has a provisional quality very unlike the intense if short-lived faith of Rex Warner or Day Lewis, let alone the tenacity of Isherwood's closest friend, Edward Upward.

The insufficiency of Marxism in the Auden-Isherwood outlook is painfully apparent in *The Ascent of F6,* where it is at the root of the confusion that virtually all critics deplore in the play.[70] The Marxist message is clear enough, but there is a parallel Freudian message separate and not entirely consistent with it, and neither of the morals so explicitly and contradictorily presented at the end of the play quite accounts for some of the questions that have been raised in the course of the action. This ambiguity may partly explain why *The Ascent of F6* is the Auden-Isherwood play that continues to receive more attention than the others, but it also explains why it was ineffective as propaganda.

More conventionally constructed than the two previous plays, *The Ascent of F6* has a straightforward and suspenseful plot, and the central set of characters, as distinguished from the personified types who serve as villains and chorus, are developed in an obvious effort to achieve a degree of audience identification, even empathy, Epic theory to the contrary notwithstanding.[71]

The drama recounts a doomed attempt by British mountaineers to climb a supposedly haunted mountain that is strategically located somewhere vaguely in the East. The idea of the ascent has been conceived by Sir James Ransom, a clever young politician who hopes to further his career through achieving a diplomatic success in the game of imperialism which England is playing with the mythical Ostnia, a rival capitalist power that appears in all the Auden-Isherwood dramas. The expedition is underwritten financially by Lord Stagmantle, who sees it simply as an opportunity to sell his newspapers, and it receives the enthusiastic support of the Blimpish General Dellaby-Couch and Lady Isabel Welwyn, who appears to have been

[70] C. E. M. Joad was an exception. Calling it a "great play," he praised its lack of clearcut answers to all the problems it raised, its sense that not all is known, that "the right conduct of life has not yet been discovered, and being alive is, accordingly, like a public performance on the violin in the course of which one must learn the instrument as one goes along" ("Notes Along the Way," *Time and Tide,* XVIII, No. 19 [May 8, 1937], 604).

[71] Brecht did not follow his own precepts with complete rigor either. See Eric Bentley's discussion of the tension between Brechtian theory and practice in *The Playwright as Thinker,* pp. 209–231.

modeled after the famous Lady "Fanny" Houston who used the *Saturday Review* during the thirties as a vehicle for her militaristic chauvinism.

The obvious choice to lead the party is James's twin brother Michael, a brilliant scholar, skillful mountaineer, and natural leader of men who bears some resemblance to T. E. Lawrence. His companions are a kindly middle-aged doctor, an unworldly young botanist, and two strongly contrasting mountain climbers who are friends of Michael's (Martha and Mary types, as the *New Statesman and Nation* reviewer identified them): Shawcross is a brave, loyal, clean, insufferably priggish youth who has never recovered from being Captain of his School, and Gunn, something of a cad and a scamp, is a constant irritant to Shawcross but more reliable in a crisis. The expedition fails, largely because news that the rival Ostnian climbing party is nearing the summit by employing various unsporting devices forces the British party to take unnecessary risks. Only the doctor, who has been left behind at the last camp, survives; the other climbers die, Michael alone on the summit.

It is a simple, exciting, and swiftly moving story that is punctuated by the satirically handled comments of the villains, who are pompous, grandiose, sentimental, and transparently hypocritical; by the rimed doggerel of Mr. and Mrs. A., who represent the "common people" (not the proletariat but the suburban lower middle class) reacting to the press and radio accounts of the expedition; and by various offstage voices. Although Michael uses blank verse in soliloquy or in conversation with his mother, and the "interruptions" are in various verse forms, the scenes that further the plot are generally in natural, colloquial prose, and the climbers are "characterized" in some detail. Thus the play is more "realistic" than *The Dog Beneath the Skin.* It is only the phantasmagoric last scene that moves into pure expressionism, and it is this scene that causes all the confusion.

The action is apparently to be taken as occurring inside Michael's mind just before his death. It reveals his final recognition of the motive behind his willingness to undertake the expedition, despite his awareness of its sordid purpose, and to lead his devoted followers to their destruction. As the Chorus says, "At last the secret is out. . . ."[72]

[72] W. H. Auden and Christopher Isherwood, *The Ascent of F6: A Tragedy in Two Acts,* pp. 120–121.

The ambiguity of the ending lies in the fact that besides the "private reason" there is also a public reason. The *New Statesman and Nation* reviewer offered the perfectly tenable political interpretation of the play as demonstrating "the exploitation by imperialists of all that is best in the youth of the Empire, with the help of their love of adventure and the influence of their parents."[73] This message is explicitly stated by the Chorus in the final lines of the play as the curtain falls on the tableau of Michael's body at the summit:

> Whom history has deserted [i.e. the imperialists]
> These have their power exerted,
> In one convulsive throe;
> With sudden drowning suction
> Drew him to his destruction
> (*Cresc.*) But they to dissolution go.[74]

The message is clear enough, but there are various elements in the drama that a strictly political interpretation leaves out of account. "The influence of their parents" is not merely a means for imperialist exploitation but the climactic revelation, and a political interpretation does little to explain why the hero identifies himself totally with the chief villain. For a more coherent reading of the whole play, it is necessary to abandon Marx for that exponent of subjectivist bourgeois idealism, Sigmund Freud.

The Freudian reading is more elaborate than the Marxist, but it explains more. In the opening soliloquy, Michael muses on the passage in Dante where Ulysses, "a crook speaking to crooks," urges his old comrades to go with him to "follow virtue and knowledge." Michael wonders, "who was Dante, to speak of virtue and knowledge?" No, he contends, what Dante wanted was neither of these, but power, the power to revenge all slights,

> with a stroke of the pen to make a neighbour's vineyard a lake of fire and to create in his private desert the austere music of the angels or the happy extravagance of a fair. Friends whom the world honours shall lament their eternal losses in the profoundest of crevasses, while he in the green mountains converses gently with his unapproachable love.[75]

[73] *New Statesman and Nation*, XIII, No. 315 N.S. (March 6, 1937), 368.

[74] Auden and Isherwood, *Ascent of F6*, p. 123.

[75] *Ibid.*, pp. 13, 14.

Michael is glumly dubious of the existence in this world of virtue and knowledge, and he finds the solitude of mountain tops a relief from "the valley and all its varieties of desperation."[76]

Although he has dreamed since boyhood of climbing F6, he first refuses his brother's proposition simply because it is James's, and James embodies for him everything he hates—his propositions are "concerned with prestige, tactics, money and the privately pre-arranged meanings of familiar words. I will have nothing to do with them." At James's instigation, however, their mother shames Michael into acceptance. She tells him that her apparent preference for James was simply part of an heroic effort to teach Michael to have the "power to stand alone," not to depend, as James does and their father did, "upon the constant praises of the little." But now his "brother's hatred" is keeping him from choosing the "greatest action of his life."[77] Michael succumbs to his mother's arguments and sets forth with her promise to be with him to the end.

In a monastery halfway up the mountain, Michael talks with the wise old Abbot, or Lama, and reveals that he too is strongly tempted to seek the "praises of the little." The Abbot tells him that this is the temptation of the Demon, for the Demon reputed to live atop the mountain is indeed real: he simply takes different forms for simple peasants and for the "complicated and sensitive." Michael's temptation, he suggests, is "to conquer the Demon and then to save mankind." But, he warns,

> As long as the world endures, there must be order, there must be government: but woe to the governors, for, by the very operation of their duty, however excellent, they themselves are destroyed. For you can only rule men by appealing to their fear and their lust; government requires the exercise of the human will: and the human will is from the Demon.[78]

Michael does not accept the Abbot's counsel to seek "complete abnegation of the will," but he now sees himself as "corrupt," like his brother, in his urge to power. When his companions, caught up in

[76] *Ibid.*, p. 14. Here, as they consistently do in Auden's poetry, mountains symbolize effort and decision and valleys passivity. Spears discusses these and other recurring symbols on p. 142 of his *Poetry of W. H. Auden.*

[77] Auden and Isherwood, *Ascent of F6,* pp. 42, 48.

[78] *Ibid.*, p. 74.

nationalistic enthusiasm, clamor to change their scientific and sporting expedition into a race to beat the Ostnians to the summit, he succumbs again, and for a man who worries about his impulse to power, he succumbs very readily. "I obey you. The summit will be reached, the Ostnians defeated, the Empire saved. And I have failed."[79]

In the final scene of Michael's dying delirium, he sees himself as the "deliverer" come to destroy the "Dragon," who is James. Under the direction of a veiled Figure, presumably the Demon,[80] he and James begin a chess game, using as pieces the three dead climbers and the three other villains. James mocks Michael's words of their earlier confrontation and, when he for the first time sees the Figure, claims victory. But the Figure shakes its head, and James falls, choking, "It was not Virtue—it was not Knowledge—it was Power!" Stagmantle, the General, and Lady Isabel promptly make speeches and sing a dirge mourning the death not of James but of Michael, although it is James's body that is carried off. Michael denies responsibility for his brother's death and accuses the Figure; but when the Abbot says that he was wrong to call Michael's temptation the Demon and that "if there were no Demon, there would be no temptation," Michael suddenly withdraws his accusation. It is too late: Michael rushes to stand before the Figure "*as if to protect it,*" but the Chorus points to the Figure and shouts "Guilty." The lights go out, leaving in view only Michael and "*the Figure, whose draperies fall away, revealing Mrs. Ransom as a young mother.*" He falls with his head in her lap, and she sings a sentimental lullaby. He is, as he visualized Dante's dream, "on the green mountains conversing gently with his unapproachable love."

The Freudian message here is as clear as the Marxist and as explicitly stated by the Chorus, in the stanza immediately preceding the one quoted earlier as the Marxist moral:

> Now he with secret terror
> And every minor error
> Has also made Man's weakness known.[81]

The Demon is not, as would have been expected in view of Auden's

[79] *Ibid.*, p. 79.

[80] This Figure cannot but remind Auden's readers of the "giantess" who calls the returning hero "Deceiver" in the Prologue to "The Orators" (*Poems*, p. 89).

[81] Auden and Isherwood, *Ascent of F6*, p. 123.

earlier poems, the spirit of fascism, but the Oedipus complex. Michael has been driven to his futile heroism by a desire to please his mother, to displace in her affections the brother who has been described as just like his father. Michael's temptation to be a Great Man, a secular savior, springs from his knowledge that this is what she wants of him. She is the real villain of the play. Because of her he has led his friends to their death and has brought about his own; but what he has done is what he most deeply wanted, and at the end he has found annihilation and a return to innocence as a good little boy at his mother's knee.

The trouble with these two parallel messages is that, as Spears "fliply" put it, "the Freud and Marx . . . don't jell."[82] If, as the Freudian interpretation suggests, any hero turns out to be a man driven by excessive love for his mother to perform actions that destroy himself and those who follow him, then the sordid machinations of the rulers of bourgeois society are rather beside the point; yet the Marxist interpretation, upon which the play ends, tells us that they *are* the point. The only way to have it both ways is to argue that Oedipus complexes afflict only the bourgeois. Then we could look upon Michael Ransom as the kind of doomed bourgeois hero that Caudwell saw in T. E. Lawrence and could hope that a future classless society would be as free of Oedipal conflict as of other bourgeois ills.[83] It is hardly possible that Auden and Isherwood had anything of this sort in mind.

More likely they simply had not resolved in their own minds the questions raised in the play. To judge by their later development, neither of them was concerned as much with the psychological or political problems of heroism as with the religious.[84] Michael is an exceptional man, gifted far beyond the common people for whom he feels a contempt that is not always kindly. The question of how

[82] Spears, *Poetry of Auden*, p. 102.

[83] Brecht's Galileo says a healthy society would not need heroes, but this idea is nowhere clearly implied in *Ascent of F6*.

[84] Isherwood wrote humorously of Auden's tendency to have characters "flop . . . on their knees" and to "turn every play into a cross between grand opera and high mass" ("Some Notes on Auden's Early Poetry," *New Verse*, November 1937, p. 9). Isherwood's own adoption of Vedanta within a few years indicates that he was also, despite his bitter anti-Christianity, highly susceptible to religious impulses.

he is to use his gifts may well have been what most interested the playwrights, and one is inclined to agree with the several critics who considered that the ending of the play evaded its central issue. Either the Marxist or the Freudian reading seems too pat, and their being combined but not synthesized solves nothing.

The difficulty under which both writers were laboring in the mid-thirties was the question of how to use their own gifts. They were at the same time profoundly suspicious of the springs of action—"will Man's negative inversion"[85]—and painfully convinced of the necessity for it. Addressing Isherwood in a 1935 poem, "August for the People," Auden calls upon him to use his "strict and adult pen" to "make action urgent and its nature clear,"[86] but for neither writer was the nature of appropriate action clear enough for him to make its urgency unequivocal. The flippancy of *The Dance of Death* and *The Dog Beneath the Skin* and the evasiveness of *The Ascent of F6* reflect this uncertainty, which was to grow more, not less, intense in the next two years.

The Spanish Civil War did not simplify Auden's thinking. He and Isherwood were strongly pro-Loyalist and remained so, but Auden's visit to Spain early in 1937 was profoundly unsettling. He was surprised to find that the closing of the churches in Barcelona distressed him, not simply as illiberal and intolerant but as revealing that "the existence of churches and what went on in them had all the time been very important to me."[87] This experience helped initiate his return to Christianity, which was not to be completed until some four years later but which was already beginning to color his outlook on political as on other matters.

Isherwood too was becoming increasingly unsure of his attitudes, and he has written of his deep confusion during 1938, the year in which his last play with Auden, *On the Frontier,* was produced. It is paradoxical that this play is entirely free of the ambiguities of its predecessors; its message is clear and simple, "altogether too simple in every respect" for Spears.[88] In the light of what both authors have

[85] W. H. Auden, "Petition," in *Poems*, p. 55.

[86] W. H. Auden, *Look, Stranger*, pp. 64, 66.

[87] W. H. Auden, untitled essay (now out of print) in James A. Pike, ed., *Modern Canterbury Pilgrims,* quoted by Spears, *Poetry of Auden*, p. 176.

[88] Spears, *Poetry of Auden*, p. 102.

since written of their thinking during this period, *On the Frontier* can be taken as a final gesture for the Popular Front before the authors resigned in despair.

On the Frontier is the most topical of the Auden-Isherwood plays and perhaps for that reason the most dated. It is straightforward and essentially negative; there is no call to join the movement of masses toward a brave new world, only a summoning of resistance to fascism. Although the analysis in the play of the nature and origins of fascism is Marxist, there is none of the buoyant confidence in the inevitability of revolution which marks so many leftist works, including some of Auden's poems of earlier years.

This last play is the culmination of a progress away from deliberate Brechtian looseness of construction toward tight formal structure. It is positively symmetrical. The chief set is the "Ostnia-Westland room," which is divided in the middle to "*convey the idea of the Frontier*."[89] This is not the Mortmere-derived Frontier of *Journey to the Border, The Wild Goose Chase*, or *The Dog Beneath the Skin*, the metaphoric frontier between past and future, bourgeois and worker; it is a frontier between nations. The characters representing bourgeois families of Ostnia (a reactionary monarchy of central Europe which is also reminiscent of France) and Westland (obviously Germany) are shown simultaneously and their speeches are often antiphonal, but they are unaware of each other except for the star-crossed lovers, Eric of Westland and Anna of Ostnia, who speak to each other in a kind of dream-communication although separated by the Frontier. The other set is the study of Valerian, the almost all-powerful capitalist who is the real force behind Westland's Leader. A Prologue and four Interludes are performed before the curtain, in which choruses of workers, political prisoners, dancers, soldiers, and English newspaper readers offer comment on the action, which shows the descent of the two nations into war and revolution, with the faintest possible hope implied for an eventual triumph of peace and justice.

Valerian, the chief figure of the play although hardly the hero, is a kind of Shavian superman, witty, cultivated, clear-eyed, and ruthless, but not given to purposeless cruelty. He believes, like Bombardone, in the Law of Personal Gravitation:

[89] W. H. Auden and Christopher Isherwood, *On the Frontier: A Melodrama in Three Acts*, p. 43.

The truth is, Nature is not interested in underlings—in the lazy, the inefficient, the self-indulgent, the People. Nor, for that matter, in the Aristocracy, which is now only another name for the Idle Rich. . . . The world has never been governed by the People or by the merely Rich, and it never will be. It is governed by men like myself—though, in practice, we are usually rich and often from the People.[90]

His ruling motive is to express his creativity in a way suitable to the present era: "Nothing is worthwhile except complete mastery." In earlier days, the hermit could master himself, and, later, the artist could master his art; but the industrial revolution has made these kinds of mastery obsolete: "To be an artist or a saint has ceased to be modern. . . . Yes, for the man of power, there can now be but one aim—absolute control of mankind."[91]

His tools for mastery are financial power and the demagogic talents of the Leader, whom Valerian has manipulated into removing his economic competitors without daring to touch the Valerian Trust. Valerian has no fears of revolution, confident that the workers, all "patient sheep, or silly crowing cockerels, or cowardly rabbits" pose no threat in a nation dominated by adulation for the Leader who appears to them, and to himself, a kind of Suffering Servant who bears their burdens, defends their rights, and will redeem their lost national honor. Neither does Valerian fear war, confident that since the industrialists prefer to profit by a continuing arms race, the politicians fear losing their supremacy to the military, and the military themselves are already "perfectly happy playing at mechanization," there will be no war despite the militaristic speeches he encourages the Leader to make on behalf of "national unity."[92]

Valerian's sanguine and perfectly rational expectations are proved wrong. Ostnia and Westland blunder into war, and a few months' experience with the reality of war quickly weakens public enthusiasm. The soldiers at the front begin to fraternize, then to mutiny against their officers, and revolutions break out in both countries. Valerian is still not alarmed. Having seen the example of Spain, he muses about the hopeful revolutionaries:

[90] *Ibid.*, pp. 24–25.
[91] *Ibid.*, p. 26.
[92] *Ibid.*, pp. 32, 78.

You poor fish, so cock-a-whoop in your little hour of comradeship and hope! I'm really sorry for you. You don't know what you're letting yourselves in for, trying to beat us on our own ground! You will take to machine-guns without having enough. You will imagine that, in a People's Army, it is against your principles to obey orders—and then wonder why it is that, in spite of your superior numbers, you are always beaten. You will count on foreign support and be disappointed, because the international working-class does not read your mosquito journals. . . . We shall expose your lies and exaggerate your atrocities, and you will be unable to expose or exaggerate ours. The churches will be against you. The world of money and political influence will say of us: "After all, they are the decent people, *our* sort. The others are rabble." A few of the better educated may go so far as to exclaim: "A plague on both your houses!" Your only open supporters abroad will be a handful of intellectuals, who, for the last twenty years, have signed letters of protest against everything from bi-metallism in Ecuador to the treatment of yaks in Thibet.[93]

Valerian does not live to see whether his prophecies will be proved true. He is shot by an embittered Shock Trooper who has just finished assassinating the Leader. Again Valerian has underestimated the power of unreason.

The play ends with the issue of revolution still unresolved. A chorus of five reads alternately from readily identifiable British newspapers —a conservative government organ, a reactionary yellow journal, a liberal, and a Communist paper, and "one of those sensational and alarming news-letters which give the 'low-down' on the international situation."[94] This last interlude permits a final flash of humor in the excellent parodies of the news coverage given the Spanish Civil War, before the somber closing scene in which Eric and Anna, both mortally wounded, speak together of the "good place" where their love could be possible.

Throughout the play Auden and Isherwood have been making the Marxist point that fascism and war are simply the logical extensions

[93] *Ibid.*, p. 108.

[94] Claud Cockburn's *This Week,* which followed the Party line, was the first of these mimeographed sheets, and gained such a wide audience that it was widely imitated by others interested in similar freedom from official censorship and similar financial success. Graves and Hodge suggest that some of the news-letter writers were also concerned to present "inside information" from other than Communist sources (*Long Weekend*, pp. 413–414).

of capitalism. In the final scene, however, there is a notable absence of red flag waving. The message is a clear but qualified call for resistance to fascism and persistence in the struggle for the "good place." Eric, who had been imprisoned as a pacifist, had apparently broken jail to man a barricade where he was shot. He offers the argument against pacifism:

> Believing it was wrong to kill,
> I went to prison, seeing myself
> As the sane and innocent student
> Aloof among practical and violent madmen,
> But I was wrong. We cannot choose our world,
> Our time, our class. None are innocent, none.
> Causes of violence lie so deep in all our lives
> It touches every act.
> Certain it is for all we do
> We shall pay dearly. Blood
> Will mine for vengeance in our children's
> happiness,
> Distort our truth like an arthritis.
> Yet we must kill and suffer and know why.
> All errors are not equal. The hatred of our
> enemies
> Is the destructive self-love of the dying,
> Our hatred is the price of the world's freedom.
> This much I learned in prison. This struggle
> Was my struggle. Even if I would
> I could not stand apart.[95]

The final duet is a tribute to the "thousands" who "have worked and work to master necessity."

> ANNA. Pardon them their mistakes,
> The impatient and wavering will.
> They suffer for our sakes,
> Honour, honour them all.
> ERIC. Dry their imperfect dust,
> The wind blows it back and forth.
> They die to make man just
> And worthy of the earth.[96]

This is a far cry from "Red Star, arise, the wide world over!"

[95] Auden and Isherwood, *On the Frontier,* pp. 120–121.
[96] *Ibid.*, pp. 122–123.

The somberness of *On the Frontier* is reflected in the poems Auden wrote for his last collaboration with Isherwood, *Journey to a War*, a record of their tour of China during the first half of 1938. These will be considered in the next chapter. Isherwood's "Travel-Diary," the prose component of the book, is excellent reporting but somewhat remarkable in its freedom from political speculation or interpretation. This may be because, in the state of mental confusion he has since described himself as experiencing during 1938, Isherwood simply did not know what to write. The Chinese journey had affected him deeply, but it was not until he and Auden were crossing the Atlantic to settle in the United States in January of 1939 that his confusion was finally resolved. While still in England, he continued to address Popular Front meetings and repeat the slogans that had lost their meaning for him, and there is considerable irony in that at the very time he was coming to "realize" he was a pacifist, *On the Frontier* was on the boards proclaiming the false individualism of pacifism and the necessity of fighting for "collective security."

Isherwood stresses that he did not "become" a pacifist but simply realized that he had always been one and that "my whole political position, left-wing anti-fascist, had been based upon the acceptance of armed force. All the slogans I had been repeating and living by were essentially militaristic. Very well: throw them out. But what remained?"[97] For the moment, the individualistic skepticism of E. M. Forster,[98] with its emphasis on personal integrity and its distrust of ideology, remained:

> the visit to China brought me back from a world of political principles to a world of human values which I had temporarily lost. . . . War starts with principles but it ends with people. . . . I found I didn't dare to say that these [Chinese] people ought to die in defense of any principles whatsoever, no matter how noble or right. In fact, balanced against this suffering and death, all such questions of right and wrong seemed academic and irrelevant. My own acceptance of armed force as a permissible means of political action had been due simply to a lack of feeling and imagination. . . . I couldn't speak for others. . . . But for the future I myself must be an avowed pacifist.[99]

[97] Isherwood, *An Approach to Vedanta*, p. 10.

[98] See Chapter III. Auden's opening sonnet for *Journey to a War* is a dedication to Forster.

[99] Isherwood, *An Approach to Vedanta*, pp. 8–9.

Whatever else the departure of Auden and Isherwood meant, and it was much discussed in England,[100] it indicated that they had lost faith in the efficacy of any political action they might take. Neither was to find Forsterian skepticism fully satisfying: before long Auden, with the assistance of Kierkegaard and Reinhold Niebuhr, had returned to Christianity; and Isherwood, assisted by Gerald Heard and Aldous Huxley, whom he joined in Hollywood, soon moved beyond simple pacifism to acceptance of Vedanta. Their geographical and spiritual exodus may have been a good move for them, but the left-wing literary movement in England was never to be the same again.

By 1939, leftist experimentation in the British theater had largely run its course, and not merely because Auden and Isherwood had gone to America. With war imminent, criticism of English institutions became less fashionable, and the tone, even among intellectuals, began to change toward celebration. As the Left grew steadily more disillusioned about Russia and communism, and as the threat of actual physical attack upon England became clearer, even those who had most bitterly condemned the evils of English society began to join home-guard units to aid in the defense of their sceptr'd isle.

[100] In his *I Am My Brother: Vol. II of an autobiography,* John Lehmann describes the reaction, largely angry, of British intellectuals to the "flight" of the two writers.

Chapter VI

ON THE LEFT: POETRY

Of the departure of Auden and Isherwood for America in 1939, Julian Symons writes, "that this marvelous monster of poetry and his coadjutor, the most sensitive prose writer of his generation, would be prepared for a lengthy exile" was profoundly discouraging to the English intelligentsia. "It is possible," he suggests, "that, had they stayed, the Thirties movement might have had a less ignominious end," because "in a very real sense, Auden's devices of style and habits of feeling *are* the Thirties, or a large part of the Thirties."[1]

Auden and his friends and followers were less fully dominant in the intellectual life of Britain during the thirties than either their admirers or detractors tended to assume. Rayner Heppenstall, who was of the Auden generation and contributed to the magazines associated with the group, wrote later that the popular stereotype of intellectuals of the thirties as following the lead of Auden was false: "Auden, Spender and Day Lewis did not, from any point at which I found myself, in the least appear to dominate the age."[2] Such able poets as Robert Graves and Laura Riding scorned the "movement," and the young William Empson, who was among the few with wit enough to attack Auden with his own weapons, derided the "revolu-

[1] Julian Symons, *The Thirties: A Dream Revolved*, pp. 163–164.
[2] "Decade Talk," *New Statesman and Nation*, LI (April 14, 1958), 377.

tionary romp,/ The hearty uproar" of the left-wing poets.[3] His "Just a Smack at Auden" is a wickedly apt parody of Auden at his heartiest:

> What was said by Marx, boys, what did he perpend?
> No good being sparks, boys, waiting for the end.
> Treason of the clerks, boys, curtains that descend,
> Lights becoming darks, boys, waiting for the end.
>
> Waiting for the end, boys, waiting for the end.
> Not a chance of blend, boys, things have got to
> tend.
> Think of those who vend, boys, think of how we
> wend,
> Waiting for the end, boys, waiting for the end.[4]

Nevertheless, what is generally called the "Thirties movement" was made up very largely of those who, consciously or by coincidence, wrote poetry revealing the "devices of style and habits of feeling" of Auden and his friends.[5] The leading members of this group have taken some pains to deny that they were a movement; "We did not know we were a Movement," writes Day Lewis, "until the critics told us we were."[6] Certainly there was no movement in the sense of a group of writers working out together a program for some clearly defined new approach to writing and thinking: no manifestoes were

[3] "Autumn on Nan-Yueh," (c. 1939), in *The Collected Poems of William Empson*, p. 79.

[4] *Collected Poems of William Empson*, p. 65. W. H. Auden and Louis MacNeice mildly twitted Empson in their "Last Will and Testament," bequeathing him "a terrible double entendre in metre or in prose" (*Letters from Iceland*, p. 253).

[5] The first important British poem with a Communist message was the "First Hymn to Lenin" by C. M. Grieve ("Hugh MacDiarmid"), published in 1931, well before *New Country*. Grieve continued to write hymns to Lenin and other revolutionary verse, chiefly in the "Synthetic Scots" dialect he had invented which often produced excellent poetic effects. However, his attitude toward the English Orthodox Left was one of scorn and resentment: he contended that they deliberately ignored and excluded him, not because he generally wrote in dialect, but simply because he was a Scot and a genuine working-class Communist (*Lucky Poet: A Self-Study in Literature and Political Ideas, Being the Autobiography of Hugh MacDiarmid*, p. 169). Since the focus of this chapter is upon the Orthodox Left, the interesting work of this erudite and dogmatic Scot has been omitted from discussion.

[6] Cecil Day Lewis, *The Buried Day*, p. 217.

issued. The critics' assumption was based partly on the accident that these poets' early works were published about the same time in the same magazines, partly on their references to each other within their poems, more on the recurrence of certain themes and techniques, and chiefly on the political attitudes that the poets appeared to share and that represented a sharp break with both Georgian pastoral and the school of Eliot.

The 1932 *New Signatures* and the 1933 *New Country* volumes, both edited by Michael Roberts, were generally supposed to have introduced the movement to the general, or at least to the poetry-reading, public. Auden, Spender, and Day Lewis had published volumes before this, but to all appearances only other poets had read them. Both Spears and Symons have noted that *New Signatures* was in no way dominated by these poets, including as it did considerable verse by poets quite outside the movement, such as Empson and Julian Bell,[7] both far from sympathetic to the communism that strongly attracted the poets of the movement in the early thirties. *New Country*, however, opens with a highly revolutionary introduction by Roberts, and the contributors wave the red flag vigorously. Auden's "A Communist to Others" appears in this volume, and the editor and the other contributors speak of him as their revolutionary leader. He was to prove something of a disappointment over the next years, as his interest in psychological and religious questions became evidently stronger than his Marxism.[8]

As we have seen, the Left, which seemed so monolithic to its opponents, was full of dissent throughout the thirties, united in antifascism but divided on matters like the use of force, the proper

[7] The liberal Julian Bell, son of Clive Bell and nephew of Virginia Woolf, is often mentioned among those who died for the Communist cause in Spain. He was indeed killed there, after only a month of service as an ambulance driver, but he had gone to Spain not as a revolutionary militant but out of general sympathy for the Republic. He had sought also, as he wrote home, "the usefulness of war experience in the future and the prestige one would gain in literature and—even more—in Left politics" (quoted in Hugh Thomas, *The Spanish Civil War*, p. 463 n). *Journey to the Frontier*, by Peter Stansky and William Abrahams, is an interesting double biography of Bell and John Cornford.

[8] Auden's disciples set austere standards for their leader. Symons describes the deep shock among them when he accepted the King's Gold Medal for Poetry in 1936 (*The Thirties*, p. 62).

attitude toward Russia, or the ideal relation of art to politics. This dissension is reflected in some of the magazines that printed poetry. Geoffrey Grigson's *New Verse* (1933–1939) welcomed unOrthodox poets as well as Orthodox, applying no standards beyond the aesthetic, while the *Left Review* (1934–1939), of which the editors, all Communists, included Montagu Slater, T. H. Wintringham of later International Brigade fame, and Edgell Rickword, viewed poetry as a weapon in the class war and selected its contributions accordingly. Symons describes the movement as "one many-headed monster, the split in [its] personality . . . nakedly shown in the paths taken in these two magazines, with Auden moving over to the humanist unpolitical *New Verse* side, Day Lewis plumping emphatically for the Communist *Left Review*, Spender wavering lyrically between, and all the little Audens, Day Lewises, and Spenders taking up their appropriate poetical-political positions."[9] Symons' own *Twentieth Century Verse* tended toward the "humanist unpolitical," and John Lehmann's *New Writing*, first published in 1936, was less Orthodox than the *Left Review*, although its original manifesto sternly closes its pages to writers of Fascist or reactionary sentiments.

Probably the best explanation for the influence of the "many-headed monster" was that it answered a felt need. The young would-be writers fresh out of University in the early thirties found in the style and subject matter of these slightly older poets a way to express the revolutionary and anti-Fascist feeling they had developed at least as much from the objective historical situation and the journalism of Communist and anti-Fascist publicists as from the often obscure and difficult verse of Auden, Spender, and Day Lewis. For many younger writers, the Auden group did not lead them to the Left: their leftism led them to the Auden group. The poems of Auden's imitators during the later thirties are often more revolutionary than his own, and some of their other activities must have amused if not embarrassed him.

Charles Madge is a good example of a young admirer of Auden who carried to somewhat absurd extremes the principles that he understood Auden to have enunciated. In a *New Country* poem, Madge tells of the electrifying effect upon him of Auden's early poetry:

[9] *Ibid.*, p. 74.

But there waited for me in the summer morning
Auden, fiercely. I read, shuddered and knew
And all the world's stationary things
In silence moved to take up new positions.[10]

The new positions had been more explicitly described by Marx and Lenin than by the riddling poet, and Madge appears to have been particularly taken by the "science" of communism. Not only did he become one of the most rigidly dogmatic and simplistic of Communist poets, and one of the most ferocious denouncers of heresy; he also branched out, sharing some responsibility for the curious Mass Observation movement and bearing full guilt for the "Oxford Collective Poem."[11]

Auden is not to be held responsible for the direction his disciples took, nor should he be credited with having singlehandedly set in motion a literary revolution. His special kind of originality has always lain in his use of the innovations of others, and Robert Graves had some basis for his caustic description of him as "a synthetic writer . . . [who] perhaps never wrote an original line," and who succeeded because "modern literature was so extensive that his communistic use of contemporary work was not at first suspected."[12] Graves, who felt that Auden had poached on his own preserves, is

[10] Charles Madge, "Letter to the Intelligentsia," in *New Country: Prose and Poetry by the Authors of* New Signatures, ed. Michael Roberts, pp. 231–232.

[11] Mass Observation, founded early in 1937, was based on the "scientific" belief that a sufficient accumulation of raw fact must necessarily produce the truth that is power. The hope was that by means of the detailed accounts of the observations of hundreds of fact-gatherers, using interviews, questionnaires, applause meters, and similar devices, social engineers could "discover the nature of the mass-life of the mass-man from the cradle to the grave" (Neal Wood, *Communism and British Intellectuals*, p. 64).

The "Oxford Collective Poem" (1937) was also based on the assumption that the mass is more "real" than the individual and that anything a single man can do, a committee working on democratic principles can do better. Symons describes the elaborate system by which the observations of twelve Oxford undergraduates working as a team were transmuted into a poem totally free of egocentric individualism.

[12] Robert Graves and Alan Hodge, *The Long Weekend: A Social History of Great Britain, 1918–1939*, p. 288. Symons tells of meeting a "Gravesian" who offered to exegise Auden's "Spain 1937" line by line to show "its multifold debt to Graves and other writers" (*The Thirties*, pp. 143–144).

not a completely unbiased critic; besides, Eliot had established the respectability of "synthetic" composition well before Auden practiced it. In any case, the sponge-like quality of Auden's mind predisposed him to accumulate influences, and the success of his results amply justified the means he employed. To paraphrase Eliot, Auden was too good a poet to borrow: he stole.

The sources for many of the modes that came to be considered Audenesque are the very mixed group of earlier poets whom Auden and his friends called "ancestors," those of whom Spender thought continually: Eliot, Hopkins, Skelton, Dickinson, Hardy, Owen—in fact anyone the young poets happened to admire. However, some of the most characteristic themes and images were of more private origin, springing from the Mortmere fantasies. Before considering some of the poetry that was directly concerned with the Spanish Civil War and concomitant events of the later thirties, it seems advisable to look briefly at the extent to which the Auden group could properly be called a movement and to trace its main figures up to the time the war broke out in 1936.

The Auden group was held together primarily by ties of personal friendship, and these in turn were largely based on similarity of age and background. The oldest members (Day Lewis, Isherwood, Upward, Warner) were only five years older than the youngest (Spender). All, including the Irish MacNeice, attended English public schools and the great Universities: Isherwood and Upward went to Cambridge, all the others to Oxford. All were born to the high-bourgeois professional class: Auden was the son of a distinguished physician, a retired medical officer; Isherwood's father, who was killed in World War I, was a professional army officer; Spender's was a wealthy and respected Liberal journalist; the rest of the group were sons of Anglican churchmen. Day Lewis, Auden, Warner, and Spender met at Oxford; Isherwood and Auden had been friends since preparatory school. The group never met *as* a group—Day Lewis points out that the first time he, Auden, and Spender were together in the same room was in 1947—but they saw each other frequently and they appear to have corresponded voluminously. Their talk and letters were, apparently, predominantly literary shoptalk, and of course they read each other's work closely and critically. In view of all this, it is hardly surprising that similar themes and techniques should recur in their work.

From the accounts of Day Lewis and Spender, Auden would appear to have been the dominant figure. Day Lewis, who met him in 1927, ascribes his magnetism less to his unquestionable intellectual power than to his immense vitality.

> a vitality so abundant that, overflowing into certain poses and follies and wildly unrealistic notions, it gave these an air of authority, an illusion of rightness, which enticed some of Auden's contemporaries into taking them too seriously. His exuberance redeemed too, for me, the dogmatism, the intellectual bossiness, and the tendency to try and run his friends' lives for them, all of which were by-products of this excess of life.[13]

Day Lewis, who describes himself as having been an extremely impressionable undergraduate, wisely decided to take Auden in "smallish doses," but this precaution and his three years' seniority still did not prevent his verse's becoming "for a time pastiche-Auden."[14]

"Intellectually bossy" though he may have been, Auden seems to have been respectful to the point of deference toward the opinions and suggestions of Isherwood, who in turn relied heavily on Edward Upward. John Lehmann, who met Spender in 1930 and was to prove extremely useful to the group as a publisher at Hogarth Press and later of *New Writing*, describes the hierarchy as Spender pictured it.

> It was part of the romantic mythology in which Stephen delighted to cloak his contemporaries, to present himself as a learner at the feet of Auden, the great prophet, but to suggest that behind both of them stood an even greater Socratic prophet, cool in the centre of the stormy drama of remote Berlin: Christopher Isherwood. . . . Later I heard with the tremor of excitement that an entomologist feels at the news of an unknown butterfly sighted in the depths of a forest, that behind Auden and Spender and Isherwood stood the even more legendary figure of an unknown writer, Edward Upward.[15]

There is no question that many of the obscurities of Auden's early poetry, at least as late as "The Orators," can be clarified by Isherwood's description in *Lions and Shadows* of the Mortmere fantasies Isherwood developed with Upward and later shared with his other friends. The school settings; the confusion of sport and war; the sense that any given poem has been excerpted from some larger,

[13] Day Lewis, *Buried Day*, p. 176.

[14] *Ibid.*, p. 178.

[15] John Lehmann, *The Whispering Gallery: Autobiography I*, pp. 179, 195.

continuing work; the atmosphere of conspiracy[16] and the heroes who seem to be spies or saboteurs; the metaphor of the frontier between past and future, dreams and action, bourgeois and proletarian—all of these, most notable in early Auden but also present here and there in Day Lewis and Warner, are traceable to Mortmere. Symons deprecates this element in these writers, seeing it as proof of their fundamental lack of seriousness. Certainly *The Dance of Death* and *The Dog Beneath the Skin* lose force, as they gain charm, through their playfulness; but when Symons specifically includes the fantasies of Rex Warner and the later Auden-Isherwood plays as proof that these writers "(with the honourable exception of Spender) still made no attempt to treat Fascism as anything but a subject for farce,"[17] he is off the mark. Lack of serious conviction is the last charge that could be made against the young Warner, nor is fascism funny in *On the Frontier*, although the Leader is. Mortmere, as Isherwood describes it, was more than a private joke; partly an escape from reality, it was also a real effort, however firmly tongue was kept in cheek, to provide a symbolic structure that would enable these young men to think constructively about the reality they knew.[18] It was not entirely incomparable to Yeats's similar efforts. It seems, in fact, to have served chiefly as a kind of bridge in their thinking to the next symbolic structure they were to adopt, with varying degrees of conviction: Marxism.

The English public school, which underlies the Mortmere fantasies, served for these writers as a convenient metaphor for the larger political-social situation as they saw it at about the turn of the decade. Auden generally made affectionate references to his public school, but he wrote in 1934 that "the best reason I have for opposing Fascism is that at school I lived in a Fascist state."[19] The public school, with its authoritarianism, its demand for conformity, its sexual prudery and prurience, its narrow "patriotism," and its encouragement of the bully and the informer, perfectly embodied the

[16] The title of Isherwood's first novel, *All the Conspirators,* is significant.

[17] Symons, *The Thirties*, p. 154. He writes of *The Wild Goose Chase*, "Warner's master here was less Kafka than Bunyan, but it is a Bunyan who turns the horror of his time to comedy" (p. 153).

[18] See Chapter IV.

[19] "Honour (Gresham's School, Holt)" in Graham Greene, ed., *The Old School* (London, 1934), quoted by Symons, *The Thirties*, p. 28.

"Enemy" for the young rebels.[20] As Spears observes, several of these kickers against the pricks found themselves very much in the position of spies and saboteurs when they became schoolmasters. Auden, Day Lewis, Warner, and Upward were all, in the early thirties, in the ambiguous situation of working for the "Enemy" they hoped to overthrow. The step from Mortmere to Marxism was easy. The "Enemy" could now be clearly identified as the capitalist ruling class, and the rebels, who had been the nonconforming schoolboy, then the artist among philistines, could now aspire to join the happy few described in the Communist Manifesto, those members of the ruling class who "break away to make common cause with the revolutionary class, the class which holds the future in its hands."

In Auden's early work, before 1933, the political direction he was taking was not yet clear. Symons notes that he and many of his friends found the "Airman's Journal" (in "The Orators," 1932) disturbingly fascistic.[21] Although many of the poems of the 1930 edition, as well as *Paid on Both Sides* and "The Orators," can be read in a conventionally Marxist way, they do not demand such an interpretation, nor do they always support it. The "farer" who will "throw away the key and walk away," the seeker for "new styles of architecture, a change of heart," is clear enough about what he is leaving and about the necessity for "death of the old gang," but he is considerably less explicit about where "your country and the home of love" is to be found.

By *The Dance of Death* (1933) and *Poems* (1934), it is obvious that the "new styles" are to be Communist and that the "new country" is the classless society envisioned by Marx. "Love," a concept that appears in many and changing forms through Auden's poetry and eventually proves to be God, is shown in the 1934 "Our Hunting Fathers" to be making it "his mature ambition/ To think no thought but ours,/ To hunger, work illegally,/ And be anonymous." The last two lines are a reference to Lenin. Love is, at this point, the "Saviour" symbolized by Warner's Wild Goose, a force that works for health and sanity in the individual and for peace and justice in the State but that is human and secular and at least partly identi-

[20] Monroe K. Spears gives an excellent reading of "The Orators" in this light, *The Poetry of W. H. Auden: The Disenchanted Island,* pp. 45–58.

[21] *Ibid.*, pp. 17–18.

fiable with History as hypostatized in Marxism. The "Love" invoked in the chorus of *The Dog Beneath the Skin* seems to be the same.

The period from 1933 to 1935 appears to have seen the highest point of Auden's enthusiasm for Marxism, yet even at that time he was not a "true-red" Marxist in the way that many of his contemporaries were; that is, he did not find in Marx sufficient and satisfactory answers to all the questions that concerned him. He wrote twenty years later:

> Looking back, it seems to me that the interest in Marx taken by myself and my friends . . . was more psychological than political; we were interested in Marx in the same way that we were interested in Freud, as a technique of unmasking middle-class ideologies, not with the intention of repudiating our class, but with the hope of becoming better bourgeois.[22]

It is to be expected that a man will, perhaps unconsciously, tend to minimize the degree of commitment he once had to a position he has since abandoned, but Auden does not seem to have taken undue advantage of hindsight, at least in regard to himself, in this statement. Even though his non-Communist readers often considered him Communist in every sense, British Communists were angrily aware of his failures in orthodoxy.

Cecil Day Lewis, who did commit himself fully, though briefly, to communism, was writing in 1936 of the conflict between the "revolutionary mass-movement" and the "liberalism of Freud," suggesting that the poet could not serve both masters;[23] yet Auden had been serving both for years. He also followed several other masters, such as the psychosomatic Groddeck and Homer Lane and the decadent individualist Rilke, all of whom were at least as incompatible with Marxism as Freud was. It is true that the mixture of Freud and Marx did not work in *The Ascent of F6*, but during the thirties Auden managed to use these and other conflicting perspectives to great effect in separate poems if not always in combination. The favorite critical adjective for Auden is "protean" and it is accurate. Spender

[22] "Authority in America," *The Griffin*, March 1955, quoted by Spears, *Poetry of Auden*, p. 86, who comments that Auden's Marxism, "which was always unorthodox, was essentially another dimension added to his psychological analysis, which was itself always potentially religious."

[23] Cecil Day Lewis, "The Revolution in Literature," *A Time to Dance, Noah and the Waters, and Other Poems, with an essay, Revolution in Writing*, p. 69.

says that in "A Communist to Others" Auden was expressing a point of view "not his own,"[24] and Isherwood speaks of "Weston's" fondness for assuming roles, often with hats to match.[25] The role of militant Communist clearly attracted him at times during the thirties, but he was as often seen as the poet-as-physician, diagnostician and healer of a sick society; or as puzzled liberal, seeking solutions but skeptical of all those being offered; or even as "lunatic clergyman." By 1936, in his "Letter to Lord Byron," he is cheerfully acquiescing in the charge of his more Orthodox friends that his aversion to all forms of authority, even the dictatorship of the proletariat, makes him hopeless as a revolutionary:

> Your fate will be to linger on outcast
> A selfish pink old Liberal to the last.[26]

Day Lewis was more strongly and lastingly committed to militant Marxism than Auden ever was. This was partly a matter of temperament. The eclectic and ironic Auden freely appropriated to his uses whatever struck him as interesting—"a poet does not have to believe in what he says, only entertain it as a possibility"[27]—but Day Lewis, agnostic son of a clergyman, was actively seeking a faith to which he could entirely devote himself. In his autobiography, he speaks of his youthful "weakness for taking everything too much to heart," which led him as an undergraduate to accept unreservedly one contradictory philosophical system after another.[28] Later he was to continue the search for "positive beliefs . . . to plug 'the hollow in the breast where a God should be' . . . a faith which would fill the void left by the leaking away of traditional religion, would make some sense of our troubled times and make real demands on me."[29]

The theme of Day Lewis' early *Transitional Poem* (1929) is the search for "the single mind." Auden's air of certainty probably explained much of his attraction for the young Day Lewis, who was eager for certainties but, as he put it, "clueless." His poems of this

[24] Stephen Spender, *World Within World*, p. 225.

[25] Christopher Isherwood, *Lions and Shadows*, p. 182.

[26] W. H. Auden and Louis MacNeice, *Letters from Iceland*, p. 203.

[27] "Religion and the Intellectuals," *Partisan Review*, XVII, No. 2 (February 1950), 127.

[28] Day Lewis, *Buried Day*, p. 167.

[29] *Ibid.*, p. 209.

period are full of references to Auden as guide and arbiter. In *Transitional Poem*, when he announces that "it is becoming now to declare my allegiance" and lists his fiancée and his friends, he reserves the place of honor for "the tow-haired poet . . . whose / Single mind copes with split intelligence,/ Breeding a piebald strain of truth and nonsense."[30] Again, in *From Feathers to Iron* (1931), the Epilogue, addressed to Auden, begins, "A mole first, out of riddling passages/ You came up for a breather in my field," and among images of young men exploring a new country Auden is described as having "pulled/ The rusty trigger summoning the stragglers."[31] The tone of lyrical admiration is almost shrill in *The Magnetic Mountain* (1933), which is dedicated to Auden. The prophet is frequently invoked, as thus: "Look West, Wystan, lone flyer, birdman, my bully boy!"[32] This enthusiasm was not, however, remarkable among the other encomia of Auden in the volume, *New Country*, in which this passage was first printed.

Auden was by no means the only influence on Day Lewis. His early poems, particularly, hold many echoes of Donne, Eliot, Hopkins, Owen, and D. H. Lawrence. Some are excessively derivative. This section from *The Magnetic Mountain* shows the poet only too close to one of Auden's less interesting manners:

> Scavenger barons and your jackal vassals,
> Your pimping press-gang, your unclean vessels.
>
> . . . .
>
> Don't bluster, Bimbo, it won't do you any good;
> We can be much ruder, and we're learning to shoot.
> Closet Napoleon, you'd better abdicate,
> You'd better quit the country before it's too late.[33]

Day Lewis has disarmed his critics by saying harsher things about his political verse of the thirties than they could:

> The only two political poems of any value which I wrote—"The Conflict" and "In Me Two Worlds"—though they end with confident statement of the choice made, are poems of the divided mind, while the shrill, schoolboyish

[30] Cecil Day Lewis, *Collected Poems 1929–1954*, p. 21.
[31] *Ibid.*, pp. 76–77.
[32] *Ibid.*, p. 97.
[33] *Ibid.*, p. 102.

derisiveness which served for satire in other political verse of mine demonstrates the unnatural effort I had to make to avoid seeing both sides.[34]

This requires some comment. The lines quoted above are a glaring enough instance of "shrill, schoolboyish derisiveness," besides reading like extra stanzas for Auden's "Beethameer, Bethameer, bully of Britain," but if Day Lewis really means to repudiate all his political poems of the thirties with the exception of the two he mentions, one cannot concur. (For that matter, he reprinted a good selection of this verse in his 1954 edition.) Many of these poems are poor indeed, but others have, in Clifford Dyment's phrase, "May-time freshness partnering May-day energy"[35] that has not lost its attractiveness despite the deflation of the revolutionary impulse. "Consider these, for we have condemned them," from *The Magnetic Mountain*, for instance, is certainly arrogant and one-sided when considered as a political argument, but it is a poem of swinging vigor and considerable beauty of sound.

The Magnetic Mountain is full of such passages. The Mountain that magnetizes the young rebels, "Wystan, Rex, all of you that have not fled"—fled, that is, into barren subjectivism—is communism; and the central image, of an armored train racing through a decaying countryside toward the mountains of effort and achievement, reflects the heroic accounts of the use of such trains in the Bolshevik revolution. Auden was never more than a temporary straphanger on the revolutionary train, but Day Lewis was to stay on almost to the end of the decade. The armored train, with its connotations of the humanly directed power of modern technology, is an apt symbol for the Communist movement as it seemed to some of its adherents. The poet hails the oppressed and exploited: "Collect your forces for a counterattack,/ New life is on the way, the relief train." The comic aspect of a trainful of gently reared young bourgeois intellectuals confidently roaring to the rescue of the proletariat was less apparent in 1933 than it was to seem later. The final exhortation is quite stirring:

> Now raise your voices for a final chorus,
> Lift the glasses, drink tomorrow's health—

[34] Day Lewis, *Buried Day*, p. 213.

[35] Clifford Dyment, *C. Day Lewis*, p. 32.

Success to the doctor who is going to cure us
And those who will die no more in bearing wealth.
On our magnetic mountain a beacon burning
Shall sign a peace we hope for, soon or late,
Clean over a clean earth.

. . . .

This is your day: so turn, my comrades, turn
Like infants' eyes like sunflowers to the light.[36]

Francis Scarfe called *The Magnetic Mountain* "certainly the heartiest piece of Left propaganda written in the 'thirties'."[37] In the hearty vein Day Lewis is more successful than Auden, whose cheerleading poems have always a faint flavor of parody. Day Lewis tells us that he, as well as his friends, "treated the slogans and rigid ideology of the extreme Left with considerable levity and scepticism";[38] as late as 1935, the skepticism, at least, shows in his prose, but neither skepticism nor levity toward communism is detectable in his verse. The pattern of most of the poems is that of "'The Conflict" as he described it, the presentation of a mind divided which ends with "confident statement of the choice made." Any doubts that remained after the choice do not show in the poems. The unsympathetic Robert Graves had grounds for saying, "Day Lewis' sentiments were those of a simple-minded Red."[39]

A simple-minded, or at least a single-minded—and the distinction between the two terms may not be great—Red is what Day Lewis was at least trying to be at this stage in his life. In his own account of his choosing communism as a faith, he speaks for a fair number of his contemporaries as well.

My susceptibility to the heroic, played upon by Russian films in which the worker, mounted upon his magnificent tractor, chugged steadily towards the dawn and the new world,[40] joined with my natural partisanship of the underdog to create a picture, romantic and apocalyptic, of the British worker at last coming into his own. . . . No less romantic was my idea of the Enemy [of whom he knew few representatives personally] . . . a sort

[36] Day Lewis, *Collected Poems*, pp. 120–121.

[37] Francis Scarfe, *Auden and After: The Liberation of Poetry*, p. 7.

[38] Day Lewis, *Buried Day*, p. 218.

[39] Graves and Hodge, *Long Weekend*, p. 288.

[40] Upward's tutor in *Journey to the Border* sees a worker on a steamroller as symbol of the new world.

of composite caricature, simplified and melodramatic. . . . In my derision of the bourgeois I was encouraged too by W. B. Yeats' rather theatrical contempt for that vast segment of humanity which lies between the aristocrat and the peasant . . . my leaning toward Communism came less from any intellectual conviction . . . than from my heritage of romantic humanism, a bent of mind quite incompatible, as I would discover, with the materialism and rigidity of Communist doctrines.[41]

Day Lewis had been wanting to join the Party for some time before he actually did in 1935, but he suffered from "a refinement of bourgeois subjectivism by which I was unwilling to join . . . until I was making enough money to be able to assure myself that I was joining from disinterested motives, not as one of the lean and hungry who would personally profit by revolution."[42] What permitted him to take the decisive step was the discovery of a knack for writing murder mysteries. From 1935 on, he was able to live on the proceeds of one mystery written under the name of Nicholas Blake each year. With this security, he quit his schoolmastering and openly joined the Party.

He was, as he later realized, an "extremely odd recruit," with his scruples about disinterestedness and his "gentlemanly refusal" to indoctrinate his pupils or conceal his Party membership. His reason for leaving the Party three years later was also rather odd, or perhaps he is just oddly frank. Although later—he does not say when or on what grounds—he became disillusioned with communism, he was still in full sympathy with it when he withdrew: "I felt no antipathy for Communist theory, and not much for Communist practice." At the time, he "could believe it permissible to do evil that good might come," and it was not any evil done by the Communists in Russia, Spain, or England which led him to abandon political activism, but simply a realization that his Party work was taking too much time, attention, and energy away from his poetry, and that the poetry was beginning to show it. As he describes his Party cell meetings, "more of a combined study group and nonconformist chapel than . . . a revolutionary body,"[43] and his propaganda activities, which could be and were being done as well by non-Party sympathizers, it is easy

[41] Day Lewis, *Buried Day*, p. 210.
[42] *Ibid.*, p. 211.
[43] *Ibid.*, p. 211.

to see how this work might have seemed "unimportant and unreal beside the exacting demands of poetry."[44] His conclusion, which he admits was not notable for logic or morality, was that "It is a right thing to do, but I am a wrong person to be doing it"; and he simply faded out of the Party by moving to an area where there was no active cell.[45]

It is apparent that the division in Day Lewis' mind during the thirties came not, as one might at first have thought, from a question of intellectual conviction but from a matter of personal temperament. Although he speaks of unspecified mental reservations, he never mentions any doubts that furthering the Communist cause was other than "the right thing to do," but only that, as a hopelessly bourgeois gentleman by mental habit and a poet by choice, he was not "the person to be doing it." His reticence on why he later became "disillusioned" leaves a very noticeable lacuna in an autobiography that often seems perfectly candid.

Stephen Spender, the third member of the triumvirate, is much more open, and was so also in the thirties. John Lehmann was impressed by Spender at the first meeting as "the most rapidly self-revealing person I had ever met, in fact . . . apparently devoured by a passion for presenting his *coeur mis à nu*."[46] Such a passion is very endearing to those who seek out the mental states of poets over a distance in time and space. Where Auden is ironic and mysterious and where Day Lewis shows surprising reticences, Spender fights out his internal conflicts publicly. At least as fervidly revolutionary in his early poems as Day Lewis, Spender did not hesitate to reveal his doubts as they developed. The incident of his letter to the *Daily Worker*, which simultaneously announced his joining the Communist Party and listed all his objections to its policies, is typical.[47]

In his autobiographical novels (which are themselves notable for their combination of apparently total candor with impermeable reserve) Christopher Isherwood speaks rather caustically of the enor-

[44] *Ibid.*, p. 223.

[45] He was to have difficulty twenty years later explaining to a United States Embassy official why he had not publicly denounced the Party on leaving it and why the Party had made no effort to recapture him. The visa he was requesting did not come through for nine months (Day Lewis, *Buried Day*, p. 225).

[46] Lehmann, *Whispering Gallery*, p. 176.

[47] See Chapter III.

mous self-centeredness of "Stephen Savage," yet this intense introversion may well have been Spender's greatest strength in the confusing days of the thirties. Always preoccupied with his own responses and resolved to be true to them above all, Spender was basically incapable of the degree of "living in the future, and in abstractions"[48] that led some of his friends to travel far from the liberal humanism to which they later returned in some disarray but which Spender really never quite left.

Spender speaks much in his autobiography of his susceptibility to the influence of others, and the favorite term of contemporary critics for him was "sensitive," in contradistinction to the "toughness" of Auden and Day Lewis. Yet he proved himself extremely resistant to pressures that threatened his individuality. In reading his early poetry along with that of his friends, one is struck with how quickly he developed a voice entirely his own. He recognized the same "ancestors" as the others did, and some of his poems can be very readily traced to their models: his 1934 *Vienna* sometimes sounds like a parody of Eliot, and his debts to Auden and, particularly, to Wilfred Owen, are clear enough. Still, despite occasional sorties into manners that did not suit his gifts, he soon discovered, and thereafter reverted in his best work to, the special kind of melodious free verse that, although recognizably influenced by Lawrence, is always unmistakably Spender. It is significant that very few Mortmere elements appear in his verse.

Spender had published two small volumes of poetry while still at Oxford (he took his degree in 1931 after having broken off his studies for a period of travel, chiefly in Germany), but he was first widely noticed through his contributions to *New Signatures* and *New Country*. His *Poems* published in 1933 created a stir by their "sensitivity," their revolutionary content, and their "modern" imagery. Readers were impressed, favorably or unfavorably, by his lyrical descriptions of the paraphernalia of technological society ("Come let us praise the gasworks," he had written at nineteen). Jokes abounded on the fondness of the triumvirate for pylons, locomotives, and rusting machinery; but budding poets abandoned Georgian for industrial pastoral.

In *The Destructive Element* (1936), Spender suggested that if Wilfred Owen had not written about the war, he might have written

[48] Day Lewis, *Buried Day*, p. 218.

about "the industrial towns, and the distressed areas":[49] the important point was that he chose a subject external to himself. Spender, in peacetime, chose these subjects as his own, and he also adopted Owen's attitude: "All a poet can do today is *warn*" and "the poetry is in the pity." He was quickly identified as the Wilfred Owen of the Depression—or the Rupert Brooke, according to his harsher critics.[50] Even the disapproving Robert Graves gave grudging praise to his "poor-little-rich-boy poems, full of genuine pity for the exploited poor, and for himself."[51]

Along with the poems of sorrowful or indignant pity for the poor, the celebrations of beauty in such utilitarian things as express trains and airliners, and the entirely personal lyrics, *Poems* (1933) contains many expressions of fervent, if rather diffuse, revolutionary ardor. The poet calls "oh young men oh young comrades" to leave their fathers' houses and "advance to rebel."[52] He sings of a "new world" in which machinery will serve human needs, not capitalist profits, in which

> Our tempered will shall plough across the nations.
> The engine hurrying through the lucky valley
> The hand that moves to guide the silent lines
> Effect their beauty without robbery.[53]

In this "new country/ Where light equal, like the shine from snow, strikes all faces," one

> may wonder
> How it ever was that works, money, interest,
> building could ever hide
> The palpable and obvious love of man for man.[54]

Spender's communism is, like Day Lewis', basically a "romantic humanism," and it is love, more than justice, that moves him. But he foresees the necessity of violence:

[49] Stephen Spender, *The Destructive Element*, p. 221.

[50] W. Y. Tindall prefers to call him the Shelley (*Forces in Modern British Literature*, p. 59).

[51] Graves and Hodge, *Long Weekend*, p. 288.

[52] Stephen Spender, No. XXVII, [Untitled], *Poems*, p. 44.

[53] Spender, No. XXXVIII, "New Year," *Poems*, p. 65.

[54] Spender, No. XXIX, [Untitled], *Poems*, p. 48.

Oh comrades, let not those who follow after
—The beautiful generation that shall spring
from our sides—
Let them not wonder how after the failure of banks
The failure of cathedrals and the declared insanity
of our rulers,
We lacked the Spring-like resources of the tiger.[55]

The lovely "Not palaces, an era's crown," which closes the volume, ends with an opposition of the fruitful violence of communism to the barren violence of fascism:

—That programme of the antique Satan
Bristling with guns on the indented page
With battleship towering from hilly waves;
For what? Drive of a ruining purpose
Destroying all but its age-long exploiters.
Our program like this, yet opposite,
Death to the killers, bringing light to life.[56]

Despite his formal membership in the Party, Spender's communism was strictly lower-case for as long as it lasted. A very clear-eyed critic of literature, he was better able than many of his contemporaries to see politics steadily and see them whole. He was less inclined to overlook or deny the weaknesses and vices of his own side. He had come from a wealthy Liberal family with strong traditions of social responsibility, and he had trod the well-worn path from liberalism to socialism and then, because of the apparent failure of social democracy and the growing menace of fascism, on to communism. He admits frankly that he was attracted to communism partly by the hope of solving thereby his personal troubles, and that he felt "by being anti-fascist, I created a rightness for myself besides which my personal guilt seemed unimportant." [57] Thanks to a comfortable independent income, he had been able to travel widely and to observe the rise of fascism in Germany and Austria with his own horrified eyes. He had quite literally loved the Germany of the Weimar Republic, seeing it as the home of light and liberty, and he had many friends among anti-Nazi Germans and Austrians. The destruction of

[55] *Ibid.*
[56] Spender, No. XL, [Untitled], *Poems*, p. 69.
[57] Spender, *World Within World*, p. 173.

freedom in these countries was an intensely personal matter to him. Nor was his detestation of Nazism lessened by the consciousness that the Jewish strain in his own family, of which he had hardly thought before, would qualify him for Nazi persecution.

The long poem *Vienna* (1934) is a well-intended if not very successful tribute to the Social Democrats of that city who were crushed by the reactionary Dollfuss regime. "The Funeral" and "Van de Lubbe," in the *Poems* of 1933 were also inspired by the events Spender witnessed in central Europe, and his play *Trial of a Judge* was to be based on the downfall of the Weimar Republic. He was in Vienna when the Spanish Civil War broke out, and he at first waited glumly with his socialist friends to hear of the collapse of one more outpost of freedom. The news of the Republican resistance gave him and his friends new hope for the defeat of fascism and the triumph of a new and better system. To them it seemed that Spain "offered the twentieth century an 1848."[58]

Spender's *Forward from Liberalism* (1937) admirably expresses the spirit that was abroad, at least on the Left, at the beginning of the Spanish Civil War, and it will serve to introduce much of the poetry that was to be written during the war. The purpose of the book, which was, as might have been expected, a Left Book Club choice, was to gain support for a united Popular Front and specifically to allay the doubts and suspicions of Liberals and Labour party socialists about working with Communists.

Basing his arguments on Sidney and Beatrice Webb's sympathetic study of *Soviet Communism: A New Civilization?*,[59] Spender gives a spirited defense of the necessity for dictatorship in the Russia of 1917 and the years afterward, when the new government was under constant threat from without and within. He describes the Bolshevik excesses as understandable, if indefensible, and he expresses hope that the new Stalin Constitution of 1936 will have signaled the gradual institution of real democracy at last. Drawing upon his own experience, he argues that the social democratic forces in Germany and Austria might well have withstood the Fascist onslaught if they had

[58] *Ibid.*, p. 170.

[59] The Webbs' book was published under this title in 1934; in the second, 1937 edition, the question mark becomes a period.

been less reluctant to employ violent or unconstitutional means. Having dealt rather sharply with Wyndham Lewis' *Left Wings Over Europe,* he more gently sets about refuting the "constructive pacifism" of Aldous Huxley as misguided and irrelevant to the current crisis.

Spender is here addressing himself to bourgeois liberals, and his basic thesis is that communism is the goal of liberalism, since political freedom cannot be fully realized without "economic freedom"; capitalist democracy must by its very nature depend on the exploitation, hence the unfreedom, of the masses by the ruling bourgeoisie, whose liberty is therefore shakily grounded upon economic oppression. In Spender's view, as in Caudwell's, true democracy is impossible without socialism. He contends that it is still possible in the England of 1937 for the progressive forces in society, if they unite, to bring about socialism within the current framework of parliamentary democracy and without excessive sacrifice of the liberty even of the exploiting classes; but if war should come, he warns, the revolutionary process might well get out of hand.

Although he defends the Russian Revolution in general, Spender does not consider the Soviet Union a desirable model for English socialists, and he has deep reservations about the rigidity and dogmatism of Communists both in England and abroad. For him, communism is the proper goal of the enlightened individualist, but the liberal must not be bound by dogma:

> on the one hand [the liberal individualist] is fighting on the side of the communists for a just and secure society; on the other hand, he is fighting for disinterestedness and spiritual freedom within that society: and here he may find that political dogma is against him. Essentially, he is using political weapons to attain an unpolitical world.[60]

Spender makes no effort to excuse the Moscow purge trials, of which the news was still fairly recent at this time, and he is strongly critical of the suppression and distortion of information in and about the Soviet Union: "we should remember that whenever it becomes necessary for communism in one country to use the methods of fascism, world revolution is postponed."[61] Nevertheless, he is convinced

[60] Stephen Spender, *Forward from Liberalism,* p. 176.
[61] *Ibid.,* p. 290.

that "the alternative to international socialism is war" and that English socialists, who have the great advantage of working from a political democracy rather than an absolute monarchy, can and must learn from the mistakes of the Russians. As for Spain,

> we must give the fullest support to the actions of the Spanish Popular Front without blinding ourselves to the fact that excesses in Spain are inevitable. Our responsibility is to support the Spanish government, whilst determining that a situation in England shall not arise which would produce a similar conflict.[62]

At the outbreak of the Spanish Civil War, the chief figures of the Auden group appear united against fascism and in favor of the Spanish Republic and of socialism as the best possible sociopolitical system, but with differing attitudes on the concomitant question of how far Russia and the Communist Party are to be identified with the anti-Fascist, socialist cause. Edward Upward is ready to abandon writing entirely, if need be, for the "practical" work of the Party, and Day Lewis has fully committed his pen to the Party's uses; Rex Warner is still apparently convinced of the centrality of the Communists in the struggle; Spender is eager to work with the Communists for what he considers their common goals but already has serious reservations; Auden, and probably Isherwood, have become, if anything, more tentative in their acceptance of Marxist explanations and prescriptions than they were two or three years before.

Louis MacNeice has been mentioned only in passing so far because his inclusion as a member of the Auden group is harder to justify than that of the others. As well as age, background, and education, he also shared with the group an aversion to capitalist society and an experimental attitude toward poetic form—and he was second only to Auden in technical skill. During the early thirties he was lecturing on classics at the University of Birmingham, but he apparently spent much time in London and was associated with the Group Theatre, which produced his translation of the *Agamemnon* and his *Out of the Picture*. In 1936 he was appointed lecturer in Greek at Bedford College of the University of London, but before taking up his duties there he accompanied Auden on the trip that was the basis of their *Letters from Iceland*.

[62] *Ibid.*, p. 294.

Auden's influence can be seen in some of MacNeice's verse, particularly in the incidental lyrics of *Out of the Picture,* the whole of which seems closely derived from the Auden-Isherwood plays. The fine "Bagpipe Music" could be called Audenesque in its "piebald strain of truth and nonsense" and its effective use of slang, but it is questionable whether MacNeice needed much outside help in developing his very characteristic colloquial style. Generally the concurrence between his verse and that of Auden can be adequately explained on the basis of similarities of outlook and, perhaps, of temperament. Certainly MacNeice gives no indication that he was even aware of the world of Mortmere.

MacNeice most differs from the rest of the group in his attitude toward communism. Asked in 1942 about his politics, he replied:

> Politics: distrust all parties but consider capitalism must go. Visited Barcelona, New Years 1939, and hold that in the Spanish Civil War the balance of right was certainly on the side of the Republican government; the situation, however, much more complicated than represented in the English press.[63]

A skeptical leftist, MacNeice did not season his Nays about capitalism with Yeas about alternative systems. His brief "To a Communist" shows the extent of his enthusiasm for that ideology:

> Your thoughts make shape like snow; in one night
>   only
> The gawky earth grows breasts,
> Snow's unity engrosses
> Particular pettiness of stones and grasses.
> But before you proclaim the millennium, my dear,
> Consult the barometer—
> The poise is perfect but maintained
> For one day only.[64]

The image of communism as snow—cold, lifeless, concealing real inconsistencies and differences under a deceptive and very temporary surface unity—is a long way from Day Lewis' Magnetic Mountain.

[63] Quoted in Stanley J. Kunitz and Howard Haycraft, *Twentieth Century Authors,* p. 889.

[64] Louis MacNeice, *Collected Poems 1925–1948,* p. 78.

"The Individualist Speaks," which appears in the *Collected Poems* immediately after "To a Communist" and could be a kind of companion piece, is ironic; but it seems not unlikely that MacNeice is expressing in it his own attitude toward the "revolutionary romp":

> Crawling down like lava or termites
> Nothing seduces, nothing dissolves, nothing
> affrights
> You who scale-off masks and smash the purple
> lights
> —But I will escape, with my dog, on the far
> side of the Fair.[65]

MacNeice was not the less anti-Fascist for not being pro-Communist. His "Eclogue from Iceland" closes with the spirit of Grettir, hero of Icelandic saga, exhorting the visiting English and Irish tourists to be firm in what may be a futile resistance to fascism:

> Minute your gesture, but it must be made
> Your hazard, your act of defiance and hymn of hate,
> Hatred of hatred, assertion of human values,
> Which is now your only duty
> . . . .
> And, it may be added, your only chance.[66]

The saga spirit of resistance, the more resolute because it is doomed, permeates MacNeice's political comment. His verse of the thirties reveals his ambivalence toward the civilization he envisages as coming to an end. He considers that the end is deserved, because the gracious civilization of which he is the happy heir is based on economic injustice and the exploitation of the many for the benefit of the few; but as one of the few, he poignantly regrets the passing of the era. This is to be a recurrent theme in the *Autumn Journal* of 1938, to be examined later, but it is nowhere better expressed than in the musical "The Sunlight on the Garden":

[65] *Ibid.*

[66] MacNeice and Auden, *Letters from Iceland*, pp. 134–145. For the parallel seeker it is interesting that Peter Viereck, discussing the spirit of rebelliousness shown by young Soviet writers during 1962–1963, quoted this passage and the lines about the gun-butt on the door (below) as expressive of their attitudes ("The Conspiracy of Feeling," KPFK-FM broadcast, March 12, 1964).

Our freedom as free lances
Advances towards its end;
The earth compels, upon it
Sonnets and birds descend;
And soon, my friend,
We shall have no time for dances.

. . . .

We are dying, Egypt, dying

And not expecting pardon,
Hardened in heart anew,
But glad to have sat under
Thunder and rain with you,
And grateful too
For sunlight on the garden.[67]

Letters from Iceland ends grimly with MacNeice's "Epilogue for W. H. Auden":

Our prerogatives as men
Will be cancelled who knows when
Still I drink your health before
The gun-butt raps upon the door.[68]

The book as a whole, however, is not grim at all. If MacNeice was fairly hopeless about the future even in 1936, Auden seems not to have been; nor did MacNeice's despair materially dull his appreciation of the fleeting present. Most of the letters, in prose or verse, are lighthearted and chatty. The closing section, "W. H. Auden and Louis MacNeice: Their Last Will and Testament" is full of rimed wisecracks about their friends, acquaintances, and enemies, with a few comments on such recent public developments as the Spanish Civil War. Among various bequests, which seem a bit private for a book offered to the general public, there are some that are not at all esoteric:

all the lives by Franco gently stopped
We leave to Rome, and for the doctrines she has
spoken,
The cock that crew before St. Peter wept.

. . . .

[67] Louis MacNeice, *Collected Poems 1925–1948*, pp. 104–105.
[68] MacNeice and Auden, *Letters from Iceland*, p. 262.

And to Sir Oswald [Mosley] (please forgive the
stench
Which taints our parchment for that purulent
name)
We leave a rather unpleasant word in French.

. . . .

We leave the Martyr's Stake at Abergwilly
To Wyndham Lewis with a box of soldiers (blonde)
Regretting one so bright should be so silly.

. . . .

We leave their marvelous jorative tongue
To Englishmen, and for our intelligent island
pray
That to her virtuous beauties by all poets sung
She add at last an honest foreign policy.[69]

Auden's verse contributions to *Letters from Iceland* include such foreboding, if unpolitical, lyrics as "Journey to Iceland" and "O Who Can Ever Gaze His Fill?"; but it is his witty and pertinent "Letter to Lord Byron" that is the most striking part of the book. This fine example of Auden's light verse at its most brilliant is not included in his later collections, and it tempts to indiscriminate quotation as the poet ranges delightfully over his life and opinions on politics, morals, and literature, following the example if not the stanza of Don Juan.[70]

Auden observes, surveying the English scene, that "John Bull of the good old days,/ The swaggering bully with the clumsy jest" is no more, having "passed away at Ypres and Passchendaele." His successor is to be found in Walt Disney: "The little Mickey with the hidden grudge:/ Which is the better I leave you to judge."

He dreads the ogre, but he dreads much more
Those who conceivably might set him free;

. . . .

The ogre need but shout "Security"
To make this man, so loveable, so mild,
As madly cruel as a frightened child.[71]

[69] *Ibid.*, pp. 240, 245, 247, 257.

[70] Auden employs rime royal, modestly disclaiming the skill to sustain Byronic ottava rima.

[71] Auden and MacNeice, *Letters from Iceland*, pp. 55–56.

The modern poet credits Byron with hating injustice, though inclined to recognize it more clearly abroad than at home, and suggests that Byron today might have "walked in the United Front with Gide"

> Against the ogre, dragon, what you will;
> His many shapes and names all turn us pale,
> For he's immortal, and today he still
> Swinges the horror of his scaly tail.
> Sometimes he seems to sleep, but will not fail
> In every age to rear up to defend
> Each dying force of history to the end.[72]

Auden traces the history of the dragon back to the Pax Romana and before:

> He comes in dreams at puberty to man,
> To carry him back to childhood if he can.

Whenever men have "lost faith in choice and thought,"

> The dragon rises from his garden border
> And promises to set up law and order.[73]

Auden, too, wants to fight the dragon in his verse, and he argues that the poet must always see himself in relation to society:

> The only thing [art] must be is attendant,
> The only thing it mustn't, independent.[74]

He acknowledges the efforts at "independence" of the Art for Art's Sake writers, but he adds that only because they had enough money not to require a patron's help were the first of them able to set up what he calls the "Poets' Party." In any case, he says, the party is over now. Today poets are likely to be schoolmasters or even journalists:

> So barons of the press who know their readers
> Employ to write their more appalling leaders
> Instead of Satan's horned and hideous minions,
> Clever young men of liberal opinions.[75]

[72] *Ibid.*, p. 58. This is the Dragon of the last scene of *The Ascent of F6* and of various shorter lyrics.

[73] Auden and MacNeice, *Letters from Iceland*, p. 58.

[74] *Ibid.*, p. 104.

[75] *Ibid.*, p. 211.

As for his own opinions, Auden admits to being "a selfish pink old liberal," but among ideologies his preferences are opposite to those he ascribes to Pope Pius XII:

> The Pope's turned protestant at last and chosen
> Thinking it safer in the temporal circs
> The Italian faith against the Russian works.[76]

Auden prefers the Russian works, but he has his doubts:

> The Great Utopia, free of all complexes,
> The Withered State, is, at the moment, such
> A dream as that of being both the sexes.[77]

The "Letter to Lord Byron" is full of sharp, satirical comments on politics and people, but the tone is of relaxed good humor. This note is not to be heard in Auden's poems again through the 1936–1939 period. He is always witty, even at his most somber, but not cheerful as in this poem. His ballads about Miss Gee, Victor, and James Honeyman are funny but cruel, and his 1937 "Danse Macabre" echoes the earlier *Dance of Death* in a grimmer way. This poem is darkly ironic; the speaker who is promising to save mankind from the Devil has every intention of destroying mankind itself in the process. The Devil, he says, walks abroad "like influenza":

> O were he to triumph, dear heart, you know
> To what depths of shame he would drag you low;
>
> . . . .
>
> Millions already have come to their harm
> Succumbing like doves to his adder's charm,
> Hundreds of trees in the wood are unsound:
> I'm the axe that must cut them down to the ground.
>
> . . . .
>
> I shall ride the parade in a platinum car,
> My features shall shine, my name shall be Star,
>
> . . . .
>
> You shall leave your breakfast, your desk, and your play
> On a fine summer morning the Devil to slay.
> For it's order and trumpet and anger and drum

[76] *Ibid.*, p. 233.
[77] *Ibid.*, p. 235.

And power and glory command you to come;
The graves shall fly open and let you all in,
And the earth shall be emptied of mortal sin.[78]

The Devil represents the forces of life and freedom, that is, of Left revolution, "the disloyal machines and irreverent thinking"; and the speaker is Fascist counterrevolution, embodying the Death-Wish or Death himself. In 1937 it is less clear than it seemed in 1933 that he is to be liquidated.

Auden was in Spain from January to March 1937, apparently as a stretcher-bearer, but he was almost alone among pro-Loyalist intellectuals in refusing at the time to discuss his experiences. His 1956 essay in *Modern Canterbury Pilgrims* reveals that one effect of his Spanish sojourn was to start him on the path that was to lead him back to Christianity. In the same essay he remarks that "Nobody I knew who went to Spain during the Civil War who was not a dyed-in-the-wool stalinist came back with his illusions intact."[79] Auden's disillusion was presumably with the Communists in Spain, not with the Republican cause. His poem on Spain was published later in the year in pamphlet form, and the proceeds of its sale turned over to Medical Aid for Spain.

"Spain 1937" has been criticized for its lack of "immediacy," and it is true but irrelevant that it probably could have been written just as well without the poet's ever having gone to Spain. It is irrelevant because the poem is not about what was happening in Spain but about what Spain meant to outsiders. To Auden, Spain appears to be the embodiment of choice, for nations and individuals, and the reflection of their inmost selves. With the refrain, "Yesterday all the past," he briefly surveys European history up to the outbreak of the Spanish War. The confused and conflicting nations invoke the "life/ That shapes the individual belly and orders/ The private nocturnal terror"—that is, Auden's current symbol for the force that moves men and nations:

"Intervene. O descend as a dove or
A furious papa or a mild engineer: but descend."

[78] W. H. Auden, *The Collected Poetry of W. H. Auden*, pp. 60–61.
[79] Quoted in Spears, *Poetry of Auden*, p. 86.

The "life . . . if it answers at all," replies, "I am whatever you do," and continues,

> "What's your proposal? To build the Just City? I will.
> I agree. Or is it the suicide pact, the romantic
> Death? Very well, I accept, for
> I am your choice, your decision: yes, I am Spain."[80]

Spain, then, holds the answers, such as they are. "Yesterday all the past . . . Tomorrow, perhaps, the future . . . But today the struggle." In Spain,

> Our thoughts have bodies; the menacing shapes of our fever
> Are precise and alive. For the fears which made us respond
> To the medicine ad. and the brochure of winter cruises
> Have become invading battalions;
> And our faces, the institute-face, the chain-store, the ruin
> Are projecting their greed as the firing-squad and the bomb.
> Madrid is the heart. Our moments of tenderness blossom
> As the ambulance and the sandbag;
> Our hours of friendship into a people's army.[81]

The above two stanzas do not appear in the poem as reprinted in the *Collected Poetry* of 1945. To Symons, as to Beach, this omission is part of the poet's "determination to rewrite his own poetic past."[82] Perhaps it is; yet it could be argued that the revision of the line just preceding these stanzas to "Our fever's menacing shapes are precise and alive" makes them only restatements of what has just been said. These stanzas might well have seemed to Auden too emotional for the cold, abstract, "hard" quality of the poem which distinguishes it sharply from almost all other poems inspired by the war. The carefully unheroic, tight-lipped urgency of the closing stanzas recalls what Spears has labeled Auden's "Nordic mask," the saga-derived style that dominates *Paid on Both Sides* and some of the early poems but appears with decreasing frequency in the later ones. "Spain 1937" does not employ the alliterative verse or the kennings of these poems, but the attitude is "Nordic":

80 Auden, *Collected Poetry,* p. 183.

81 These nine lines, omitted from the *Collected Poetry,* are quoted by Symons, *The Thirties,* p. 124.

82 *Ibid.* A major thesis in J. W. Beach's *The Making of the Auden Canon* is that, in preparing the *Collected Poetry* of 1945, the poet revised his earlier poems to bring them more nearly in line with his changed attitudes.

Tomorrow, for the young, the poets exploding like bombs,
The walks by the lake, the winter of perfect communion;
                Tomorrow the bicycle races
Through the suburbs on summer evenings: but today the struggle.
Today the inevitable increase in the chances of death;
The conscious acceptance of guilt in the necessary murder;[83]
                Today the expending of powers
On the flat ephemeral pamphlet and the boring meeting.[84]

. . . .

The stars are dead; the animals will not look:
We are left alone with our day, and the time is short and
                History to the defeated
May say Alas but cannot help or pardon.[85]

For all its dry reserve, "Spain 1937" comes as close to propaganda as anything Auden wrote in this period except the choruses of *On the Frontier* because it urges a specific course of action; that is, support for the Spanish Republic and a readiness to war on fascism. Auden did not, however, consider propaganda a suitable purpose for poetry. In 1935 he wrote that

> Poetry is not concerned with telling people what to do, but with extending our knowledge of good and evil, perhaps making the necessity for action more urgent and its nature more clear, but only leading us to the point where it is possible to make a rational and moral choice.[86]

Strictly speaking, "Spain 1937" does no more than encourage "a rational and moral choice"; but the circumstance of its being published for the benefit of a Loyalist agency served to indicate which choice Auden considered rational and moral.

Auden's other poems of the late thirties follow this prescription closely. Few are entirely free of political content, but the political elements are in each poem integral to the individual moral context, not the main point. For this reason, in part, Auden's poems, which were rightly read at the time as sharply relevant to current political

[83] "The necessary murder" is revised in the *Collected Poetry* to "the fact of murder."

[84] Cyril Connolly drily noted that "copies of [Auden's] pamphlets are excessively rare" (*Enemies of Promise*, p. 99).

[85] Auden, *Collected Poetry*, pp. 184–185.

[86] W. H. Auden, Introduction, *The Poet's Tongue*, ed. W. H. Auden and John Garrett, p. ix. This passage recalls "August for the People"; see Chapter V.

issues, lose less when read out of contemporary context than do many other good poems of the time.

Francis Scarfe has written that "in his early poems [Auden] tried to express a fairly universal, and in any case a second-hand subject-matter in an intensely personal style, and since then he has moved towards a more personal subject-matter and a more impersonal style."[87] This is true, but it allows of some expansion. The "universal" and "second-hand" subject matter seems to be what Day Lewis meant when he spoke of his circle's living "too much in the future, and in abstractions"; and the "intensely personal style" was characterized by an extreme particularity that makes some of the poems Auden wrote during the first five years or so of his poetic life densely obscure without the aid of footnotes identifying historical and Mortmere personages, and personal friends.[88] The later poems of the thirties use more generalized symbols. The counterparts of Hoover, Briand, Mosley, and "loony Layard" of the earlier verse become simply "the fashionable madmen" raising "their pedantic boring cry" in 1937. The anonymous statesmen, politicians, tyrants, soldiers of the "In Time of War" sonnet sequence could be suitably named by readers in 1939, but they can be named equally well, although differently, by readers in 1969.

It is much too early to speak of "universality" in connection with Auden's subject matter of only twenty-five years ago; however, on a relative scale, his choice of material and his treatment of it in these poems have proved much less susceptible to changing historical circumstances than have some other choices, including some of his own. When he and Isherwood and Rex Warner chose the Marxist myth as basis for their scientific fairy tales, *The Dog Beneath the Skin* and *The Wild Goose Chase,* they may well have considered that myth likely to confer lasting validity; yet these fine works are already period pieces, while much of the poetry from *On This Island* (*Look, Stranger* is the English title), *Journey to a War,* and *Another Time,* which seemed and was topical in the late thirties, is just as meaningful today. A happier century may find these poems historical curiosities, but not this one.

[87] Scarfe, *Auden and After,* p. 33.

[88] It is significant that many of Auden's later revisions of his early poems are in the direction of removing the particularity and private references in them, as Beach notes (*Auden Canon, passim*).

In 1938 Auden and Isherwood toured China and produced their *Journey to a War*, which consisted of a travel-diary by Isherwood and a "Verse-commentary" and sonnet sequence, "In Time of War," by Auden. Auden's debt to Rilke, particularly in the sonnet form, has been frequently commented upon, and in this sequence he includes a tribute to the German poet (Sonnet XXIII). The mode, which usually involves an unidentified protagonist shown in the midst of some kind of unspecified situation within a symbolic landscape, is well suited to Auden's purposes in *Journey to a War*. The first sonnets present, in a sonnet apiece, certain types more readily recognizable from a Marxist perspective than otherwise: the peasant (IV), the decayed aristocrat (V), the intellectual (VI), the poet (VII), the bourgeois (VIII). There are other types too, including Man himself (I–III) and a religious leader much like Christ (X). A Marxist approach also helps in reading some of the later sonnets. For instance, Sonnet XII ("And the age ended, and the last deliverer died") can be read as a poetic treatment of the dangers to capitalist society of the economic forces it fails to recognize in their bourgeois disguises. Again, Sonnet XV can, though it need not, be read as implying a Marxist view when the poet describes the Japanese bomber pilots as ignorant of the meaning of their acts:

They will never see how flying
Is the creation of the ideas they hate,
Nor how their own machines are always trying
To push through into life.[89]

Although a Marxist interpretation is often useful in reading these sonnets, they are basically liberal humanist, not "scientific." The central concept is love, not yet identified with God. Organized religion is associated in Sonnets X and XI with compulsion and tyranny, although the religious leader of X and the capitalized "He" of XI are figures of love. The suggestion in this sequence is that man is the sole source of love. Sonnet XXV tells us of the "little workshop of love," long neglected and hardly acknowledged:

We can't believe that we ourselves designed it,
A minor item of our daring plan
That caused no trouble; we took no notice of it.

[89] Auden, *Collected Poetry*, p. 327.

Disaster comes, and we're amazed to find it
The single project that since work began
Through all the cycle showed a steady profit.[90]

Possibly the most moving sonnet of the sequence, testimony that the cold and abstract "Spain 1937" was not the only tone Auden could strike in writing of war, is number XVIII, on a dead Chinese soldier:

No vital knowledge perished in his skull;
His jokes were stale; like war time, he was dull;
His name is lost forever like his looks.

He neither knew nor chose the Good, but taught us,
And added meaning like a comma, when
He turned to dust in China that our daughters

Be fit to love the earth, and not again
Disgraced before the dogs; that, where are waters,
Mountains and houses, may be also men.[91]

The last sonnet reaffirms the necessity for "rational and moral choice," using Auden's customary symbol for decision:

We live in freedom by necessity,
A mountain people dwelling among mountains.[92]

The "Commentary" shows Auden at his most "classical," fluent, easy, witty, discursive, without great emotional tension achieved or sought—writing the kind of expository verse that is easier to criticize as facile than to imitate. Here Auden tries to place the Chinese war in historical context, along with the concurrent battles in Spain and, now underground, in the rest of Europe: the age-old struggle between totalitarianism and freedom. In 1938 he sees men wandering "in search of home" and weeping for "the lost ages/ Before Because became As If, or rigid Certainty/ The Chances Are."[93] The "violent/ Who long to calm our guilt with murder" respond in Spain, in Germany, in China, with their "brazen offer":

[90] *Ibid.*, p. 333.

[91] *Ibid.*, pp. 328–329. Lines four and five as quoted here are a revision, typically in the direction of greater reserve, of those which in the first publication of this sonnet (July 2, 1938, *New Statesman and Nation*) read: "Professors of Europe, hostess, citizen,/ Respect this boy. Unknown to your reporters . . ."

[92] Auden, *Collected Poetry*, p. 334.

[93] *Ibid.*, p. 341.

"Man can have Unity if Man will give up Freedom.

. . . .

Leave Truth to the police and us; we know the Good;
We build the Perfect City time shall never alter;
Our Law shall guard you always like a cirque of mountains,
Your ignorance keep off evil like a dangerous sea;
You shall be consummated in the General Will,
Your children innocent and charming as the beasts."[94]

On the side of "their principle of Nothing Private," Auden sees among others Genghis Khan, Diocletian, Plato "the good," Machiavelli, Hobbes, "generalizing Hegel and quiet Bosanquet." "And every family and every heart is tempted," in Asia, Europe, England, "in the Far West, in absolutely free America,/. . . Thousands believe, and millions are halfway to a conviction."[95]

Yet all the same we have our faithful sworn supporters
Who never lost their faith in knowledge or in man,

. . . .

Some looked at falsehood with the candid eyes of children,
Some had a woman's ear to catch injustice,
Some took Necessity, and knew her, and she brought forth
Freedom.[96]

These "supporters" have an answer to the "brazen offer," and "if we care to listen, we can always hear them":

"Men are not innocent as beasts and never can be,
Man can improve but never will himself be perfect,
Only the free have disposition to be truthful,
Only the truthful have the interest to be just,
Only the just possess the will-power to be free.

. . . .

Now in the clutch of crisis and the bloody hour
You must defeat your enemies or perish, but remember,
Only by those who reverence it can life be mastered;
Only a whole and happy conscience can stand up
And answer their bleak lie; among the just
And only there, is Unity compatible with Freedom.[97]

[94] *Ibid.*, pp. 341–342.
[95] *Ibid.*, p. 343.
[96] *Ibid.*, p. 344.
[97] *Ibid.*, pp. 346–347.

The "Commentary" ends with a prayer to the best in man to help us unfreeze our hearts, clear our heads of "impressive rubbish," and rally our will to construct "a human justice."[98] This work of construction must be free of "doing evil that good may come." It is significant that this volume is dedicated to that prophet of individualistic "political quietism," E. M. Forster.

Auden's plea for a "human justice" is noble and inspiring, but short on specifics. There is no such vagueness in the poems composed during the later thirties by Day Lewis. He sees the way to this ideal as complete identification with the proletarian cause, a dedication stronger than the religious, which "offers no compromise, means far harder/ Visions than valley steeples call to, a stricter vow."[99]

The central image of the long title poem in *A Time to Dance* is the difficult and dangerous flight in a patched-up old airplane from England to Melbourne by two Australians in 1920. For Day Lewis, this flight symbolizes the way to a new world. He anticipates and answers the objections of his little-man audience:

> "Those were free agents: we are tied"—Listen,
> *Freedom is knowledge of necessity*:
> It is using the currents of air to waft your wings
> . . . .
> It is the will to prove
> Your case, though that last word
> And clinching argument should be your death.
> . . . .
> Sirs, you are that world
> Shall make a new world and be all the world.[100]

At this point in the poem appears the irregular sonnet that was to give such wicked delight to the detractors of the Auden group:

> Yes, why do we all, seeing a Red, feel small? That small
> Catspaw ruffles our calm—how comes it?
> . . . .

[98] So the poem ends as printed originally in *Journey to a War* (p. 301). In revising it for the 1945 edition, Auden changed the object of the prayer to God, who is then personified as "that Justice . . ./ Whose uplifting, loving, and constraining power" contains "all human reasons" (*Collected Poetry*, p. 347).

[99] Day Lewis, "Moving In," in *A Time to Dance*, p. 10.

[100] *A Time to Dance*, pp. 54–55. See discussion of Caudwell, Chapter III.

Here it is. There fall
From him shadows of what he is building.
. . . .
It is the future, walking to meet us all.
Mark him. He is only what we are mortal. Yet for the night
Of history, where we lie dreaming still, he is wide awake:
Weak, liable to ill luck—yet rock where we are slight
Eddies. . . .
Mark him, workers and all who wish the world aright:
He is what your sons could be, the road these times should take.[101]

This passage was one of several in "A Time to Dance" which Day Lewis was to regret and to omit from his *Collected Poems* of 1954. There is, however, considerable excellent verse in the *Time to Dance* volume as a whole, and much of it is in the title poem. The Audenesque ballad, "I've heard them lilting at loom and belting," is musical and touching, the narrative sections are stirring and vivid, the parodies are pertinent though unimportant, the closing passages dignified and impressive.

A Time to Dance includes the only two political poems Day Lewis still liked nearly twenty years later, "In Me Two Worlds" and "The Conflict," both of which deal, as he says, with the "divided mind." The first leaves the issue of the poet's "psychomachia"—the conflict between his bourgeois habits and loyalties and his new revolutionary faith—somewhat in doubt:

So heir and ancestor
Pursue their inveterate feud
Making my senses' darkened fields
Their theatre of war.[102]

"The Conflict," which is probably Day Lewis' best political poem, poses the impossibility of neutrality—"private stars fade in the blood-red dawn/ Where two worlds strive"—and states the poet's choice in persuasive terms:

The red advance of life
Contracts pride, calls out the common blood,
Beats song into a single blade,

[101] Day Lewis, *A Time to Dance*, p. 55.
[102] *Ibid.*, p. 16 .

Makes a depth-charge of grief.
Move then with new desires,
For where we used to build and love
Is no man's land, and only ghosts can live
Between two fires.[103]

This poem well indicates what Day Lewis found most imaginatively stimulating in his political commitment during the thirties, the intermingling of public and personal concerns which made both seem more meaningful. The fullest expression of this is his *From Feathers to Iron,* which celebrates simultaneously the gestation and birth of his first child and the gestation and coming birth of the new society.

Day Lewis apparently did not like the most explicit of his divided-mind poems, "Johnny Head-in-the-Air," a ballad-like description of a signpost in the form of a man with his arms pointing in opposite directions: right, toward the valleys of sloth, escapism, decay, the past; left, toward the mountains of duty, effort, freedom, the "living dawn." The "skyward man" in his attitude of crucifixion offers choice to the travelers seeking direction but he cannot himself join them on their way:

That cannot be till two agree
Who long have lain apart
Traveller, know, I am here to show
Your own divided heart.[104]

The theme of division is treated at greatest length, although not to best effect, in the verse morality play, *Noah and the Waters.*[105] The epigraph is the passage from the Communist Manifesto about the farsighted bourgeois who break away to join the party of the future. Noah symbolizes the bourgeois intellectual uncertain whether to join the Burgesses in their efforts to stop the coming Flood, the wave of the future, or to join the Flood. Two Voices, apparently Eros and Thanatos, offer him counsels respectively of hope and despair as the past and the future, heir and ancestor, contend for his allegiance.

The Burgesses bluster about the "criminal and alien degenerate" rain that has come to corrupt "pure stay-at-home English waters."

[103] *Ibid.*, p. 12.
[104] *Ibid.*, p. 24.
[105] This play appears in *ibid.*, pp. 97–145.

They plead for compromise with the Waters: "Let 'each for the other and all for the school' be our motto," since their interests and those of the waters are really the same.[106] They appeal to Noah's old loyalties, "The little brown jug and the thin red line/ . . . prayers at our mother's knee/ . . . Fireworks at the mortgaged country seat." They warn him that the Flood will level "all to plumb monotony" with no respect for the "subtle whorls of the solitary conscience/ For country house cricket or the classic style."[107]

The Voices in the Flood reply to the Burgesses: they have not been corrupted by foreign elements, since "all waters [are] our brothers"; compromise is impossible with the Burgesses, whose "profit is our loss [and whose] life is our death/ . . . Only the dying make terms with decay." When the Burgesses threaten to call in foreign intervention, the Waters respond, "Waters of the World, unite!"[108]

Noah elects to join the Flood, and his own Voices offer him animal companions symbolizing the virtues he will need. Among these are the single-minded gannet, which can dive "deep to take the moral" where the moral may be obscure, and the sheepdog, who is apparently Marxist doctrine, "The directed wisdom,/ The controlled initiative,/ The heart-felt system."[109] As Noah and the Waters drive the Burgesses offstage, the Chorus tells us the future is uncertain, but if Noah and the Waters maintain their "stern and rhythmic assault" on the Burgesses' hearts of stone, they will yet discover "a land greener, more great with growth and ease/ Than dreams dared imagine," where Noah will delight to "live among these/ Who shared his exile, to work with, to have for enduring fellows/ All rivers, rains, and seas."[110]

This morality play has a faint similarity to Auden's *Dance of Death* except that here there is no question of the author's dead seriousness; hence its effect of solemn caricature, too crude to be taken to heart yet obviously meant to be so taken. Despite some mildly funny passages, the play is an artistic error, and the realization of this, encouraged by bad reviews, was important in Day Lewis' decision that his poetry was deteriorating through his concentration on politics and

106 Cf. the Rev. Hamlet's speech in *The Wild Goose Chase,* Chapter IV.
107 Day Lewis, *A Time to Dance,* pp. 118–133.
108 *Ibid.*
109 *Ibid.,* p. 140.
110 *Ibid.,* pp. 144–145.

that he would do better to leave the Party and give more attention to being a poet.

Although Day Lewis' work during the years of the Spanish Civil War was uneven at best, the sheer quantity of it inspires a certain respect for his energy and devotion. From 1935 on, he produced one Nicholas Blake mystery a year to keep the pot boiling;[111] he also wrote two novels under his own name, both conventional, competent, and not very interesting; he edited *The Mind in Chains,* wrote articles and reviews for various periodicals, and carried on vigorous polemics in the Letters columns; he attended conferences and addressed meetings despite a native shyness; he boned up earnestly on Marxist texts for his "political education" duties in the Party;[112] and he composed two sizable volumes of poetry and a verse play.

Probably Day Lewis' most valuable contribution to the cause of the Spanish Republic was his poem "The Nabara," published in the 1938 *Overtures to Death.* He had wanted to join the International Brigades but, as he says with the candor that generally characterizes his autobiography, lacked the nerve. The hero of his novel *Starting Point* takes this action symbolically for him. Whether his possibly dying in Spain would have been more useful to the Republic than his writing this excellent poem is very doubtful.

"The Nabara," based on G. L. Steer's story in *The Tree of Gernika* of the sea battle between a small Basque trawler and a Nationalist cruiser, is heroic narrative verse of a high order. It can hardly have failed to gain sympathy for the Republican cause, which was its immediate purpose; beyond that, it stands comparison with the best narrative poems in English. Day Lewis has written of his "susceptibility to the heroic"; in this poem he achieves the delicate and difficult—difficult particularly in a period when the heroic tended to be associated with the Fascist—task of sustaining a lofty and solemn rhetoric without inflation or embarrassment. The events of the battle are described with color, suspense, and force, and the moral is stated with considerable nobility:

[111] John Strachey considered Nicholas Blake a better writer than C. Day Lewis (quoted in Kunitz and Haycraft, eds., *Twentieth Century Authors,* p. 359).

[112] He describes his lecturing on Marxism to real workers as a "signal instance of the blind leading the short-sighted" (*Buried Day,* p. 215).

Freedom is more than a word, more than the base coinage
Of statesmen, the tyrant's dishonoured cheque, or the
dreamer's mad
Inflated currency. She is mortal, we know, and made
In the image of simple men who have no taste for carnage
But sooner kill and are killed than see that image betrayed.
Mortal she is, yet rising always refreshed from her ashes:
She is bound to earth, yet she flies as high as a passage
bird
To home wherever man's heart with seasonal warmth is stirred:
Innocent is her touch as the dawn's, but still it unleashes
The ravisher shades of envy. Freedom is more than a word.[113]

The fact, which the poet later recognized, that "freedom" was as much "base coinage" for the Party to which he had committed himself as for the Non-Intervention statesmen he attacks in this poem does not detract from the effectiveness of his celebration of those who did indeed live their beliefs.

Day Lewis essayed, and in "The Nabara" achieved, the heroic; and Auden managed it, too, in his different way; but Stephen Spender never really made the effort in his poems about Spain, despite his obsessive devotion to the Loyalist cause. Of this obsession he later wrote that the "public emotion which had become a private one . . . invaded my personality rather than sprang out of it."[114] He worked tirelessly for the Republic. Never greatly tempted by the idea of combat, he worked furiously behind the lines. It was certainly Spender whom Cockburn had most sharply in mind when he sneered at the "intellectually photogenic" Communists whose privileged position so irritated the rank and file.[115] Everyone's picture of the poet—so young, so tall and slim, with his mass of curls topping a face that looked much more like Shelley's than any disappointing contemporary portrait—Spender was in great demand at rallies and public meetings and the innumerable writers congresses of the period, and he earnestly did his bit. His account in *World Within World* of all these activities captures both their idealistic and their comic aspects.

[113] Day Lewis, *Collected Poems 1929–1954*, p. 191.

[114] Spender, *World Within World*, p. 173.

[115] Claud Cockburn, *In Time of Trouble: An Autobiography*, p. 239. See Chapter III.

Yet when he wrote poems about Spain, Spender was stubbornly true to his own feelings, and these were far from the militant ardor conveyed in the revolutionary poems of his 1933 volume. He was in Spain for fairly lengthy visits at least twice during the war, and what he saw there did not stimulate him to heroics; on the contrary, he wrote angrily from Barcelona:

The dead in wars are not heroes: they are freezing or rotting lumps of isolated insanity . . . to say those who happen to be killed are heroic is a wicked attempt to identify the dead with the abstract ideas which have brought them to the front, thus adding prestige to those ideas, which are used to lead the living to similar "heroic" deaths . . . not the least of [war's] crimes is the propaganda which turns men into heroes.[116]

Spender was sickened by the reality of war and startled to discover the paucity of "undivided hearts" among the English volunteers of the International Brigades and the extent of ignorance of the issues among the soldiers of both sides. He was also deeply distressed by the ability of Communists and fellow travelers in Spain and in England to overlook or condone distortions of the truth by their side, and he was quite unable to share the spirit in which his friend Edward Upward could say of the Moscow trials, "What trials? I've given up thinking of such things long ago."[117]

To paraphrase his own youthful poem, what he expected of the Spanish War was "Some brightness/ To hold in trust,/ Some final innocence/ To save from dust"; what he saw in it was "the gradual day/ Weakening the will/ Leaking the brightness away."[118] Not all the brightness leaked away: still in 1939 he could quote Keats on Peterloo in reference to Spain—"No contest between Whig and Tory—but between Right and Wrong."[119] But in explaining why he did not "strike a more heroic note" in his Spanish poems, he insisted "that a poet can write only about what is true to his own experience, not about what he would like to be true to his experience."[120] The truth of

[116] Stephen Spender, "Heroes in Spain," *New Statesman and Nation,* XIII, 323 N.S. (May 1, 1937), 715.

[117] Spender, *World Within World,* p. 225.

[118] Spender, "What I Expected," in *Poems,* p. 25.

[119] Stephen Spender, Introduction, *Poems for Spain,* ed. Stephen Spender and John Lehmann, p. 9.

[120] Spender, Foreword, *Ruins and Visions: Poems 1934–1942,* p. 11.

Spender's experience was that all he could write about Spain was "the pity of war."

In only two of the ten poems about Spain is any villain but war itself apparent. The subjects are the dead, the defeated, the frightened; he offers no heroes. One would not expect to find in Spender the kind of glorification of the gallant dead that appears in *Flowering Rifle* or even "The Nabara," but "War Photograph," "A Stopwatch and an Ordnance Map," and "Ultima Ratio Regum" lack even the degree of heroic spirit that is conveyed in Auden's sonnet on the dead Chinese. "Ultima Ratio Regum," like that sonnet, describes an unknown, insignificant soldier killed in a cause he did not comprehend; but there is no suggestion that his death has any meaning or value at all:

> The guns spell money's ultimate reason
> In letters of lead on the spring hillside.
> But the boy lying dead under the olive trees
> Was too young and too silly
> To have been notable to their important eye.
> . . . .
> Consider his life which was valueless
> In terms of employment, hotel ledgers, news files.
> Consider. One bullet in ten thousand kills a man.
> Ask. Was so much expenditure justified
> On the death of one so young and so silly
> Lying under the olive trees, O world, O death?[121]

There is some anger directed specifically toward the enemy, as in "The Fall of a City," a description of a city captured by the forces of reaction:

> All the lessons learned, unlearnt;
> The young, who learned to read, now blind
> Their eyes with an archaic film;
> The peasant relapses to a stumbling tune
> Following the donkey's bray;
> These only remember to forget.[122]

Typically, the reference to the Nationalists is in the secondary meanings of "archaic film" and "donkey's bray," not in explicit statement

[121] Spender, *Ruins and Visions,* p. 43.
[122] *Ibid.*, p. 49.

like the last lines of "Ultima Ratio Regum." Again, political issues appear in the closing stanza of "At Castellon," in which Nationalist bombers are seen unloading

Cargoes of iron and of fire
To delete with blood and ire
The will of those who dared to move
From the furrow, their life's groove.[123]

"The Bombed Happiness," which employs with painful effectiveness almost surrealist images to describe children caught in an air raid, places the responsibility for the suffering firmly upon the enemy, but the tone is less angry than pathetic:

The bomb's victoried drumming enters
Above the limbs of bombed laughter
The body of an expanding State
And throbs there and makes it great
But nothing can recall
Gaiety buried under these dead years,
Sweet jester and youth playing fool
Whose toy was human happiness.[124]

The least militant of all the poems is "Two Armies," which describes the opposing forces dug in on a winter plain "to destroy each other." They are seen as kept in their lines only by the habit of discipline,

Yet when they sleep, the images of home
Ride wishing horses of escape
Which herd the plain in a mass unspoken poem.
Finally, they cease to hate: for
. . . .
who can connect
The inexhaustible anger of the guns
With the dumb patience of these tormented animals?
Clean silence drops at night when a little walk
Divides the sleeping armies. . . .
When the machines are stilled, a common suffering
Whitens the air with breath and makes both one
As though these enemies slept in each other's arms.[125]

[123] *Ibid.*, p. 52.
[124] *Ibid.*, p. 53.
[125] *Ibid.*, pp. 41–42.

Cyril Connolly produced a massive understatement when he referred to "Mr. Spender's not very martial muse";[126] no absolute pacifist wrote more convincing antiwar poems during the thirties than this fervent apologist for collective security.

One of Spender's last services to the Spanish Republican cause was to assemble with John Lehmann the anthology *Poems for Spain.* By the time it was published in 1939 it was a kind of memorial volume, for the cause was clearly lost. In his introduction, Spender describes the Spanish War as "a heroic and tragic spectacle" in which the fall of the Republic represented "the real and entire destruction of a life and a principle by the death-bearing force that opposes them," and thus a fit subject for poetry.[127]

The selection he and Lehmann made from the vast body of verse bearing on the war is on a notably high level of technical competence, however derivative some of the poems seem. There is a sizable group of Spanish poems in translation, but most of the contributors are British, chiefly from the Orthodox Left. The triumvirate is represented, Auden by "Spain 1937," Spender by four poems (not including "Two Armies"), and Day Lewis by his "Bombers," which is not as good as "The Nabara" but better for inclusion because shorter. A section from MacNeice's *Autumn Journal* is excerpted.

The anthology has a section devoted to satire which is rather disappointing, but then it was hard for most pro-Loyalists to be very funny about the war. Most of the pieces included are rather heavy-handed, none of them any better than and not many as good as the brief occasional verses "Sagittarius" (Mrs. Hugh Miller) regularly published in the *New Statesman and Nation* as a running commentary on events throughout the period. The chief interest in this section is in the proof offered by the Chilean Pablo Neruda's "Almería" that a pro-Loyalist poet could match Roy Campbell in sheer bloodiness.

There is another section devoted to poems about García Lorca. Spender was to object later, in *World Within World,* to the way Communists claimed as a martyr to their cause this Catholic and traditional poet whom they would have attacked as a reactionary but for the accident of his murder by Fascists.[128] The laments Spender and Leh-

[126] Cyril Connolly, "Today the Struggle," *New Statesman and Nation,* XIII, No. 328 N.S. (June 5, 1937), 926.

[127] Spender, Introduction, *Poems for Spain,* p. 9.

[128] Spender, *World Within World,* p. 227.

mann selected for this volume mourn Lorca as a poet rather than as a revolutionary.

Thirty-one poets are represented in the anthology, some by several poems, and there is considerable variety in both style and attitude. Some, like Ruthven Todd's "Poem for Joan Miró," T. A. R. Hyndman's "Jarama Front," Sylvia Townsend Warner's two brief lyrics, and Herbert Read's "Bombing Casualties," are as nonideological as Spender's. Read's "The Heart Conscripted" tells of his having given up "the ulcer of poetic pride/ . . . the owl's indifferent mood" to join the Republican cause largely because "Lorca was killed, singing,/ And Fox, who was my friend."[129] The very unOrthodox Read also contributed "A Song for the Spanish Anarchists."

Truly fire-eating verse is rare in this anthology, not surprisingly in view of the debunking war had received during the previous fifteen years. John Cornford comes closest, and it must be remembered that he wrote his poems early in the war and was killed before he could see any of the "brightness leaking away." At eighteen he had already proven himself so brilliant and efficient as a Communist organizer at Cambridge that he was head of the Federation of Socialist Societies, and at the time of his death only three years later he had become a kind of symbol of youthful communism. He was mourned for his political as well as for his poetic promise, and his admirers wondered at the skill with which he managed to write verse at once aesthetically pleasing and ideologically correct. "Full Moon at Tierz: Before the Storming of Huesca" is both of these. Beginning with the proclamation that "We are the future" who will "swing [history] to its final course," Cornford celebrates the rapid growth of Communist forces:

> Three years Dimitrov[130] fought alone
> And we stood taller when he won.
> But now the Leipzig dragon's teeth
> Sprout strong and handsome against death
> And here an army fights where there was one.

It is curious to see Wilfred Owen's poetic innovations put to such militant purposes. After naming other heroes, Cornford tells how,

[129] Herbert Read, "The Heart Conscripted," *Poems for Spain*, p. 40.

[130] Dimitrov was the Bulgarian-born leader of the German Communists whose trial for alleged complicity in the Reichstag Fire proved to be a major propaganda blunder for the Nazis.

for him as for many others, communism offered an escape from—or better, a transcendence of—his personal problems:

Then let my private battle with my nerves,
The fear of pain whose pain survives,
The love that tears me by the roots,
The loneliness that claws my guts,
Fuse in the welded front our fight preserves.

Asserting that the International Brigades are fighting as much for England and for anti-Nazi resistance in Germany as for Spain, he closes triumphantly:

Freedom is an easily spoken word
But facts are stubborn things. Here, too, in Spain
Our fight's not won till all the workers in all the world
Stand by our guard on Huesca's plain,
Swear that our dead fought not in vain,
Raise the red flag triumphantly
For Communism and for liberty.[131]

This and the other poems Cornford wrote are all very promising, although it is doubtful whether they would have been so highly praised if they had not been dignified by his death. They do have, as Symons observes, a "sort of eager innocence" and "an exquisite simplicity of feeling" that is rare in the works of those who lived to see more of the war.

T. H. Wintringham's poems also convey intense conviction, but what is likely to strike the student of the Spanish War as most remarkable about them is the rather elegant artfulness of these lyrics written literally under fire by the tough Brigade Commander. "Granien" gracefully opposes those "who are in love with death" to those who love life. Wintringham, describing a doctor operating in a field hospital by the light of a flashlight, contends,

Our enemies can praise death and adore death;
For us endurance, the sun; and now in this night
The electric torch, feeble, waning, but close-set
Follows the surgeon's fingers; we are allied with
This light.[132]

[131] John Cornford, "Full Moon at Tierz: Before the Storming of Huesca," in *Poems for Spain*, pp. 27–29.

[132] T. H. Wintringham, "Granien," in *ibid.*, p. 41.

Wintringham's poems and many of the others written either by actual participants in the fighting or by close observers have considerable "immediacy," but perhaps the bulk of the verse in *Poems for Spain* expresses the feelings of sympathetic outsiders, awed by the courage and endurance of the fighters, guilty about their own safety, and indignant over the policies of the British government. Margot Heinemann protests, "One nation cannot save the world forever."[133] Edgell Rickword, addressing himself "To the Wife of Any Non-Intervention Statesman," denounces her husband as a blood-soaked hypocrite.[134] Brian Howard implores "Those with Investments in Spain: 1937" to think less of their money and "spare a thought . . . for a people in danger."[135] Rex Warner rages with his customary vigor against "Arms in Spain":

> So that the drunken General and the Christian millionaire
> might continue blindly to rule in complete darkness,
> that on rape and ruin order might be founded firm,
> these guns were sent to save civilization . . .
> and to root out reason, lest hope be held in it . . .
> these guns, these tanks, these gentlemanly words.[136]

Warner's "The Tourist Looks at Spain" is perhaps the best of the large number of poems stressing the "indivisibility of freedom." It begins, "Spain has torn the veil of Europe," and ends:

> See Spain and see the world. Freedom extends
> or contracts in all hearts.
> Near Bilbao are buried the vanguard of our army.
> It is us too they defended who defended Madrid.[137]

On the whole, *Poems for Spain* stands as a fine, if futile, tribute to a cause that engaged the hearts and consciences of a great many talented Englishmen. In its reflection of the variety of responses to the sad and stirring events in Spain, it is probably the best single

133 Margot Heinemann, "The New Offensive (Ebro, 1938)," in *ibid.*, p. 25.

134 Edgell Rickword, "To the Wife of Any Non-Intervention Statesman," in *ibid.*, pp. 74–76.

135 Brian Howard, "Those with Investments in Spain: 1937," in *ibid.*, pp. 77–78.

136 Rex Warner, "Arms in Spain," in *ibid.*, p. 50.

137 Rex Warner, "The Tourist Looks at Spain," in *ibid.*, p. 69.

volume for reference. There were many poems inspired by the war which were not included, but most of the best are there.

One extremely interesting poem about the war which was excluded, probably because of its length, is *Calamiterror* by George Barker, who is represented in *Poems for Spain* by a good sonnet, "O Hero Akimbo." *Calamiterror* is more ambitious, however, and it is of particular interest for this study because it is a very different kind of poetry from that of the Auden school which is generally associated with political and social comment. Barker's masters are the Surrealists and Dylan Thomas. Thomas called himself a Communist,[138] and the Surrealists, like their French counterparts, professed revolutionary politics, but their poetic principles precluded political verse; hence their omission from this study. The curious thing about *Calamiterror,* which appeared in 1937, is that it employs Thomas' back-to-the-womb approach and surrealistic imagery to offer the same kind of message that is to be found in the more rational and colloquial poems of the Auden imitators.

Calamiterror is often obscure and confusing in detail, but its theme is easy enough to follow. In Francis Scarfe's words, it works through some fifty-odd pages "towards an immense deliverance, a delivery, as it were, from the womb of self into a universal sympathy."[139] The chief midwives are "three women weeping in Irun's ruins," who reappear at intervals and help the laboring poet to achieve an apocalyptic vision. Finally, "On Sunday the 12th April . . . over the Thames at Sonning," he saw "William Blake large and bright like ambition. . . ./ His soul like a cinema in each of his eyes,/ And Swedenborg labouring like a dream in his stomach./ . . . And saw myself the minor bird on the bough."[140] In a mystic trance he hears

[138] Thomas told Augustus John that he had joined the Party but left it upon being directed to write propaganda verse (William Y. Tindall, *A Reader's Guide to Dylan Thomas,* p. 50). Tindall's readings of two of Thomas' 1934 poems, "Our eunuch dreams . . ." and "All all and all . . .," convincingly suggest Marxist revolutionary meanings among the many, but certainly neither of these poems nor the broadly political but nonpartisan "The hand that signed the paper . . ." (1936) resembles propaganda verse as the Orthodox Left understood it. Thomas' political ideas seem to have had very little effect upon his poetry.

[139] Scarfe, *Auden and After,* p. 127.

[140] George Barker, *Calamiterror,* p. 38.

"the ancestral voice" prophesying war, the "air like newsboys shrieking/ Instances of insult, aggravation,"

> I met seven saints in Salisbury with cotton wool
>   in their ears,
> I remembered with shame my own music.
> The splitting of the central pillar like aural lightning,
> I felt it crack my abdomen, the world.[141]

He feels himself "embroiled like/ The Egyptian corpse in images of self./ . . . I scratch the itch of self to make it swell." But "the bird at my eyelids [is] beating to awaken/ The free and easy fellow in me"; and soon "like the phoenix snake from beetle skin/ I feel the free one in me move." In the next stanza, the freed one has become the speaker, the self become "him" whose "corpse lies there": "But phoenix, beetle, snake, from his blood,/ I rose and felt the throes of Spain." Having through dream reached responsibility, the freed man now mourns his egotistic predecessor, "who made/ The myriad of human mean less than his one," but in his new freedom

>   How can he cease
> From political fight, how can his word sleep in his hand,
> When a dark time in a dark time
> Inundates and annihilates the mind?[142]

Now he sees the world in true perspective:

> London lies like a huge rot along the Thames, and Rome
> Roars. O Spain, my golden red, she tears rot out
> The Franco gangs that furrow in her heart. See how
>   she stands,
> Her Madrid middle growing vague with ravage,
> Laboring to let out liberty, with the rat and the rot
>   at her heart.[143]

The poem ends with the poet fully identified with humanity and committed to struggle for its survival.

>   And my mother world, with bomb holes in her bosom,
> Goes gradually on, with the myriad of me at her breast.[144]

[141] *Ibid.*, p. 39.
[142] *Ibid.*, pp. 49–50.
[143] *Ibid.*, p. 51.
[144] *Ibid.*, p. 53.

Scarfe considers *Calamiterror* "with all its faults, . . . perhaps the most successful long poem of the 'thirties' . . . of all the poems bearing on the Spanish war, [it] will stand with the highest, next to Auden's 'Spain' and not below it."[145] *Calamiterror* may be somewhat overlong for some tastes: Barker's constant fortissimo tends to lose its compelling power as the pages pass; yet virtually any randomly chosen short passage is moving and exciting. Comparison with "Spain 1937" is difficult and probably fruitless, but the two poems do well as companion pieces, the most outward and the most inward of poems on the Spanish War.

For a final look at the debacle of the Thirties movement, three poems from the Auden group will serve. Louis MacNeice's *Autumn Journal* of 1938 captures the spirit of gloom over Munich and the last flickering of hope for Spain. This poem, which runs to fifty-six pages in the *Collected Poems*, is rather neglected today because of its length and its topicality, but for all its discursiveness and occasional longeurs, it is a remarkably intelligent, graceful, and perceptive meditation on the feelings of a skeptical and humane classics don as he watches his world fall apart.

Spain is central to the poem. An early passage (printed in *Poems for Spain*) recalls MacNeice's visit there at Easter in 1936, when Spain was "ripe as an egg for revolt and ruin," but the tourist did not realize

> That Spain would soon denote
> Our grief, our aspirations;
> Not knowing that our blunt
> Ideals would find their whetstone, that our spirit
> Would find its frontier on the Spanish front,
> Its body in a rag-tag army.[146]

MacNeice speaks here as an unattached liberal; for his Communist and fellow-traveling friends, Spain found their ideals very sharp indeed and left them badly blunted. Symons has commented on the "double, and contradictory, process" by which, in the course of the Spanish War, once militant men like Auden and Isherwood turned increasingly away from "political attachments" toward the "political

[145] Scarfe, *Auden and After*, pp. 127–128.
[146] MacNeice, *Collected Poems*, pp. 130, 132.

quietism" of E. M. Forster, while the individualistic and detached MacNeice and others like him came to regard their earlier aloofness with shame and to see fascism as "a threat before which all individualism must seem finicky."[147]

MacNeice describes his reaction to the Munich agreement:

once again
The crisis is put off and things look better
And we feel negotiation is not vain—
Save my skin and damn my conscience.
And negotiation wins,
If you can call it winning,
And here we are—just as before—safe in our skins;
Glory to God for Munich.
And stocks go up and wrecks
Are salved and politicians' reputations
Go up like Jack-on-the-beanstalk; only the Czechs
Go down and without fighting.[148]

But his lost confidence in human courage and decency is restored by a visit to Barcelona just before New Year's 1939:

Though the old order is gone and the golden calf
Of Catalan industry shattered;
The human values remain, purged in the fire,
And it appears that every man's desire
Is life rather than victuals.
Life being more, it seems, than merely the bare
Permission to keep alive and receive orders.
. . . .
For here and now the new valkyries ride
. . . .
To maim or blind or kill
The bearers of the living will,
The stubborn heirs of freedom
Whose matter-of-fact faith and courage shame
Our niggling equivocations—
We who play for safety,
A safety only in name.

147 Symons, *The Thirties*, pp. 160–161.
148 MacNeice, *Collected Poems*, p. 137.

Whereas these people contain truth, whatever
Their nominal facade.
Listen: a whirr, a challenge, an aubade—
It is the cock crowing in Barcelona.[149]

The poem closes on a note of decision:

Tonight we sleep
On the banks of the Rubicon—the die is cast;
There will be time to audit
The accounts later, there will be sunlight later
And the equation will come out at last.[150]

MacNeice was to stand by his decision. Like Auden and Isherwood, he went to the United States in 1939 with the intention of settling there, but, although a citizen of neutral Ireland, he returned to England in 1940 to volunteer for military service.

Auden was in New York when World War II came, and he wrote the epitaph of the "low, dishonest decade" just ending, in his "September 1, 1939":

Into this neutral air
Where blind skyscrapers use
Their full height to proclaim
The strength of Collective Man,
Each language pours its vain
Competitive excuse:
But who can live for long
In an euphoric dream;
Out of the mirror they stare,
Imperialism's face
And the international wrong.[151]

He looks gloomily at himself and his contemporaries,

Lost in a haunted wood,
Children afraid of the night
Who have never been happy or good.

[149] *Ibid.*, pp. 170–173. The American correspondent Vincent Sheean also speaks of going back to Spain after Munich and there finding hope in the continuing resistance of the Loyalists, "the force of light struggling against the turbulent onrush of the engulfing dark" (*Not Peace But a Sword*, p. 341).

[150] MacNeice, *Collected Poems*, p. 175.

[151] Auden, *Collected Poetry*, p. 57.

Pursuing his theme that "international wrong" is the reflection of individual failures of love, he wonders, "Who can reach the deaf?/ Who can speak for the dumb?" And he replies:

All I have is a voice
To undo the folded lie,
The romantic lie in the brain
Of the sensual man-in-the-street
And the lie of Authority
Whose buildings grope the sky;
There is no such thing as the State
And no one exists alone;
Hunger allows no choice
To the citizen or the police;
We must love one another or die.[152]

Defenseless under the night
Our world in stupor lies;
Yet, dotted everywhere,
Ironic points of light
Flash out wherever the Just
Exchange their messages:
May I, composed like them
Of Eros and of dust
Beleaguered by the same
Negation and despair
Show an affirming flame.[153]

As Europe descended into war, the ardent if sometimes absurd idealists of the Left went into exile or uniform. As Spender wrote, they had already lost their battle, "a battle against totalitarian war, which could have made the war unnecessary."[154] During the war that followed, there were some who felt the lack of poems celebrating the struggle, poems that would treat war as terrible but ultimately noble and valuable—the kind of poems that Cornford, Wintringham, Day Lewis, and some others had written about the Spanish conflict. To the question, "Where are the war poets?" the wit replied, "Killed in

[152] Auden dropped this stanza in his 1945 edition, but the entire poem as written is printed in Oscar Williams, ed., *A Little Treasury of Modern Poetry*, pp. 703–706.

[153] Auden, *Collected Poetry*, p. 59.

[154] Spender, *World Within World*, p. 238.

Spain."[155] A better answer, and one suitable to end a chaper, was made by Day Lewis. Disillusioned, but unrepentant and unreconciled, he spoke his scorn for those who had, he felt, brought on the war and were now asking for poetic celebration of it. "It is the logic of our times," he observes, "That we who lived by honest dreams/ Defend the bad against the worse."[156]

[155] Symons, *The Thirties,* p. 136.
[156] Day Lewis, "Where Are the War Poets?" in *Collected Poems,* p. 228.

Chapter VII

CONCLUSIONS

The questions that arise about the politically oriented writings of the later thirties are, first, what effect if any they may have had upon the events they were intended to shape, and, second, what effect this venture into politics had upon the authors of these works.

It can be said of the right-wing writers here considered that they won in the short run and lost in the long run. The British government did not, as they wished it to, overtly support the Spanish Nationalist cause, but its policies were instrumental in assuring the Nationalist victory. Most of the writers discussed in Chapter II must have shared the satisfaction with the outcome of the Spanish War and with British policy toward Spain which was expressed in the London *Times* leader of May 29, 1939:

> It does not seem unreasonable to hope that in the new Spain the name of Great Britain will be accorded a respect forfeited by those Powers that associated themselves with the fallen regime, and perhaps an affection not easily retained by those who presume too far upon the assistance they have given the victors. Hard things are always spoken of neutrals while war rages, but an honourable and consistent neutrality comes to be appreciated when peace is won.

The satisfaction of pro-Nationalists was short-lived. Within a few months they found themselves supporting war against the very powers whose intervention in Spain they had defended and, in most cases, applauded. They do not appear to have been deeply discomfited by this rather sudden shift in alliances, however, and in looking back on the Spanish War they tend to stress their anti-Communist motives rather than their temporary collaboration with fascism. Since for most of them the second sprang from the first, this emphasis cannot be called incorrect. Wyndham Lewis was alone—as he often was—in completely repudiating his political attitudes of the thirties. Within a few years the pro-Nationalists in England were forced to take what poor comfort they could find in recalling their early recognition of the evils of communism, since the elections of 1945 brought into power in their own country the very forces of social democracy which they had rejoiced in seeing suppressed in Spain.

As for the pro-Loyalists, their short-run defeat was almost total. The Spanish Republic was destroyed, and the anti-Fascist propaganda effort, of which support for the Republic was only a part, failed to achieve any stiffening of British resistance to Fascist aggression until it was very nearly too late—if indeed their efforts played any significant part in the Government's final decision to honor its pledges. The British public may have been the more ready for war because of the writings of the anti-Fascists during the previous several years; but history indicates that governments rarely have any difficulty arousing hatred of the enemy, and the prewar propaganda might well have been dispensed with on this score. Of course those works that attacked fascism abroad without strongly implying the existence of Fascist tendencies within Britain were grist to the wartime propaganda mill and reached much larger audiences than they had during the best days of the Popular Front. The entrance of Russia into the war made possible a revival of Popular Front spirit, different from but comparable to that of the thirties.

The real effectiveness of leftist propaganda was long-run. It hardly seems possible that the Labour party victory of 1945 was not due in large part to the writings of the Thirties movement. For the British electorate to abandon in overwhelming numbers the party of their wartime leader and hero Churchill in favor of socialism argues wide public acceptance of the criticism of capitalism and the praise of socialism offered by the Left during the years before the war. Symons has noted that the Pragmatists of his Pyramid were to become the makers and shapers of the postwar Welfare State; they were able to take along with them a great part of the Audience and of the masses, and for this much credit must go to the Artists. If the Left had failed wretchedly in 1936–1939, it had largely succeeded in 1945.

"Largely" is an important qualification. The Welfare State, at least so far, is a long way from the "new country" sung in the thirties—it is also a long way from the ugly realities of British life during the thirties—but by the end of that decade most of the proponents of total revolution had ceased to believe in either the possibility or the desirability of such drastic reorganization of society. Since the war, the revolutionary intellectuals of the thirties have largely been reabsorbed in the Labour party and many have become full members of the Establishment: it is symbolic that both Auden and Day Lewis have been Professor of Poetry at Oxford and that Day Lewis was named Poet Laureate in 1968.

British leftist intellectuals have been spared the anti-Communist hysteria that forced many of their American counterparts into orgies of self-humiliation and repudiation of all they strove for during the thirties. None of them, apparently, has undergone the violent revulsion of some American ex-Communists who simply turned their former attitudes inside-out and became as fanatical against communism as they had once been for it. Even in America, Auden and Isherwood continue active in "liberal causes," which is about as close as they can come in this country to the moderate social democracy of their former associates in Britain.

When veterans of the Thirties movement write of that period, they sometimes express shame for their credulity and self-deception about Russia and the Communist Party and for their intemperance and intolerance toward those who did not share their beliefs, and they may stress the comic aspects of their activities in the thirties; but the dominant tone in their reminiscences is of regret and nostalgia, melancholy not bitter. "We were singularly fortunate, compared with the young of today," wrote Day Lewis in 1960, "in believing that something could be done about the social and political evils confronting us. Had we seen all avenues blocked by mushroom-shaped spectres, we might well have thrown in our hands."[1]

What former members of the Orthodox Left most regretted losing was the hopefulness and single-mindedness made possible by the

[1] Cecil Day Lewis, *The Buried Day*, pp. 208–209.

"radiant . . . illusion that man could, under Communism, put the world to rights."[2] By the end of the thirties, most had concluded that the world was not going to be put to rights, under communism or otherwise. The confidence in their ability readily to distinguish the sheep from the goats had also vanished to be replaced by a growing suspicion that mankind could not be so easily categorized, and the war did nothing to revive their earlier assurance.

The worst fears of the leftists were not realized: they had supposed that world war could only end in the total destruction of freedom in all nations that took part; instead, they saw a large part of their program put into effect in England by democratic elections, quite free of violence or disorder. On the other hand, they had not foreseen the "mushroom-shaped spectres" blocking the avenues to the brave new world of which they had dreamed.

If the survivors of the Thirties movement recall some of their attitudes and behavior with shame and regret, they do not regret or repudiate their motives and hopes. The Right might take pride in having "seen through" communism, but the Left could point to the abundant justification of their antifascism demonstrated during and after the war. Julian Symons expresses the attitude of many of his contemporaries:

> Behind the Thirties movement . . . were the most generous impulses of humanity, impulses more valuable by far than the barren knowingness of the Fifties. It is better to be waiting for Lefty than to be waiting for Godot.[3]

The question remains, if their experience in politics left most of the writers of the thirties sadder and wiser men, did it have any appreciable effect upon them as artists? The question would be easier to answer if this group of writers had already established a direction of development before they became interested in politics; then their excursion into politics could be seen as a departure to be reversed, and each writer's work during the thirties could be considered in the light of his work before and after that period. For most of the writers of this study, this comparative approach is not possible since their political period was also their formative period as artists. Concern over the ills of society and what must be done to cure them is a major theme in their work from the beginning, and their political ideas are

[2] *Ibid.*, p. 211.

[3] Julian Symons, *The Thirties: A Dream Revolved*, p. 52.

of central importance in their development. During the years of the Spanish Civil War there were authors who wrote about politics in a brief burst of enthusiasm, or out of a sense that they ought to make some sort of comment on the exciting public events of their time, or simply in the realization that political verse and prose had become fashionable and marketable; but the writers considered here set the fashion. They were writing politically well before the Left Book Club gave them an audience, and they were doing so because they thought and felt in political terms.

Political writing is didactic by definition, and in the past century there have been plausible arguments that didacticism has no place in art. The proper esthetic emotion, Stephen Dedalus told his friends, is static; arts that incite action are improper arts.[4] The artist should cultivate an attitude of contemplative detachment toward the life about him, seeing it as material for his esthetic purposes; he may describe, express, interpret it, but any effort to change it is outside his function as an artist. From this point of view, any politically conceived work must appear an esthetic mistake whatever its incidental felicities.

This austerely esthetic attitude toward the purpose of art is a fairly recent development; the nineteenth century was well under way before artists ceased to feel they had to defend whatever in their work was *not* didactic. It is an attitude that has regularly characterized the thoroughly disaffected writer, the one who not only finds his world intolerable except as material for art but who despairs of its susceptibility to improvement. There has been much in twentieth-century life to disaffect a writer, and estheticism has had many gifted adherents. Nevertheless, the traditional view of the artist as prophet, teacher, and possible legislator of mankind has not been generally abandoned.

The belief that art can and should shape events may be stated as crudely as "Art is a weapon" or as subtly as in Christopher Caudwell's lengthy and sophisticated disquisition in *Illusion and Reality* on art as a mode of action. It traces its lineage back to the beginnings of literature and is as well exemplified by Dante and Milton as by Day Lewis. The basic assumption is that man and society can and should be improved and that the artist has a responsibility to employ his abilities toward that end. To paraphrase Marx, it is not enough to understand—or describe or express—life: the artist must try to change

[4] James Joyce, *A Portrait of the Artist as a Young Man*, p. 205.

it. Auden spoke, at least in the thirties, for this point of view. Without condemning "escape art," he valued more highly "parable art," of which the purpose is to "teach man to unlearn hatred and learn love."[5] If a writer is to set seriously about teaching, he must be fairly confident that his audience is teachable and that what he is going to teach them is true. During the thirties, most of the writers discussed here felt considerable certainty on both scores; the fact that they have written less didactically since does not demonstrate so much a change in attitude toward the function of art as the loss of certainty brought about by events at the end of the decade.

If we accept the propriety of didacticism in art—and to deny it is to remove from the category of art a good proportion of the literature of Western culture—the problem then arises of distinguishing between esthetically successful didacticism, which can be called "parable art," and unsuccessful didacticism, which can be called "propaganda." In 1935 Auden distinguished the two by suggesting that propaganda tells people what to do and art does not; rather art extends their knowledge of good and evil, perhaps stresses the urgency and clarifies the nature of right action, and leads them to the point at which they can "make a rational and moral choice."[6] The difference appears to be largely a matter of specificity: art does not present a program, but it can and should induce attitudes and emotions that will eventuate in action, not simply understanding. The end of art, as of propaganda, is action.

A reading of the politically activated works of the thirties affords support for Auden's distinction, but it suggests another factor in the difference between those works that offer only instruction or exhortation and those that give esthetic pleasure as well. The better poems, plays, and novels of the period have a richness and complexity that is often extraneous and sometimes even damaging to their didactic purposes, and they imply the working in their authors of other impulses than the didactic: the desire to express personal conflicts in artistic terms, for instance, and, perhaps even more important, the sheer delight in mastering the techniques of one's craft. The exuberant extravagance of *The Dog Beneath the Skin* or *The Wild Goose Chase* has little to do with the Marxist message for which they serve

[5] See Chapter V.
[6] See Chapter VI.

as vehicles. The ambiguities of *The Ascent of F6* enhance its literary interest as they confuse its presumed propaganda purpose. *The Revenge for Love* is less than successful as an argument against communism, but it is a fascinating examination of what politics can do to people. Louis MacNeice's *Autumn Journal* effectively argues that liberal anti-Fascists ought to join in concerted action, but the poem is still worth reading not for its lesson but for its graceful use of language and its portrait of a complicated and sympathetic man. Auden's "Spain" is a better poem than Rickword's "To the Wife of a Non-Intervention Statesman" not only because it is less specific, but also because it contains much that has little directly to do with the necessity for a change in British foreign policy. From the standpoint of propaganda, all these added dividends of pleasure could be justified as sugarcoating to make a message more palatable; but on a longer view it may seem that the best propaganda is good art, and for the artist, although the didactic impulse may perhaps be his original motivation, it cannot be his only one.

The sense that art must propagate ideas is congenial to some talents and less so to others. The gifted Edward Upward found that he could not continue writing at all as his political convictions told him he should write, and there may well have been other potentially good writers who were similarly inhibited. The masterful playwright Sean O'Casey, driven by political passion to write a work of pure propaganda, produced an artistic disaster; Roy Campbell's poetic gift was, at least temporarily, squandered in *Flowering Rifle*; much of Day Lewis' work as a Communist brought him nothing but esthetic remorse, and his best poems of the later thirties are the highly personal lyrics and "The Nabara," which is a paean to heroism that can be read without political context. Stephen Spender could write at the top of his bent when he dealt with the pity of war, but his attempt to present a propaganda message on the stage foundered at least partly because what his political beliefs demanded that he preach was in conflict with what he most deeply felt. He was later to characterize his "public emotion" during the thirties as having "invaded" rather than sprung out of his personality. The stale facility of Day Lewis' poorer work toward the end of the decade may well reflect a diminution into dutifulness of the Marxist enthusiasm that is fresh and vigorous in *The Magnetic Mountain.* It is this freshness and vitality that make Rex

Warner's first novel, however naïve, more thoroughly satisfying than his later, shapelier, more responsible books.

Auden, Isherwood (both in his collaborations with Auden and in his novellas),[7] and MacNeice were less subject to the kind of strain that appears sometimes in Spender and Day Lewis, perhaps because they were less deeply committed than their friends were to the necessity of making their writing serve the class struggle. Whatever effect their political concerns had upon their talents must have been beneficial because none of them has since surpassed the best work he did during the thirties.

On the evidence of the politically oriented writing of the thirties, no sweeping generalizations come to mind on the merits or demerits of political and social ideas as an impetus to literature. Much very bad writing was done during the period, but whether the proportion of bad to good books was any higher then than at any other time would require a vast and systematic study beyond the powers of a single scholar. Political passion demonstrably leads to oversimplification and overstatement, which are not usually more desirable in imaginative than in informational writing, but passion in itself can be very productive in art, and when political passion has become as fully internalized as it was in the better writers of the thirties, it can contribute heavily to whatever mysterious force engenders good art. The worst drawback to writing from political impetus is practical: when the political situation has changed, the works it inspired may lose much of their interest. If longevity is a criterion of artistic excellence, the writer who chooses to deal with contemporary social and political problems is taking a heavy risk. Some admirable products of the literary-political ferment of the thirties have already dwindled into quaintness.

But any writer takes a risk. There is no question that the authors considered in this study would have written, and written well, if they had begun their work at a point in history when politics was a less insistent influence. Whether they might have written better is a meaningless question. What they did write, we have: and it includes some fine poetry, some interesting if not entirely satisfactory plays, and a

[7] Isherwood's best work was in fiction, but since his province was Berlin and he was not given to general political statement in his stories, they have been omitted from consideration here.

few good novels. Compared with similar periods in this century, the thirties were less fruitful in literary achievement than the twenties, but the other decades do not look markedly better.

Viewed from a perspective of thirty years, the Thirties movement seems often misguided, purblind, even absurd, but also generous, humane, fresh, and hopeful. There has been nothing like it since in England, although in the United States a similar spirit may be seen in the young, and not so young, whites who have taken as their own the Negro cause, as the young bourgeois of 1932 took as their own the proletarian cause, in the name of freedom and justice. Whether the parallel will continue, in letters or in action, remains to be seen.

APPENDIX

The Issues of the Spanish War[1]

The Republic against which the Nationalist revolt was directed was still very new in 1936. It had come into being only five years before with the departure of Alfonso XIII in April, 1931, and the election of a Constituent Cortes two months later. The monarchy had been steadily losing popular support for some years. In 1923 the King had concurred in the institution of a military dictatorship under General Miguel Primo de Rivera, a move then welcomed by most Spaniards as necessary to combat the extreme chaos and disorder into which the nation had fallen. Primo enjoyed wide public backing for his first three years, during which he was able to conclude a costly and unpopular war in Morocco and, aided by unprecedented postwar prosperity, to achieve remarkable advances in modernizing and Europeanizing the country. Furthermore, the relative order that he maintained permitted the contending interests within the nation a short breathing spell that they utilized to prepare for further conflict. However, Primo, although a man of great energy and considerable good will, was unable to make the kind of economic improvements sought by his supporters

[1] I have relied chiefly on Gerald Brenan's *The Spanish Labyrinth* for information on Spain before the War, on Franz Borkenau's *The Spanish Cockpit* for detailed information about the Republic during the War, on Sir Robert Hodgson's *Spain Resurgent* for a representation of the Nationalist point of view, and on Hugh Thomas' *The Spanish Civil War* for the most nearly complete account of the War itself. Brenan and Borkenau are sympathetic to the Republic, Hodgson to the Nationalists, although all three achieve considerable objectivity. Thomas has had access to documents not available to the others and, perhaps because he was not in Spain during the War, as they were, his work has an impartiality rare among studies of this subject.

among the large industrialists because he was still more dependent upon the good will of the Church, the wealthy landowners, and the Army, all of whom were, for different reasons, deeply inimical to modernization. The rural and urban proletariat, who were sharing very little in the postwar prosperity and were putting their hopes in strongly political trade unions of conflicting ideology, generally socialist in central and northern Spain and anarcho-syndicalist in the east and south, had been nearly exhausted by the often bloody struggles of the previous decade, and they dissipated much of their force in battling each other; however, they were more or less united in opposition to the dictatorship.

Between these upper- and lower-class groups stood the Republicans, a rather small but active and articulate party made up largely of the lower middle class of the towns and strongly supported by many intellectuals and journalists. Like the leftist parties, the Republicans were antimonarchist and anticlerical, but they were also capitalist in their economic outlook. Although they approved of much of Primo's economic program, they grew increasingly restive as the dictator, probably against his personal inclinations, felt forced to take ever more repressive measures to secure his rule. Liberal intellectuals like Miguel de Unamuno, José Ortega y Gasset, and Pío Baroja protested as Primo discarded the constitution, curtailed freedom of speech, suppressed critical newspapers, and began arresting his critics. By January of 1930, the King found it necessary to replace Primo de Rivera, but he had taken full responsibility for the dictator's actions, and his efforts to continue in power through new civilian cabinets headed first by General Berenguer and then by Admiral Aznar merely added to popular discontent, which had been growing against Alfonso ever since a particularly disastrous military blunder in Morocco in 1921 that public opinion correctly attributed to the King's meddling.[2] Under pressure from the Republicans, the King finally called municipal elections. Although the rural districts, thanks to the traditional system of political bosses working for the local landowners (the caciques), voted monarchist,

[2] Alfonso, impatient with the slow progress of efforts to pacify the Berbers, had ordered a favorite general to disregard War Office instructions and march his column from Melilla to Alhucemas, arranging his arrival there to coincide with a speech the King planned to make on St. James Matamoros (Kill-Moors) Day, June 23. The column was ambushed. Ten thousand Spanish soldiers were killed, four thousand taken prisoner, and all their military supplies captured. Soon afterwards, and apparently as a result, seven thousand more Spaniards were massacred at another fortified position and their officers taken for ransom. Melilla was held only with great difficulty. It was widely believed that the institution of Primo's dictatorship was an attempt by the Army to cover up the King's responsibility for these military disasters (Brenan, *Spanish Labyrinth*, pp. 74–75, 82).

the cities voted so heavily Republican that Alfonso was forced to abdicate and go into exile.

The Constituent Cortes of the Second Republic, elected two months later, was dominated by the Left and Center. How far it reflected popular opinion in Spain was subject to much subsequent debate. Spanish elections had for a hundred years been notoriously corrupt, a fact that partly explains the scorn in which Anarchists and left-wing Socialists on the one hand and the Army on the other held such implementations of democracy. The official records of these June elections were never released.[3] Since the Anarchists, who probably represented the majority of working-class people in Catalonia and southwestern Spain, boycotted elections on principle, and the caciques guaranteed firm control by the anti-Republican landowners of much of the rural vote, it is fairly safe to conclude that popular sentiment for the Republic was even greater than the election returns indicated. Certainly evidence suggests that the new Republic began life with strong public support and much enthusiasm among Spanish intellectuals.

The balance of power in the Cortes was moderate.[4] The strongest forces were the liberal capitalist Republicans and the Socialists, who were at that time thoroughly committed to gradual, legal reforms. Their central problem was to achieve the reforms needed to alleviate the desperation of the poor, who were growing daily more revolutionary, and at the same time avoid arousing violent reaction from the upper classes, as represented by the large landowners, the industrialists, the Church hierarchy, and the Army, all of whom, the Republicans rightly foresaw, were likely to resist any reforms at all. Further difficulties could be anticipated from the long-standing demands for local autonomy in the Catalan and Basque provinces and from the impatience of many anticlericals to reduce the power of the Church hierarchy. Furthermore, all these problems had to be faced and dealt with at a time when Spain was suffering even more than the rest of Europe from the international economic depression.

It is doubtful whether any government could have found a peaceful solution to these problems. Moreover the troubles of the Spanish Republic were multiplied by what commentators appear to consider a special national trait, which Brenan calls the "crusading impulse," generated by the eight hundred years' struggle to evict the Moors. Under the influence of the Church, Brenan observes, "Spaniards became accustomed to thinking that

[3] *The Times* (London), July 29, 1932.

[4] Gerald Brenan estimates (*Spanish Labyrinth*, pp. 232–233) that the Left Republicans elected 150 deputies, the Right Republicans just over 100, the Socialists 115; the anti-Republican parties elected 52 deputies, only about half of these confirmed monarchists.

all differences of opinion were crimes and all wars were ideological."[5] This singleness of vision goes far to explain both the selfless courage and the ruthless cruelty that marked both sides during the war that was to follow, and it also helps explain how the most earnest efforts of intelligent and humane men were to come to nothing. Speaking of the admirable Republican constitution, Brenan writes:

These able, cultured and disinterested men who came forward to build a new constitution for their country were building in sand. With skill and foresight they prepared a document that was to be the charter of Spanish rights and liberties for generations to come. . . . Everything that could be thought of was thought of—except that the people for whom it was designed might not want it.[6]

Between 1931 and 1933, the Republican government attempted to right some of the wrongs that virtually all elements of the Cortes acknowledged to exist. Steps were taken toward agrarian reform, not enough to do more than whet the desires of the landless poor but enough to convince the largely absentee, wealthy landowners that the Republic was fully bolshevized and determined on liquidating them as the Russians had done the kulaks. Similar efforts to improve the wretched conditions of industrial labor failed to achieve much beyond raising the workers' hopes and the owners' fears of expropriation. In an attempt to reduce the likelihood of military *pronunciamentos,* of which Spain had had many, and to raise the notoriously low level of Spanish military efficiency,[7] the government instituted mild reforms in the Army, abolishing the military courts that had previously had jurisdiction in any crime involving "disrespect" for the military, and requiring all officers to choose between swearing allegiance to the Republic and retiring with pay. Less moderate deputies were unhappy over this gentle treatment of potential troublemakers, and the major effect of the policy did seem to give the retired officers greater time and leisure to concoct plots. Even before the new constitution had been approved, General Sanjurjo, who had helped establish the Republic by his refusal to place his forces at the King's disposal, attempted a rising in Seville. It was, however, easily put down, partly because of a general strike called

[5] Brenan, *Spanish Labyrinth,* p. xi. He notes the long and disastrous series of Spanish wars in the seventeenth and eighteenth centuries and the Carlist civil strife of the nineteenth, which were all fought with religious fervor and disregard for the practical interests of the nation.

[6] *Ibid.,* p. 261.

[7] Aside from their short and humiliating encounter with the United States in 1898, the Spanish armed forces had for a century made war only upon North African tribesmen or other Spaniards.

by the Anarchist CNT (Confederación Nacional del Trabajo) in support of the government that its principles had kept it from voting for.

Perhaps the Republic did itself most damage in its relations with the Spanish Church. Over the previous century the Church had completely abandoned its historic role as protector of the poor and had become "the chief support and maintainer of reaction."[8] The Church had identified itself with the monarchy, and during the election campaigns Archbishop Cardinal Segura of Toledo, Primate of Spain, had issued a militant pastoral letter calling for Catholic resistance to "the enemies of Christ," which had brought on church burnings all over Spain.[9] It is worth remembering that church burning was not a Bolshevist innovation but the time-honored response of the Spanish poor when roused. Over perhaps half a century, working-class Spaniards had generally come to see the Church as hypocritical and oppressive and had channeled their religious passion into the revolutionary doctrines of anarchism and socialism; in moments of crisis it had become customary to attack the local church to destroy it or perform acts of blasphemy within it. Although most Republicans were not at all antireligious, they were strongly anticlerical and were eager to reduce the influence of the Church hierarchy. In view of the religious disaffection of the masses and of the fact that not over twenty per cent, most of them women, of the Spanish population were practicing Catholics in 1930, the government apparently felt safe in moving toward secularization. They passed legislation closing convents and church schools, except seminaries, and cutting off the payment of government salaries to priests.

In retrospect, this rather moderate action seems to have been unwise. The Republicans may have been justly dissatisfied with the high rate of illiteracy that the almost entirely Church-controlled educational system had allowed to continue, but they closed the Church schools without having made any serious arrangements to replace them, and the result was that Spain soon had few schools of any kind. Throughout its existence, the Republic worked hard and often effectively to provide adequate education, but it was a poor start, and conditions for improvement did not become

[8] Brenan (*Spanish Labyrinth*, p. 237) ascribed this change of role largely to the misdirected efforts of the nineteenth-century anticlerical Liberals who, in trying to break the temporal power of the Church, had deprived it of its vast landholdings. The Church, which had until then enjoyed a large measure of autonomy, now began to identify itself with the interests of those who were able and willing to support it financially; thus from being the champion of the poor and friendless, it came to be the ally of the rich and powerful (*ibid.*, pp. 37–57). At the time of the Republic it was not, as foreign leftists often claimed, the largest landowner in Spain, but it was the largest capitalist (Borkenau, *Spanish Cockpit*, p. 9).

[9] Brenan, *Spanish Labyrinth*, p. 236.

any more favorable. As for the cutting off of clerical salaries, it was politically disastrous. Wealthy though the hierarchy and the monastic orders were, the parish priests were generally poor, and many of them had voted for the Republic against the orders of their superiors. The abrupt termination of their already barely adequate salaries turned these priests against the government throughout Spain. (The Basque priests, for a variety of reasons, remained fervent Loyalists, and during the Civil War some of them were to die for the Republic.) Finally, the spirit in which the reforms were made was characterized by the Republican Salvador de Madariaga as "the maximum of ill-will and the minimum of courtesy."[10]

There were genuinely antireligious elements in the Spanish Left, but they were not in the government. The Anarchists represented a large proportion of the Spanish masses, but they refused, of course, to have anything to do with governments; and the Communists had denounced as "Trotskyists" all who counseled cooperation with Socialists and Republicans at this time.[11] The Spanish Communist Party was, in any case, so small and insignificant that Primo had not even bothered to suppress its newspapers during his regime.[12] Still, the government's actions against the Church, coupled with its difficulties in preventing antireligious mob attacks, were taken by its enemies, either through conviction or expediency, as proof of a Marxist plot to destroy Spanish Christianity, and the defense of religion against the anti-Christ became their rallying cry. The Spanish Falange, modeled on European Fascist parties, was no more devoted to the preservation of Christianity than the Anarchists were, but the Falangists manfully swallowed their antireligious scruples to cooperate with the Catholic and Traditionalist parties in opposition to the government, and they even brought themselves to speak feelingly of the sanctity of the Church. The Falangists were not, however, at this time any more potent within the anti-Republican camp than were the Communists in the Republican.[13]

One of the few actions of the Republican government that was to prove useful in the ensuing Civil War was its grant of a degree of autonomy to Catalonia, the richest and most industrially advanced province of Spain. Although anarcho-syndicalism was strong among the Catalan working classes, the effective power was in the hands of conservatives who might have been expected to sympathize with the Franco revolt but for the unyielding resistance of the Spanish Nationalists to all separatist movements. In the crisis the Catalans as a group stood for the Republic. Much of the support that the Republic was to receive from the devoutly Catholic

[10] Quoted by Hodgson, *Spain Resurgent*, p. 25.

[11] Brenan, *Spanish Labyrinth*, p. 296.

[12] *Ibid.*, p. 223.

[13] *Ibid.*, p. 309.

Basques can also be ascribed to its willingness to grant autonomy to those provinces, although the Basque statutes did not come to a vote before the Cortes was dissolved in 1933.

The first two years of the Republic were marked by attempts at reform that were consistently watered down before passage and held up in implementation because of differences within the government, usually between Republicans and Socialists, on the means for putting them into effect. The masses whom the reforms were intended to help grew increasingly impatient for results while the classes that saw their privileges threatened grew increasingly alarmed. The period was characterized by risings on both Right and Left, and the government, in suppressing them with even-handed severity, heightened its unpopularity with both extreme groups.

The forces of the Right chose the election campaign of 1933 to form a united front, and they were voted into office despite a plurality of votes for the disunited parties of the Left. Although far from unanimous (they ranged from the Carlist "Traditionalists" through various monarchist and Catholic parties to the revolutionary Falange), they were able to agree on broad policy, which was simply to undo the work of the first two years of the Republic. They were not able to do this without strenuous popular resistance: in addition to scattered Anarchist risings and a Catalan separatist attempt (the new government had withdrawn the autonomy statute), there was a climactic rebellion by the Asturian miners in October, 1934. Unlike the Anarchist revolts, in which the principles of spontaneity and individual action prevented fanatical courage from having any lasting practical effect, the Asturias rebellion was carefully organized by the orderly and well-disciplined Socialists, who had previously been reluctant to take illegal action. The Socialist organizers were able to win cooperation not only from the Asturian Anarchists but also from the Communists of the area, who had only recently been informed by the Comintern that joint action in a "popular front" was no longer Trotskyist but respectable Party doctrine. The revolt was remarkably successful: the miners actually occupied several towns, Oviedo the largest, and administered them through workers' committees representing the different parties. The full force of the government was used to suppress the revolt, but the miners held out for nearly three weeks, and it required the Foreign Legion and Moorish troops to crush them.[14]

The repercussions of the rising and its suppression were important. The

[14] Some seventy thousand miners rose, forty thousand from the Socialist UGT (Union General de Trabajadores), twenty thousand from the Anarcho-Syndicalist CNT, and nine thousand Communists. Official records listed three thousand dead and seven thousand wounded, less than three hundred of the dead being soldiers (Brenan, *Spanish Labyrinth*, p. 286).

rightist press produced endless accounts of the most bloodcurdling atrocities alleged to have been committed by the miners, and the failure of independent journalists and deputies of the party then in power to find any substantiation embarrassed them not at all. This press campaign undoubtedly helped build fear of the "Red Menace" and "produce an atmosphere in which a terrible vengeance could be taken."[15] Yet the unexampled brutality with which the revolt was crushed, the thousands of prisoners shot, and the institution of a torture squad by the police[16] elicited more horror than satisfaction from the general public.

For Spaniards not yet firmly committed politically, probably the most unsettling aspect of the affair was the use of the Foreign Legion and the Moorish troops against the miners. This seems to have been made necessary by the reluctance of regular Spanish troops to fire on their fellow Spaniards, but it was an unpopular move. The Legion or Tercio (which was made up largely of Spaniards) had never been used before within Spain, and for eight centuries "the crusade against the Moors had been the central theme of Spanish history." Brenan contends, "by this single act the Spanish Right showed that neither tradition nor religion—the two things for which they professed to stand—had any meaning for them."[17] For the working classes,

> The rebellion in Asturias, which from a military point of view had been such a fiasco, had, thanks to the stupidity of the Right, been turned into an enormous moral and political success. The entire proletariat and peasantry of Spain had been thrilled by the miners' heroism and roused to indignation by the vengeance taken against them. The Anarchists [particularly] . . . were jealous of the success of the despised Socialists and ashamed of the small part they had played in it themselves.[18]

The government, which had already caused wide public dismay over its cruelty, further lost favor through revelations of graft and corruption, traditions of Spanish government from which the Left Republicans had been refreshingly free. But what really decided the electoral triumph of the Left in 1936 was the formation of the Popular Front. Having learned from the victory of the rightists' united front in 1933, the Left for the first time

[15] *Ibid.*, p. 286. He notes (p. 284 n) that the later rightist charge that the rebellion was armed by the Russians was invented for foreign consumption; all the arms used by the miners bore the Toledo Arms Factory stamp, as newspapers of all shades of opinion reported at the time.

[16] This was apparently not rightist policy but the inspiration of a local police major, whom the government dismissed once it accepted as true the accounts of his acts (*ibid.*, p. 289).

[17] *Ibid.*, p. 288.

[18] *Ibid.*, p. 292.

temporarily shelved their differences; even the Anarchists, although offering no candidates of their own, voted this time, mainly on the strength of a Republican promise of amnesty for the thousands of political prisoners still in jails. The result was a narrow but decisive victory for the Popular Front, and a coalition of eighty-nine Socialists, eighty-four Left Republicans, thirty-seven Republican Unionists, and sixteen Communists took power.

The number of deputies for each party represented pre-election agreement, not voting strength. The Communists, for instance, were still stronger in influence than in numbers, but they were beginning to grow.[19] Their participation in the Asturias rebellion—especially the fact that the heroine of the Asturias, Dolores Ibarurri "La Pasionaria," was a Communist—offered a solid basis for their skillful propaganda. Once committed to the Popular Front, the Communists proved far more flexible than the other leftist parties, more willing to work with the new-dealing Republicans, consistently more "conservative." During the elections, the Socialists had joked, "Vote Communist to save Spain from Marxism,"[20] and events proved it was no joke at all.

The new Republican government differed from that of 1931. Some of its eminent proponents, disgusted by the first term in office, had abandoned politics (like Ortega y Gasset) or gone over to the Right (like Unamuno),[21] and the Socialist policy was to vote with the government but take no part in it.[22] The Republicans had to take office alone. They set out to reinstate the reforms that had been reversed during the rightist tenure of office (the *bienio negro,* as Republicans called it) but were, if anything, even more hesitant than before about putting their words into action.

The Right, however, had abandoned hope of winning elections and changing the constitution legally. The Army began at once to prepare a

[19] The Communists claimed twenty thousand members in 1935, but General Krivitsky, who as Soviet Military Intelligence Chief for Western Europe was in a position to know, gave the membership as three thousand in 1936, and two hundred thousand in January 1937. Borkenau (*Spanish Cockpit*) and Brenan (*Spanish Labyrinth*, p. 306) accept these figures.

[20] Brenan, *Spanish Labyrinth*, p. 307.

[21] As Rector of the University of Salamanca, Unamuno was in the territory of the Nationalists when war broke out, and as late as mid-September he was quoted as supporting their "struggle for civilization against tyranny"; but he dramatically repudiated the Movimiento a month later in an address before the assembled Nationalist dignitaries. He was placed under house arrest and died "broken-hearted" on December 31, 1936 (Thomas, *Spanish Civil War,* pp. 353–355, citing Luis Portillo's *Unamuno's Last Lecture,* which was published in *Horizon*).

[22] Borkenau, *Spanish Cockpit*, p. 61.

rising and negotiate for foreign assistance, and the small Fascist party, the Falange Espanola, began to grow in numbers and support under the leadership of the dashing José Antonio Primo de Rivera, son of the dictator. The urban and rural masses, their impatience with promises fast becoming overpowering, found their enthusiasm for "direct action" enormously heightened by the Asturias rising. The Socialists had moved leftward since 1934 but were still unwilling to reject parliamentary methods and lead a mass movement to enforce the social changes they desired; the Anarchists, however, were inflamed with visions of *comunismo libertario* just around the corner.

Between February and July of 1936, while the government appeared unable to take any decisive action in its own defense, peasant risings were ever more frequent and violent, and the forces of the Right were solidifying their plans for revolt. In some districts peasants were taking agrarian reform into their own hands, church burnings proliferated, as did street brawls among various armed extremist groups of Left and Right, and assassinations were becoming commonplace. Finally,

> As a reprisal against the assassination of a republican police officer, a group of shock police [the Assault Guards] killed Calvo Sotelo, the intended leader of the insurrectional movement of the Right. This sped things up. The generals got frightened that, while the government was treating them with velvet gloves, uncontrollable elements from among the masses of the people might not allow them to live long enough to rise against the Republic. They decided to rise immediately, though the change of date upset all their preparations. On 17 and 18 July they rose, confident of immediate success.[23]

The initial advantage certainly seemed to lie with the rebels. Led by Generals Franco, Mola, and Goded,[24] they had four-fifths of the infantry and artillery officers, the Civil Guard (federal police), the Foreign Legion, a division of Moorish troops, some regiments of Spanish troops from reliable northern districts, the Carlist private armed forces (Requetés), which had been drilling secretly for some time, and the promise of Italian and German tanks and airplanes if needed. The government had only the Assault Guards (a separate federal police force set up at the beginning of the Republic) and a small, poorly equipped Air Force. Many officers who remained loyal to the Republic were shot at the start of the revolt for unwillingness to join the uprising. The planned rebellion in the Navy did not, however, succeed: the enlisted men, many of them Socialists who honored the memory of the sailors of Kronstadt, re-enacted that feat by

[23] *Ibid.*, p. 62.

[24] General Sanjurjo, one of the chief conspirators, was killed in an airplane accident before the coup was under way.

killing their officers and throwing them overboard.[25] Nevertheless, the preponderance of rebel forces was so obvious that the government had only two alternatives, to surrender or to arm the populace. The decision was as much forced upon them as chosen.

Inspired by the Asturian example and fired by hope of revolution, the Socialist and Anarchist trade unions with their mass following resisted the generals' revolt with whatever weapons they had on hand and demanded arms from the government. These were granted after a short delay, and the rebellion was crushed in Madrid, Barcelona, and about half of the rest of Spain, with the workers' committees becoming, for a period of about three months, "the real rulers of the country and the organizers of the war."[26] During this time, the Madrid government, now under the leadership of Largo Caballero,[27] did, and could do, little to maintain central control over the Republican armed forces, which consisted mainly of the party militias of the CNT, the UGT (soon in the northeast merged with various Communist groups to form the PSUC or Partit Socialista Unificat de Catalunya), and the POUM (Partido Obrero de Unificación Marxista), a small "left-deviationist" Marxist party;[28] these shortly were joined by the International Brigades. The government was able, with the assistance of leftist party leaders, to slow down and, by the end of 1936, end the large-scale and often indiscriminate mass killings of actual and suspected rebel sympathizers within Republican territory which Nationalists and their adherents called the "Red Terror."

The Red Terror was matched by a White Terror behind the Insurgent lines, where middle-class freemasons and liberals were as liable to summary execution as Communists, Socialists, and Anarchists. Which side achieved the greater savagery is still a point of controversy. There were horrifying and often substantiated tales of atrocity on both sides, and the Church, which might have tried to moderate the excesses, consistently applauded the White Terror and deplored the Red.[29] The Nationalists have had some historical advantage in that, as victors, they were able to try "war

[25] Brenan, *Spanish Labyrinth*, p. 316.

[26] *Ibid.*, p. 317.

[27] This Socialist leader, so "moderate" as to have served in Primo de Rivera's cabinet, had moved to the Left by 1936, and Communist propagandists called him the "Spanish Lenin."

[28] Although rigidly Marxist, the POUM had elected to work with the Bakuninist CNT rather than the Marxist UGT on the grounds that the latter were insufficiently revolutionary (Brenan, *Spanish Labyrinth*, p. 296).

[29] *Ibid.*, p. 322. Salvador de Madariaga quotes one priest, just escaped from Barcelona, where Anarchist mobs were killing priests by the hundreds, as saying, "The Reds have destroyed our churches, but we first had destroyed the Church" (*Spain*, p. 377).

criminals" after the war and offer official lists of Republican atrocities without acknowledging any similar crimes by their own forces. Brenan "suppose[s] that for every person executed in Government territory, two or three more were executed in the Rebel zone during the first six months of the war" and "for Andalusía the proportion was probably even higher."[30] He contrasts the total absence of protests on the Nationalist side with the continuing denunciations by government officials and party leaders of Loyalist excesses: "the leaders of the Left parties often protected people who were in danger and facilitated their escape. The Communists, who to annoy the Anarchists had adopted a protective attitude toward the Church, took on themselves the task of sheltering priests," and the Anarchist editor Juan Peiró attacked almost daily the "modern vampires," "fascists in a latent state," "thieves and assassins guilty of a crime against the honour of revolutionaries" in his own party.[31] Among the Nationalists,

> executions without trial took place every day in the prisons . . . until the prisons had several times been filled and emptied. If this did not happen to any great extent on the other side that was because the Republican authorities were strongly opposed to terrorism and put an end to it as soon as they were able, whereas on the Nationalist side the terrorists themselves —that is the Falangists and the Carlists—were in charge of the Home Front and remained so throughout the war. And though as time passed . . . the number of executions diminished, they broke out again whenever a new tract of territory was conquered. The will to exterminate their enemies never failed the Nationalists.[32]

Hugh Thomas, although agreeing that almost all Republican mass killings took place during the first weeks of the war, concludes that there were so many of these that they may have totaled actually higher than the more systematic and prolonged executions by the Nationalists.[33] Whatever the figures and however much allowance is made for the propaganda distortions of both sides, there was ample factual basis for revulsion.

As the fighting wore on, both sides abandoned their early practice of simply shooting all prisoners as a matter of course, not through any lessening of hatred but because eminent prisoners were useful for exchange, because captured foreigners gave evidence of outside intervention on behalf of the enemy, and because recruits from one side could often be found willing to join the army of their captors if the alternatives offered were unappealing enough. The rapid and steady growth of the Communist and

[30] Brenan, *Spanish Labyrinth*, p. 322.

[31] *Ibid.*, p. 323 n.

[32] *Ibid.*, pp. 322–323.

[33] Thomas, *Spanish Civil War*, pp. 169, 173.

Falangist party memberships reflected the policy of redemption by enlistment.

The Civil War began as a Spanish affair, but it did not remain so for long. When the generals first rose, all the nations of Europe except Portugal, which joined later, agreed on strict non-intervention as the policy best calculated to localize the conflict, and the United States revised its 1935 Neutrality Act, which did not apply to internal struggles, to suit the Spanish situation, for the same reason. But the intervention of Italy and Germany from the very beginning of the war and of Russia not long afterward made the policy meaningless. Neither of the Spanish contenders approved the Non-Intervention Pact: the Government claimed that the Pact, in forbidding shipments of supplies to either side, violated its right to buy materials to defend itself against rebellion; the Nationalists, denying that the Republic was the legal government of Spain, demanded belligerent rights, particularly in the matter of naval blockade. The other powers either observed or ignored the Pact as it suited their convenience. Something of the farcical nature of the Non-Intervention Pact appears in the assignment of Italian ships to watch Nationalist ports for evidence of foreign intervention. As the extent of foreign participation in the Civil War became clearer, criticism of Non-Intervention within the democratic signatories grew, but it was without effect.

The Insurgents had been promised Italian assistance as needed, and within a few days after the revolt began Italian ships and planes had been identified by neutrals as taking part in military actions. Although there is no evidence of prior arrangements with Germany, German planes piloted by regular air force Germans had joined the Insurgent forces by mid-August,[34] and in September the Nazi Minister in Italy, Hans Frank, spoke of the two forces in Spain as "on the one side the Germans and the Italians; on the other, the French, Belgians, and Russians."[35] The Nationalists also received help from Portugal, which secured the western border, turned over fleeing Republicans to their pursuers, and provided some 20,000 volunteer troops (of whom 8,000 were lost). In addition, there was an Irish unit of 730 men recruited by General O'Duffy "In Defense of Christianity." The Irish were not popular with their Spanish allies, being known as the "Gasoline Brigade" for their excellent transport, which permitted them to cover much of Nationalist Spain without ever getting involved in any serious fighting. When they voted by 654 to return home, at Nationalist expense, they were allowed to go, seemingly without regrets on either side.[36] According to Hugh Thomas there were also a right-wing

[34] Hodgson, *Spain Resurgent*, p. 74.

[35] *Ibid.*, p. 67, citing Count Ciano's *Diplomatic Papers.*

[36] *Ibid.*, pp. 70–71.

French brigade in the Tercio and a company of White Russians fighting with the Carlist Requetés, as well as a few individual volunteers from Great Britain and Eastern Europe and perhaps one American.[37]

The number of "volunteers"[38] from Germany and Italy is not certain. Sir Robert Hodgson, who was assigned to the Nationalists as agent of the British government, estimates a total of thirty to forty thousand, most of them Italian.[39] Relations between the Italians and the Spanish were early strained in the capture of Malaga by Italian troops; the Italian general objected to the mass slaughter of Republicans by the Nationalists. Relations did not improve: Mussolini's personal envoy, Roberto Farinacci, made no effort to disguise his disapproval of the non-Fascist elements (the Carlists and the Catholic enthusiasts) on his side, and the Spanish in turn referred to their Italian allies as *Macaronistas.*[40] However, aside from the Moors and the Tercio, the Carlists were the only reliable Spanish forces, so the uneasy alliance with foreign volunteers was maintained despite the friction. The Spanish also had mixed feelings about the Germans.

> German aid to Spain, though numerically far inferior to Italy's from the practical point of view, was much more valuable. . . . The "Condor Legion," commanded by General Hugo Sperrle and, afterwards, by General Baron von Richthofen . . . was formed of technicians of various kinds, mainly airmen, ground staff, and anti-aircraft gunners. Numerically it never exceeded 5,000 at any one time . . . Moreover, the Legion's mission being to acquire experience which would be turned to account later on a wider front, the Legionaries only stayed in Spain for a few months, being systematically relieved by new arrivals, and the Spaniards profited greatly by their tuition. On the termination of the war in Spain some 15,000 Legionaries paraded in Berlin.[41]

The motive for aid to Franco was similarly stated by Portugal, Italy, and Germany: to save Spain and Western civilization (and Christianity as well, according to the Catholic governments) from imminent bolshevization by the Moscow puppets in Madrid. Dr. Salazar may also have felt he would be more comfortable sharing the Iberian peninsula with a government more like his own than with the kind of liberal welfare state the

[37] Thomas, *Spanish Civil War,* p. 635.

[38] Borkenau notes (*Spanish Cockpit,* p. 270) that at least some of the Italian troops were not aware that they had volunteered to fight in Spain. Hundreds of the Italians captured at Guadalajara claimed that they had surrendered voluntarily, furious because they had enlisted for work service in Abyssinia, not war in Spain.

[39] Hodgson, *Spain Resurgent,* p. 61.

[40] *Ibid.,* pp. 63–65.

[41] *Ibid.,* p. 68.

Spanish Republicans were trying to establish. A later, and possibly franker, statement of Italian motives was made by the Stefani Agency in 1941: Italy had intervened in Spain "for reasons of national, revolutionary, and Mediterranean policy" for the purpose, among others, of "preventing Spain from becoming, as a consequence of the interference of various popular fronts, a military and naval base for Britain and France against Italy."[42] Germany too was concerned with the strategic advantage of having a friendly government on the Mediterranean with whose help the axis powers could isolate France and exclude England, and Hitler had specific designs on mineral and industrial concessions.[43]

The Republic also received decisive foreign support, although not in the form of regular military units. Almost all the foreigners fighting with the Loyalists were individual volunteers, largely recruited by agencies of the Comintern and assigned to units of the famous International Brigades according to their countries of origin.[44] Of these volunteers, the most numerous were the twenty to thirty thousand French, who made up several brigades, often in combination with Belgians; there were also brigades of anti-Nazi Germans (the Thälmann), anti-Fascist Italians (the Garibaldi), Americans (the Lincoln and Washington brigades, combined after heavy losses at Brunete), Canadians, Poles and other Slavs, and British (English, Irish, and Scots), among others. The total number of volunteers during the existence of the International Brigades is not certain. Franco spoke of "more than 100,000 Communists," but Hodgson, no Republican apologist, considers the total to have been well less than half that, and they were by no means all Communists.[45]

Although recruitment for the Brigades, which began in September of 1936, was done chiefly by the Comintern, either directly or through "front" organizations, the proportion of their membership that was actually Communist has not been established. Franco's willing identification of his cause with Italy and Germany persuaded many anti-Fascists in Europe

[42] Quoted in *ibid.*, p. 66.

[43] *Ibid.*, p. 69. Hodgson notes the intense resentment of the Spanish over German demands that they were not in a position to reject. Thomas cites the German delivery of heavy arms in August of 1936 as decisive in Franco's successful Catalan campaign; without these, a negotiated peace might have been inevitable. But the price was German participation in all important iron ore projects in Spain (Thomas, *Spanish Civil War*, p. 612).

[44] Even before the Brigades were formed, some foreigners in Spain at the outbreak of fighting had joined the various militias, among them European athletes in Barcelona for the "People's Olympiad" organized as a counter to the Olympic Games then being held in Berlin (Hodgson, *Spain Resurgent*, p. 47).

[45] *Ibid.*, pp. 55–60. Thomas lists (*Spanish Civil War*, pp. 638–639) the names and composition of the International Brigades.

and America that the fight for the Spanish Republic was a battle for freedom and democracy against Fascist dictatorship. This was, of course, the Popular Front line of the Communists, who since 1934 had soft-pedalled talk of class war and proletarian dictatorship and now spoke as fervently as any Congressman of the virtues of parliamentary democracy. But certainly antifascism was not an exclusively Communist cause. The Brigades included a high proportion of Jews and other Europeans of many shades of political opinion who saw in Spain the first instance of an entire population rising in spontaneous resistance to the very kind of reactionary and racist[46] dictatorship that had triumphed in their own countries, and they welcomed the opportunity to join the battle. Many volunteers from France, Britain, and the United States, enraged and ashamed by what they considered the appeasement policies of their governments, felt the Spanish War offered them a chance to redeem, in their own persons, their lost national honor. And of course the Brigades also attracted refugees with nowhere else to go and nonpolitical adventurers, as well as not a few who enlisted simply because they had been unemployed for years.

For about two years the International Brigades were the heart and head of the Republican forces, bearing the brunt of the fighting in the early months of the war and then continuing to serve as crack troops while they molded an effective regular Spanish army. By September of 1938, the Prime Minister, Juan Negrín, was able to propose to the League of Nations that all foreign combatants be withdrawn from Spain under League supervision. Like the Nationalists, the Loyalist Spanish were grateful for foreign help but eager to be rid of the foreigners. Negrín was aware that his enemies were by this time relying much more heavily upon foreign troops than the Republic was, and he also hoped by this proposal to disprove Nationalist claims of Moscow domination of the Republican government and so make it easier for the western democracies to abandon Non-Intervention. The League did send a commission to supervise withdrawal of Loyalist foreign volunteers, and in January of 1939 it reported that all of the 12,673 foreigners fighting for the Republic at the time it began its work the preceding October had been withdrawn and were being repatriated.[47] However, the withdrawal did not have the hoped-for effects: the Non-Intervention policy remained unchanged, and although Mussolini withdrew some thousands of Italian troops, the Nationalists refused League supervision, and many thousands of Italians were still fighting on the Nationalist side when the war ended the following spring. There were also

[46] Queipo de Llano, the Nationalist "Radio General" always referred to the French premier as "that Jew, Blum."

[47] Norman J. Padelford, *International Diplomacy in the Spanish Civil Strife*, pp. 114–116.

some 6,000 Germans on hand for a farewell parade in León six weeks after the peace.[48]

The USSR was able to exercise powerful influence in the Republic through the Spanish Communists and especially the foreign Stalinists within the International Brigades, but no Russian nationals were allowed to join the Brigades. Some five or six hundred of the original members came from Russia, but they were all nationals of other countries (or "stateless persons") who had been living in exile there. The some two thousand Red Army men sent to Spain were kept separate from the Internationals. These were chiefly technicians—general-staff men, gunners, engineers, chemical warfare specialists, military instructors. "Only pilots and tank officers . . . saw active service."[49]

The Russian interest in Spain was, said Stalin in a message of October, 1936, "to liberate Spain from oppression by Fascist reactionaries . . . not the duty of Spaniards only, but the common task of advanced and progressive humanity."[50] History casts as much doubt on this assertion as on those of Hitler and Mussolini in the same connection. There is no question that the International Brigades, Communist organized and led, and the Spanish troops under Communist leadership were the best-disciplined and most effective forces the Republic had, nor that the heroic action of the half-trained Internationals had saved Madrid and the Republic during the first months of the war. (Although only half-trained, most of the Internationals had at least done military service in their native countries, whereas a good part of the Spanish militiamen were workers and peasants who had never held a rifle before and were at least as dangerous to themselves and their comrades as to the enemy). It is further beyond dispute that Russian material aid made the continuation of the war possible for the Republic. Aside from a little French aid at the very beginning of the revolt, before the Non-Intervention Pact, the Republic depended almost entirely on the Russians for arms and supplies. Most of these were not of Russian manufacture but were bought, with Spanish gold paid in advance, by Comintern agents in Europe (France, Belgium, Czechoslovakia, the Scandinavian countries, and even, at first, Germany) and America. Delivery was usually by Russian ships or through France. Since the French border

[48] Thomas, *Spanish Civil War,* p. 604.

[49] General W. G. Krivitsky, *I Was Stalin's Agent,* cited by Hodgson in *Spain Resurgent,* p. 52. Krivitsky broke with Stalin in 1937 and fled to the United States where he died mysteriously in 1941. Thomas says (*Spanish Civil War,* p. 263 n) Krivitsky's "evidence must be regarded as tainted unless corroborated" (as the above statement is elsewhere) since his book was "probably partly written by a well-known American Sovietologist, often thought to be helped in what he writes by the FBI."

[50] Hodgson, *Spain Resurgent,* p. 51.

was closed from time to time during the war in obedience to British pressure, and since some local French officials of Nationalist sympathies put obstacles in the way of Loyalist shipments, the overland route was uncertain at best.[51]

Because of the Non-Intervention policy of Britain and France and the embargo of the United States, the Republic depended for its survival on the good will of Stalin, and the Communists in Spain were able to exercise great leverage by threatening the withdrawal of Russian aid. The bulk of Soviet assistance came during the last three months of 1936, and from that point on, further help was well paid for both in gold and in Communist power within the Republic. The Nationalist charge that the Republic was from the first simply a front for a Moscow-directed conspiracy to create a Soviet Spain, a charge that can hardly have been made seriously, simply will not bear examination.[52] The Spanish Communists were few and powerless before the revolt, but after six months of civil war, matters were different. The period of workers' committees and social revolution and terror was over, and the Communists had grown in numbers and prestige on the strength of the exploits of the International Brigades, for which they took full credit, of the vital arms being brought in on Russian ships, of their excellent propaganda, and of their own very real virtues of courage, discipline, and efficient action. At this point, early in 1937, there were rumors that the Communists would perform a coup d'état.

Instead, they combined with about half the Socialists and all the Republicans in the government to offer a new, conservative program for winning the war: an end to party and trade-union militias in favor of a regular army organized on traditional military lines, an end to all revolutionary measures, greater centralization of authority, and a more efficient conduct of the war.[53] The moderates could hardly worry about growing Communist influence within the government, since these policies proposed

[51] Brenan, *Spanish Labyrinth*, p. 329. When French bankers sympathetic to Franco made payments difficult, the greater part of the Bank of Spain gold reserves, about 574 million dollars, was sent to Russia, where any that was not spent during the war remained.

[52] Arthur Koestler, a Comintern agent during the Civil War, describes the indignation among Communists over the Nationalist claims that they had acted simply to forestall a Communist revolution in Spain. Using the figure of a professional burglar facing a bum rap, Koestler notes that while the Communists could not honestly deny (although they did deny) that they were plotting revolution, they had in fact "not been planning a revolution in that particular country at that particular time. . . . It was humiliating to serve as an involuntary midwife at the birth of one Fascist dictatorship after another" (*The Invisible Writing*, p. 335).

[53] Brenan, *Spanish Labyrinth*, p. 327.

by the Communists were precisely the ones that seemed most reasonable to the moderates themselves. Almost all agreed that the first and most pressing problem facing them was to forge an army reliable, well-disciplined, and trained in the most modern military tactics; the popular militias had shown themselves capable of the most reckless courage and heroic self-sacrifice one day and disorderly flight from an unfamiliar situation the next. Secondly, almost to the end the Republican government refused to give up hope that if the Western democracies were reassured as to the essentially legalistic, democratic and unrevolutionary nature of the Republic, they would come to its aid or at least stop helping its enemies, which was the effect of Non-Intervention. To the end of proving their respectability to England, France, and America, the Republicans (who did not want social revolution anyway) and the Socialists (who felt it would have to wait until the war was won) joined with the Communists to return expropriated land and factories and break up the collectives established during the first three months of the war by peasant and worker committees. The slogans were "Respect the property of the peasants," "No interference with the small business man," and "No socialization of industry."[54]

The Anarchists and the POUM resisted this move to the Right, convinced as they were that the war should be not primarily a defense against a reactionary putsch but rather a means to revolution and that if they surrendered the advances made during the first chaotic months of civil war they were unlikely to retrieve them under any conceivable victorious Republic. However, their leaders chose not to fight on the issue, and the Communists were unable to persuade the rest of the government to suppress the anarcho-syndicalist unions and place the Catalan police and press (the Anarchists were strongest in Catalonia) under what would have amounted to Communist control. They were more successful, thanks to the lever of Russian aid, in their assault on the small POUM, which Stalin considered Trotskyist and which was not markedly popular in any case. The other parties cooperated in suppressing the POUM and in trying its leaders on baseless charges of treason and collaboration with the enemy. The leaders were ultimately cleared, but by then Andrés Nin had been secretly murdered in a Communist-controlled prison and Joaquín Maurín was in Franco's hands; the POUM simply vanished.[55]

Communist power continued to grow through 1937 into 1938, both in membership and in government influence, and by April of 1938 the Com-

[54] *Ibid.*, p. 316.

[55] *Ibid.*, p. 328. See George Orwell's *Homage to Catalonia* for a personal account of the suppression of the POUM and of Orwell's experiences fighting in its militia.

munists were able to force the fall of the Socialist Prieto, who had resisted their efforts to gain control of the Army. Yet, despite the strategic placement of Communists within the Republican forces (almost all army political commissars were Communists, the propaganda department was under their control as were most of the police forces,[56] and they had their own police and prisons), their effectiveness began to wane as it became clear that Stalin was withdrawing from Spain, and the Socialists and Republicans regained their dominance in the government.

The history of the war indicates that the other elements in the Republic accepted the aid and submitted to the influence of the Communists because their ideas on how best to conduct the war coincided, because the Communists provided discipline and efficiency not to be found elsewhere on the Republican side, and because non-intervention made the Republic solely dependent upon Russian aid, which was not to be had without compensation. The fact that Stalin proved either unable or unwilling to give sufficient aid to make possible a Republican victory renders academic the question of whether communism of the Stalin variety might have triumphed in Spain, but students of Spain tend to doubt it.

Stalin's motives in his Spanish adventure remain obscure. It was unquestionably a profitable enterprise for him. His intercession on behalf of the Republic gained Russia enormous propaganda rewards. Under the Popular Front line, best exemplified in Spain, the USSR came to be widely seen as the outstanding, indeed the only national champion of antifascism, and besides the many who actually joined the Communist parties of the Western democracies there were far more who moved from aversion or indifference to active sympathy for communism and for Russia. Among intellectuals communism became not only respectable but positively chic. For sophisticated leftists, the Russian action in Spain served to distract attention from the uglier aspects of Stalinism, which had been becoming increasingly apparent in the purge trials which began in 1935 and reached a climax with the first death sentences in August, 1936. Men like Gustav Regler, André Malraux, and Arthur Koestler, who had by this time come to recognize the extent to which Stalin's Russia resembled the Fascist dictatorships, nevertheless resolved to keep silence about their differences with the Communist Party in the interest of anti-Fascist solidarity. Many disillusioned leftists were convinced that criticism of Russia during this

[56] Under Communist control the Republican political police proved generally to be more concerned with suppressing enemies of the Communist Party than with discovering enemies of the Republic. There were few executions, but the jails were full. "Like all Spanish police, it was extraordinarily incompetent," says Brenan (*Spanish Labyrinth*, p. 329).

period, however justified, would only play into the hands of the Fascists, and Stalin profited by their restraint.

It is unlikely that Stalin ever had designs for a Communist Spain. At two points, in early 1937 and in mid-1938, conditions for a Communist coup were favorable, but Stalin did not make the effort. Non-Communist Marxists like Franz Borkenau, George Orwell, Erich Fromm, and C. Wright Mills have contended that Stalin did not want a Spanish revolution because he knew he could not control it and because he was not interested in revolution anyway but only in consolidating his own essentially counter-revolutionary totalitarian bureaucracy. Certainly his agent in Spain, André Marty, seemed far more eager to purge Trotskyists than to fight Fascists or make a revolution; both Koestler and Louis Fischer noted the frequency with which foreign Communists serving in Spain were ordered to Moscow to be shot or simply to disappear.[57]

Hugh Thomas believes that Stalin originally decided to intervene in Spain for strategic and propaganda reasons, to prevent the Republic from losing the war without helping it to win: "the mere continuance of the war would keep him free to act in any way."[58] After Munich and the end of any chance for an alliance with the British and French against Hitler, he began to abandon his Spanish adventure, and he was more than willing to permit the withdrawal of the International Brigades which the Republic desired. From this point, Russian and Comintern aid to Spain also steadily diminished.[59]

Whatever the reasons for the slackening and eventual end of Russian assistance to the Republic, whether a cynical decision that Spain had served its purpose or a simple inability to continue at a level competitive with the German and Italian aid to the other side (the Russian performance in Finland not long afterward offered poor testimony to Soviet military might), it meant the end of the Spanish War. Negrín, the last Republican Prime Minister, seems to have continued the fight during the last hopeless months only in a vain attempt to compel firmer guarantees against reprisals and more humane terms of surrender than those that were finally imposed.[60]

[57] Fischer, not a Communist himself but long a sympathizer with Russia and communism, was among the first Americans to enlist in the International Brigades. His *Men and Politics* is an interesting account of life on the Left in the twenties and thirties. Gustav Regler's *The Owl of Minerva* is still better.

[58] Thomas, *Spanish Civil War,* p. 216.

[59] *Ibid.*, p. 557.

[60] Nationalist mass executions continued long after the end of the fighting; A. V. Phillips of the *News Chronicle* estimated these as one hundred thousand

Gerald Brenan gives a succinct summary of the course of the war:

After a period of violent social revolution the "Reds" or "Loyalists" . . . began to move more and more to the Right . . . At the same time they took up a national and patriotic attitude of defense of their country against the foreign invader. What was strange was that the chief advocates of this policy were the numerically feeble but actually very influential Communist party. The "Nationalists," on the other hand, fell more and more deeply under German and Italian influence and, to give their own side something of a mass following, were obliged to hand over the greater part of the political power to the Falangists and to come out with a social program that, if it were meant seriously, was more drastic than anything ever proposed by the Republic.

The result of the war was decided by the question of foreign help. Whilst there was little to choose between the political and military competence of either side, almost all the mass support, the enthusiasm, the spirit of sacrifice was upon the Republican. The Falangists proved to be a mere Iron Guard, undisciplined and irresponsible; for a crusading spirit Franco could count only on the Carlists. But German and Italian help was enormously more powerful than Russian, and for this reason the Franco forces won.[61]

Briefly then, the Spanish Civil War was neither so clearly a confrontation of democracy and dictatorship nor of Communism and Christian civilization as the proponents of either side claimed. The Spanish Republic was neither the Marxist conspiracy its enemies called it nor quite the citadel of liberal democracy it appeared to some of its foreign supporters. The Nationalists were neither the defenders of Christian civilization that their admirers believed them nor close copies of the Nazis and Fascists with whom they were allied. As later events proved, Franco (a man "singularly lacking in all führerlike qualities"[62] who had become dictator largely through the accident of his leading co-conspirators' dying in the course of the war) was of only limited usefulness to his allies in World War II, and they did not stint expressions of their sense of ingratitude and betrayal. Franco's

---

by the end of 1939, but Thomas considers the figure of nine thousand for the same period, suggested by an escaped Republican trade-union leader, as more probable. Perhaps two million had been imprisoned for various terms by 1942, although none apparently served all of the frequently imposed thirty-year sentence. Disabled Republican veterans were also denied the small pensions granted disabled Nationalists (Thomas, *Spanish Civil War*, pp. 608–609).

[61] Brenan, *Spanish Labyrinth*, pp. 316–317.

[62] *Ibid.*, p. 331. Thomas writes (*Spanish Civil War*, p. 609): "Upon the heaped skulls of all these ideals [which had been fought for and lost in the final misery of the war], one dispassionate, duller, greyer man survived triumphant. . . . Francisco Franco was the Octavius of Spain."

Spain is as reactionary and authoritarian as his enemies had expected, but its close connections with the Spanish Church have made it seem much more like the traditional military dictatorships of other Latin countries than like a modern Fascist state.[63]

[63] Ironically, the economic structure of Franco's Spain, as described by Hodgson and others, is closer to the syndicalism proposed by his bitter enemies than to any other model, with the decisive difference that the "vertical syndicates" are placed under strongly centralized control from the authoritarian top rather than based upon the voluntary and spontaneous mass cooperation of which the Anarchists dreamed.

BIBLIOGRAPHY

Adler, Henry. Review of *Out of the Picture* by Louis MacNeice, *Time and Tide,* XVIII, No. 29 (July 24, 1937), 1018.

America, 1936–1939.

Auden, W. H., and Christopher Isherwood. *The Ascent of F6: A Tragedy in Two Acts.* London: Faber and Faber, Ltd., 1936.

———. *The Collected Poetry of W. H. Auden.* New York: Random House, Inc., 1945.

———, and Christopher Isherwood. *The Dog Beneath the Skin, or Where Is Francis?* London: Faber and Faber, Ltd., 1935.

———. Introduction to *The Poet's Tongue,* ed. W. H. Auden and John Garrett. London: G. Bell & Sons, Ltd., 1935.

———, and Louis MacNeice. *Letters from Iceland.* London: Faber and Faber, Ltd., 1937.

———. *Look, Stranger.* London: Faber and Faber, Ltd., 1936.

———, and Christopher Isherwood. *On the Frontier: A Melodrama in Three Acts.* London: Faber and Faber, Ltd., 1938.

———. *Poems.* New York: Random House, Inc., 1934.

———. "Religion and the Intellectuals," *Partisan Review,* XVII, No. 2 (February 1950), 120–128.

Authors Take Sides on the Spanish War. London: Left Review, n.d.

Barker, George. *Calamiterror.* London: Faber and Faber, Ltd., 1937.

Bates, Ralph. *The Fields of Paradise.* New York: E. P. Dutton & Co., Inc., 1940.

———. *Lean Men.* New York: The Macmillan Company, 1935.

———. *The Olive Field.* New York: E. P. Dutton & Co., Inc., 1936.

Beach, J. W. *The Making of the Auden Canon.* Minneapolis: University of Minnesota Press, 1957.

Bentley, Eric. *The Playwright As Thinker*. New York: Meridian, World Publishing Co., Inc., 1955.

Bernanos, Georges. *Les grands cimetières sous la lune*. Paris: Plon and Nourrit, 1938.

Borkenau, Franz. *The Spanish Cockpit*. London: Faber and Faber, Ltd., 1937.

Bowers, Claude. *My Mission to Spain*. New York: Simon & Schuster, Inc., 1954.

Brenan, Gerald. *The Spanish Labyrinth*. New York: The Macmillan Company, 1943.

Campbell, Roy. *Flowering Rifle: A Poem from the Battlefield of Spain*. London: Longmans, Green & Co., Ltd., 1939.

———. *Light on a Dark Horse: An Autobiography (1901–1935)*. London: Hollis and Carter, Ltd., 1951.

———. *Lorca: An Appreciation of his Poetry*. New Haven: Yale University Press, 1952.

———. *Selected Poems*. Chicago: Henry Regnery Company, 1955.

Cardozo, H. G. *March of a Nation: My Year of Spain's Civil War*. New York: Robert M. McBride & Company, 1937.

Catholic Worker, 1936–1938.

Cattell, David T. *Communism and the Spanish Civil War*. New York: Russell & Russell, Inc., 1965.

Caudwell, Christopher. *Illusion and Reality: A Study of the Sources of Poetry*. London: Macmillan & Co., Ltd., 1937.

———. *Studies in a Dying Culture*. With an Introduction by John Strachey. London: John Lane, The Bodley Head, Ltd., 1938.

Cockburn, Claud. *In Time of Trouble: An Autobiography*. London: Readers Union, Rupert Hart-Davis, Ltd., 1957.

Commonweal, 1936–1939.

Connolly, Cyril. *The Condemned Playground (Essays 1927–1944)*. New York: The Macmillan Company, 1948.

———. *Enemies of Promise*. London: George Routledge and Kegan Paul, Ltd., 1938.

———. "Today the Struggle," *New Statesman and Nation*, XIII, No. 328 N.S. (June 5, 1937), 926–928.

Crossman, Richard H. S., ed. *The God That Failed*. New York: Bantam, Harper and Brothers, 1950.

Day Lewis, Cecil. *The Buried Day*. London: Chatto and Windus, 1960.

———. *Collected Poems 1929–1954*. London: Jonathan Cape, Ltd., and The Hogarth Press, 1954.

———. *The Friendly Tree*. New York and London: Harper and Brothers, 1937.

———, ed. *The Mind in Chains: Socialism and the Cultural Revolution.* London: Frederick Muller, Ltd., 1937.

———. *Starting Point.* New York and London: Harper and Brothers, 1937.

———. *A Time to Dance, Noah and the Waters, and Other Poems, with an essay, Revolution in Writing.* New York: Random House, Inc., 1936.

Demetz, Peter, ed. *Brecht: A Collection of Critical Essays.* Englewood Cliffs, New Jersey: Prentice-Hall, Inc., 1962.

Dyment, Clifford. *C. Day Lewis.* Writers and Their Work, No. 62. London: Longmans, Green, & Co., Ltd., 1955.

Eliot, T. S. "Commentary," *Criterion,* XVI, No. 62 (October 1936), 63–69; XVI, No. 63 (January 1937), 289–293; XVI, No. 64 (April 1937), 469–474; XVIII, No. 70 (October 1939), 58–62; XVIII, No. 71 (January 1939), 269–274.

Empson, William. *The Collected Poems of William Empson.* New York: Harcourt, Brace & Co., Inc., 1949.

Fischer, Louis. *Men and Politics.* New York: Duell, Sloan, and Pierce, Inc., 1941.

———. "Soviet Democracy," *New Statesman and Nation,* XII, No. 284 N.S. (August 1, 1936), 148–150.

Ford, Hugh D. *A Poet's War: British Poets and the Spanish Civil War.* Philadelphia and London: University of Pennsylvania Press and Oxford University Press, 1965.

Forster, E. M. *Abinger Harvest.* New York: Harcourt, Brace & Co., Inc., 1936.

———. "Credo," *London Mercury* XXXVIII, No. 227 (September 1938), 397–403.

———. "The Long Run," *New Statesman and Nation,* XVI, No. 407 N.S. (December 10, 1938), 971–972.

Fox, Ralph. *The Novel and the People.* New York: International Publishers Co., Inc., 1935.

Gassner, John. *Masters of the Drama.* New York: Dover Publications, Inc., 1945.

Gollancz, Victor, ed. *The Betrayal of the Left.* With essays by John Strachey, George Orwell, Harold Laski, and the editor. London: Victor Gollancz, Ltd., 1941.

———. *More for Timothy, Vol. II of an Autobiography.* Victor Gollancz, Ltd., 1953.

Graves, Robert, and Alan Hodge. *The Long Weekend: A Social History of Great Britain, 1918–1939.* New York: The Macmillan Company, 1941.

Greene, Graham. "Alfred Tennyson Intervenes," *Spectator,* CLIX, No. 5711 (December 10, 1937), 1058.

———. *Another Mexico.* New York: The Viking Press, 1939.

———. *The Confidential Agent: An Entertainment.* New York: Sun Dial, The Viking Press, 1945.

———. *England Made Me.* Garden City, New York: Doubleday, Doran, and Co., Inc., 1935.

———. *It's a Battlefield.* London: Wm. Heinemann, Ltd., 1959.

———. *The Lost Childhood and Other Essays.* London: Eyre & Spottiswoode, Ltd., 1951.

———. *The Power and the Glory.* New York: Bantam, The Viking Press, 1954.

———. *Stamboul Train.* London: Wm. Heinemann, Ltd., 1932.

———. *This Gun for Hire.* Garden City, N.Y.: Doubleday, Doran, and Co., Inc., 1936.

Grieve, C. M. *Lucky Poet: A Self-Study in Literature and Political Ideas, Being the Autobiography of Hugh MacDiarmid.* London: Methuen and Company, Ltd., 1943.

Guttmann, Allen. *The Wound in the Heart: America and the Spanish Civil War.* New York: Free Press of Glencoe, Macmillan, Crowell-Collier, 1962.

Harrison, John. *The Reactionaries.* With a Preface by William Empson. London: Victor Gollancz, Ltd., 1966.

Heppenstall, Rayner. "Decade Talk," *New Statesman and Nation,* LI (April 14, 1958), 377.

Hodgson, Sir Robert. *Spain Resurgent.* London: Hutchinson & Co., Ltd., 1953.

Hone, Joseph. *W. B. Yeats 1865–1939.* New York: The Macmillan Company, 1943.

Howard, Brian. "Time, Gentlemen, Please," *New Statesman and Nation,* XIII, No. 309 N.S. (January 23, 1937), 122–124.

Huxley, Aldous. *An Encyclopedia of Pacifism.* London: Chatto and Windus, 1937.

———. *Ends and Means.* London: Chatto and Windus, 1937.

———. *Eyeless in Gaza.* New York and London: Harper and Brothers, 1936.

Isherwood, Christopher. *All the Conspirators.* With an Introduction by Cyril Connolly. London: Jonathan Cape, Ltd., 1939.

———. *An Approach to Vedanta.* Hollywood: Vedanta Press, 1963.

———, and W. H. Auden. *The Ascent of F6.* See Auden.

———, and W. H. Auden. *The Dog Beneath the Skin.* See Auden.

———. *Down There on a Visit.* London: Methuen and Company, Ltd., 1962.

———. *Lions and Shadows.* Norfolk, Connecticut: New Directions, 1947.

———. "Man of Honor," *New Republic,* XCVIII, No. 1266 (March 8, 1939), 138.

———, and W. H. Auden. *On the Frontier.* See Auden.

———. "Some Notes on Auden's Early Poetry," *New Verse,* November 1937.

Jerrold, Douglas. *Georgian Adventure.* London: William Collins Sons & Co., Ltd., 1937.

Joad, C. E. M. "Notes Along the Way," *Time and Tide,* XVIII, No. 19 (May 8, 1937), 604.

———. "What Is Happening in the Peace Movement?" *New Statesman and Nation,* XIII, No. 325 N.S. (May 15, 1937), 802–804.

Joyce, James. *A Portrait of the Artist As a Young Man.* New York: The Viking Press, 1956.

Kazin, Alfred. *Starting Out in the Thirties.* Boston, Toronto: Little, Brown, & Co., 1962, 1965.

Kemp, Harry, Laura Riding, and others. *The Left Heresy in Literature and and Life.* London: Methuen and Company, Ltd., 1939.

Kenner, Hugh. *Wyndham Lewis.* The Makers of Modern Literature. Norfolk, Connecticut: New Directions, 1954.

Koestler, Arthur. *The Invisible Writing.* London: William Collins Sons & Co., Ltd., 1954.

Kunitz, Stanley J., and Howard Haycraft, eds. *Twentieth Century Authors.* New York: The H. W. Wilson Company, 1942.

Kunkel, Francis L. *The Labyrinthine Ways of Graham Greene.* New York: Sheed & Ward, Inc., 1959.

Lehmann, John. *Down River.* London: The Cresset Press, 1939.

———, ed. *Folios of New Writing.* London: The Hogarth Press, 1936–1938, 1940–1941.

———. *I Am My Brother: Vol. II of an Autobiography.* New York: Reynal & Co., Inc., 1960.

———. *The Whispering Gallery: Autobiography I.* New York: Harcourt, Brace & Co., Inc., 1954.

Lewis, John. *Christianity and the Social Revolution.* London: Victor Gollancz, Ltd., 1935.

Lewis, Wyndham. *The Apes of God.* New York: Robert M. McBride & Co., 1932.

———. *The Art of Being Ruled.* New York and London: Harper and Brothers, 1926.

———. *Count Your Dead: They Are Alive: A New War in the Making.* London: Lovat Dickson, Ltd., 1937.

———. *Hitler.* London: Chatto and Windus, 1931.

———. *The Hitler Cult.* London: J. M. Dent & Sons, Ltd., 1939.

———. *Left Wings Over Europe, or How to Make a War About Nothing.* London: Jonathan Cape, Ltd., 1936.

———. *The Lion and the Fox.* London: Methuen and Company, Ltd., 1955.

———. *Paleface: The Philosophy of the Melting Pot.* London: Chatto and Windus, 1929.
———. *The Revenge for Love.* Chicago: Henry Regnery Company, 1952.
———. *Rude Assignment: A Narrative of My Career Up-to-Date.* London: Hutchinson & Company, Ltd., 1950.
———. *Time and Western Man.* Boston: Beacon Press, Inc., 1927.
Lunn, Arnold. *Come What May: An Autobiography.* Boston: Sheed & Ward, Inc., 1941.
———. *Spanish Rehearsal.* Boston: Sheed and Ward, Inc., 1937.
MacCarthy, Desmond. "The American Stage," *New Statesman and Nation,* XVI, No. 384 N.S. (July 2, 1938), 14–15.
———. "A Play of the Moment," *New Statesman and Nation,* XVI, No. 406 N.S. (December 3, 1938), 914, 916.
———. "Trial of a Judge," *New Statesman and Nation,* XV, No. 370 N.S. (March 26, 1938), 523–524.
MacNeice, Louis. *Collected Poems 1925–1948.* London: Faber and Faber, Ltd., 1937.
———, and W. H. Auden. *Letters from Iceland.* See Auden.
———. *A Play in Two Acts: Out of the Picture.* London: Faber and Faber, Ltd., 1937.
———. "The Tower That Once," *Folios of New Writing,* Spring 1941, pp. 37–41.
Madariaga, Salvador de. *Spain.* 2d ed. New York: Charles Scribner's Sons, 1942.
Malraux, André. *L'Espoir.* Paris: Gallimard, 1937.
Martin, Kingsley. "The Peace Movement," *New Statesman and Nation,* XV, No. 380 N.S. (June 4, 1938), 946–947.
———. "The Soviet System," *New Statesman and Nation,* XIV, No. 350 N.S. (November 6, 1937), 758–760.
Mitford, Jessica. *Hons and Rebels.* London: Victor Gollancz, Ltd., 1960.
Muggeridge, Malcolm. "Men and Books," *Time and Tide,* XVIII, No. 21 (May 23, 1937), 693.
New Statesman and Nation. Review of *The Ascent of F6: A Tragedy in Two Acts,* by W. H. Auden and Christopher Isherwood, XIII, No. 315 N.S. (March 6, 1937), 368.
O'Casey, Sean. *The Star Turns Red,* in *Collected Plays.* Vol. II. London: Macmillan & Co., Ltd., 1950.
———. *Sunset and Evening Star,* in *Mirror in My House: The Autobiographies of Sean O'Casey.* Vol. II. New York: The Macmillan Company, 1956.
Orwell, George. *Animal Farm.* New York: Harcourt, Brace & Co., Inc., 1946.

———. *A Collection of Essays by George Orwell.* Garden City, New York: Doubleday & Co., 1954.

———. *Coming Up for Air.* New York: Harcourt, Brace & Co., Inc., 1950.

———. "Experientia Docet," *New Statesman and Nation,* XIV, No. 34 N.S. (August 28, 1937), 314.

———. *Homage to Catalonia.* With an introduction by Lionel Trilling. Boston: Beacon Press, Inc., 1955.

———. Letter to the Editor, *Time and Tide,* XIX, No. 6 (February 5, 1938), 165.

———. *1984.* New York: Harcourt, Brace & Co., Inc., 1949.

———. Review of *The Tree of Gernika* by G. L. Steer and *Spanish Testament* by Arthur Koestler, *Time and Tide,* XIX, No. 6 (February 5, 1938), 177.

Padelford, Norman J. *International Diplomacy in the Spanish Civil Strife.* New York: The Macmillan Company, 1939.

Partridge, Eric. *A Dictionary of Slang and Unconventional English.* 3d ed. New York: The Macmillan Company, 1950.

Pike, James A., ed. *Modern Canterbury Pilgrims.* New York: Morehouse-Gorham Company, 1956.

Plomer, William. "New Chains for Old," *London Mercury,* XXXVI, No. 213 (July 1937), 299–300.

Pritchett, V. S. "New Novels," *New Statesman and Nation,* XIV, No. 344 N.S. (September 28, 1937), 448.

———. Review of *Homage to Catalonia* by George Orwell, *New Statesman and Nation,* XV, No. 375 N.S. (April 30, 1938), 734–736.

Regler, Gustav. *The Great Crusade.* Translated by Whittaker Chambers and Barrows Mussey, with a Preface by Ernest Hemingway. New York: Longmans, Green, & Co., Ltd., 1940.

———. *The Owl of Minerva.* New York: Farrar, Straus, and Cudahy, Inc., 1959.

Rice, Elmer. *Judgment Day.* New York: Coward-McCann, Inc., 1934.

Roberts, Michael, ed. *New Country: Prose and Poetry by the Authors of New Signatures.* London: The Hogarth Press, 1933.

———, comp. *New Signatures: Poems by Several Hands Collected by Michael Roberts.* London: Leonard and Virginia Woolf, 1932.

Samuels, Stuart. "The Left Book Club," *Journal of Contemporary History,* I, No. 2 (1966), 65–86.

Scarfe, Francis. *Auden and After: The Liberation of Poetry.* London: George Routledge & Sons, Ltd., 1942.

Scott-James, R. A. "Two Books by Mr. Wyndham Lewis," *London Mercury,* XXXVI, No. 212 (June 1937), 201.

INDEX